T0377714

COLONIZING OURSELVES

NEW DIRECTIONS IN TEJANO HISTORY

Alberto Rodriguez and Timothy Paul Bowman,
Series Editors

COLONIZING OURSELVES

Tejano Back-to-Mexico Movements and the Making of a Settler Colonial Nation

JOSÉ ANGEL HERNÁNDEZ

UNIVERSITY OF OKLAHOMA PRESS : NORMAN

Publication of this book is supported in part by the generous assistance of the McCasland Foundation, Duncan, Oklahoma.

Library of Congress Cataloging-in-Publication Data

Names: Hernández, José Angel, 1969– author.
Title: Colonizing ourselves : Tejano back-to-Mexico movements and the making of a settler colonial nation / José Angel Hernández.
Description: Norman : University of Oklahoma Press, [2024] | Series: New directions in Tejano history ; volume 5 | Includes bibliographical references and index. | Summary: "A history of the 'back to Mexico' movement in the late 19th century, a colonization scheme that enticed Tejanos to settle on Mexican lands near its northern border with Texas"—Provided by publisher.
Identifiers: LCCN 2024009765 | ISBN 978-0-8061-9459-2 (hardcover)
Subjects: LCSH: Return migration—Mexico—History. | Mexicans—Texas—History. | Mexicans—Migrations. | Settler colonialism—Mexico—History. | Mexico—Emigration and immigration—History. | Mexico—Emigration and immigration—Government policy. | Mexico—History—1867–1910. | BISAC: HISTORY / United States / State & Local / Southwest (AZ, NM, OK, TX) | HISTORY / United States / 19th Century
Classification: LCC JV7403 .H47 2024 | DDC 304.80972—dc23/eng/20240613
LC record available at https://lccn.loc.gov/2024009765

Colonizing Ourselves: Tejano Back-to-Mexico Movements and the Making of a Settler Colonial Nation is Volume 5 in the New Directions in Tejano History series.

The paper in this book meets the guidelines for permanence and durability of the Committee on Production Guidelines for Book Longevity of the Council on Library Resources, Inc. ∞

Copyright © 2024 by the University of Oklahoma Press, Norman, Publishing Division of the University. Manufactured in the U.S.A.

All rights reserved. No part of this publication may be reproduced, stored in a retrieval system, or transmitted, in any form or by any means, electronic, mechanical, photocopying, recording, or otherwise—except as permitted under Section 107 or 108 of the United States Copyright Act—without the prior written permission of the University of Oklahoma Press. To request permission to reproduce selections from this book, write to Permissions, University of Oklahoma Press, 2800 Venture Drive, Norman OK 73069, or email rights .oupress@ou.edu.

Dedicado a mis padres,

José Gabriel Hernández Sánchez
y
Martha Antonio Carrillo Hernández

In our humble opinion, as we have already clearly expressed, the colonization of Mexicans who are returning to reclaim their homeland and that of those who inhabit it as nomadic tribes, without organization or incentive for work, as is the case with the unfortunate indigenous race, should be given preference over foreign colonization. This is what convenience dictates and what reclaims national identity. Asian or European colonists may come later, but first, we need to colonize ourselves.

—*El Colono*, 10 April 1897

CONTENTS

ACKNOWLEDGMENTS

To echo the fundamental themes of this monograph, it seems appropriate to fashion these acknowledgments in alignment with a parallel narratological trajectory. I recognize that a significant motivator for embarking on this research project was the global pandemic that transpired from 2020 to 2022, with SARS-CoV-2 being identified as one of the primary catalysts. This period of collective upheaval deeply influenced my creative motivations and theoretical reflections. Well-worn concepts of "imagined communities," elucidated by Benedict Anderson, and the role of nineteenth-century newspapers in molding national identity gained fresh relevance as I observed mainstream media, with clear political biases, manipulating scientific research to align with their ideologies. Similarly, Michel Foucault's seeming passé ramblings on "biopower" now resonated as I witnessed surreal public debates over vaccines, prophylactics, and pharmaceuticals. Despite ongoing discussions about the declining authority of nation-states, the pandemic, aided by the very "experts" Foucault cautioned us about, affirmed the enduring presence and importance of the state. Though I could cite numerous examples, my central point is the unlikelihood, if not impossibility, of embarking on this monograph without the quarantine measures. These lockdowns compelled me to embrace writing as a productive occupation that diverted my attention from sensationalist media and grocery store altercations over toilet paper. An invisible, airborne virus emerged as the paramount historical agent in contemporary world history, transforming what I initially expected to be a brief respite during a spring break in 2020 into an unforeseen two-year period of confinement.

Having duly acknowledged the primary catalyst for historical transformation during the inception and conceptualization of this monograph, I sought solace in becoming a member of diverse writing groups. This decision not only served as a mechanism for preserving my mental equilibrium, but also provided a rare conduit for human interaction and camaraderie when everyone was masking, social distancing, and wiping down their groceries. First and foremost, I extend my gratitude to the Arizona State University–Boston College Writing Studio, founded by Christopher Jones. As of January 2024, the group continues to meet via Zoom on weekdays, and through the most trying phases of the pandemic, I found myself dedicating an average of thirty hours a week to these sessions. Here I would like to thank my fellow Fulbrighter, Patience Akpan-Obong of Arizona State for introducing me to the group and to its many wonderful hosts. In the early stages of this journey, the Collaborative Writing Group, hosted by various colleagues at the University of Houston via Teams, played a pivotal role in supporting my navigation through vast reservoirs of data. Additionally, during the most challenging stretches of the pandemic, particularly when I was diligently reviewing every annual report on colonization published by the Mexican Department of Development, Colonization, Industry, and Commerce, I also actively participated in the London Writers Salon. As I diligently filled numerous legal pads with my pencil-sketched ideas, I discovered within these virtual platforms collegial environments that aided me in the creation of initial drafts for two monographs, one of which is the current work.

In 2003, a Mellon Foundation Latin American Fellowship from the University of Chicago introduced me to the dossier of Luis Siliceo and his extensive archive at the Archivo Histórico de Terrenos Nacionales (AHTN). From its inception, this monograph owes its existence to the significant financial and institutional support provided by the Fulbright Commission. I lived in Ciudad Juárez, Chihuahua, between July 2003 and August 2005, and later in Mexico City, thanks to substantial backing from the Fulbright. During a Fulbright-Hays Dissertation Fellowship in 2004–5, I returned to the AHTN armed with a digital camera, which allowed me to meticulously copy Siliceo's entire archive. However, I had to place this research on the back burner as I worked on my dissertation and, later, my first book. One unintended consequence of technology was that I accumulated a vast repository of digital images, which I did not revisit for years.

My ability to publish this research today is a testament to the enduring support provided by a number of academic institutions. Research funding and favorable circumstances at the University of Massachusetts, Amherst (UMass), enabled me to hire two research assistants to conduct an extensive analysis of 287 declaration forms. In 2011, Sergio Rodríguez, then pursuing his doctoral studies in the Department of Economics at UMass, played a pivotal role in quantifying the data and conducting rigorous statistical analyses. His contributions greatly influenced the concluding section of this monograph, and his findings and expertise have become integral to this study. In subsequent years, Aurora Vergara Figueroa, PhD, currently serving as the minister of education for Colombia, joined the effort. She was in the final stages of her doctoral program in the Department of Sociology. Beyond verifying Sergio's findings, Aurora developed a comprehensive database centered around Siliceo, which complemented Sergio's earlier work. My collaborations with both Sergio and Aurora significantly enhanced my grasp of statistical methodologies and deepened my understanding of multivariate analysis. I am sincerely grateful for their diligent work.

In 2015, I was honored to receive a Fulbright US Scholar Award, which allowed me to conduct research in Tijuana, Baja California, and later in Coyoacán, Mexico. During challenging moments in my archival work, I sought refuge in the boxes of documents I had brought to my beachside condo in Rosarito. There, I meticulously examined *El Colono* newspaper page by page. After numerous visits to the Instituto de Investigaciones Históricas at the Universidad Autónoma de Baja California, Tijuana Campus, and extensive hours dedicated to digitizing archival documents there, I had a significant revelation. A substantial portion of the holdings had originated in other repositories, principally the Archivo General de la Nación (AGN) in Mexico City. While the Fulbright award allowed me to explore the often-overlooked westernmost region of the Mexican American borderlands, my evenings immersed in the pages of *El Colono* compelled me to return to Mexico City in the summer of 2015. The AGN held documents pertaining to some of Siliceo's other business activities, including his correspondence with the secretary of the Department of Development, Colonization, Industry, and Commerce (a department that had several names over the course of its existence).

Upon returning to the University of Houston (UH), I was fortunate to receive steadfast support from my academic department, college, and notably, the Center for Mexican American Studies (CMAS). This support extended to the organization of annual summer trips to Mexico and, later, the Philippines. In 2017, I received a Faculty Research Grant to research back-to-Mexico movements during the Porfiriato. This endeavor yielded significant findings at the Archivo Histórico de Relaciones Exteriores (AHSRE), particularly relating to repatriation requests. My time in the archives of various libraries in Mexico City, with a special focus on the Biblioteca Nacional at the Universidad Nacional Autónoma de México (UNAM), the Biblioteca Vasconcelos, and the Biblioteca Miguel Lerdo de Tejada, proved exceptionally rewarding. These hours and days were dedicated to meticulously collecting and organizing a substantial collection of memorias, bulletins, and annals from the Department of Development, Colonization, Industry, and Commerce.

During the quarantine period, my initial drafts and outlines gradually developed into rough chapters. I am grateful to the College of Liberal Arts and Social Sciences at UH for providing me with two book completion grants. These grants allowed me to engage the services of a proficient copyeditor, Daniel McNaughton of Paleograph Editing Services. His meticulous efforts were instrumental in refining and polishing the chapters, and I extend my deep appreciation for his invaluable contributions throughout this transformative process.

As I prepared a more refined but still incomplete monograph, I was in regular contact with Alberto Rodriguez, professor of history, director of the Mexican American Studies Institute at Texas A&M University, Kingsville, and co-editor with Tim Bowman of the New Directions in Tejano History series. I was intrigued by the editors' scholarly direction and the intellectual risks they were willing to take. I admire their choice of works and extend my heartfelt gratitude to them for embracing this project. Alberto kindly encouraged me to submit my monograph as the fifth installment in this esteemed series, and I owe him my sincere appreciation for his support and guidance during this endeavor.

Rodriguez and Bowman introduced me to Editorial Director Andrew Berzanskis and the exceptional team at the University of Oklahoma Press. After conducting thorough readings, Andrew provided valuable insights and suggested the title *Colonizing Ourselves*. I am grateful for his intellectual contributions, especially the title, which better encapsulates the essence of the study than the original title, *Soldiers of Progress*. As well, I would like to express my gratitude to Managing Editor Steven Baker, who diligently supervised the production process. Ben Folger, an editorial assistant who is currently pursuing a PhD in the Department of History at the University of Oklahoma, helped with the organization of the manuscript, including obtaining all the figures and permissions. Furthermore, I thank Kirsteen E. Anderson, who copyedited the monograph. Kirsteen's technical skills and extensive experience are evident in her copyediting work, and I was deeply impressed by her intellect, suggestions, and ability to distill vast amounts of information into concise sentences. Lastly, I am sincerely grateful to the two external reviewers for their kind words of encouragement regarding my work. Their feedback instilled in me faith and confidence that my research was both innovative and of historiographical significance. I have endeavored to incorporate all of their suggestions into the final manuscript.

I also express my deep gratitude to my academic colleagues for providing invaluable insights and suggestions during this project. Their recommended readings proved highly relevant. As part of my CMAS Faculty Grant requirements, I presented "The 1883 Land and Colonization Law: Race Science and Repatriation Policy in Nineteenth-Century Mexico" in February 2018. This lecture drew the attendance of several colleagues from the Department of History, including Philip Howard, Raul Ramos, Guadalupe San Miguel, and Richard Mizelle, who posed thought-provoking questions about Mexican American historiographies and the history of science and medicine in Mexico, leading to refinements in my book. However, it was a question about settler colonialism from Abdel Razzaq Takriti, the Arab-American Educational Foundation Chair in Modern Arab History, that particularly resonated with me. I promptly engaged with his recommendation to delve into Patrick Wolfe's extensive body of work. Not only was his suggestion highly pertinent, but the alignment of the settler colonial model with the internal colonial model, which I had scrutinized as an undergraduate in Mexican American Studies, persuaded me of the need to reexamine all of that literature with a fresh perspective.

I also want to acknowledge colleagues who attended the Annual Social Science History Association in Chicago in November 2019, where I presented an outline that contributed to this book. Special thanks to Juan "El Profe" Mora-Torres from DePaul University and John McKiernan González, now the Supple Professor of Southwestern Studies at Texas State University. Juan's mentorship has been invaluable over the years, and I hold his advice and professionalism in high regard. John's wise counsel to revisit the African American colonization of Tlahualilo was well received. Their advice, suggestions, and recommendations are reflected in both the narrative and footnotes of this work.

Both longstanding and newly formed friendships and connections played a pivotal role in sustaining my passion for this project. Above all, I owe a profound debt of gratitude to Professor Mihwa Choi, whose guidance was instrumental during moments of frustration and intellectual stagnation. Since our serendipitous encounter on New Year's Day in 2005, Mihwa has consistently challenged me intellectually, prodding me to refine my ideas. During one of our quarantine-era phone conversations she inquired casually about this ongoing project, pointedly offering valuable theoretical insights that dissipated my haze of frustration. In that moment I discerned a potential framework for this book, the following month I feverishly outlined it, then crudely penciled the first of the five sections. I extend my heartfelt thanks to Mihwa, my peach, for helping me crystallize these ideas.

Several close friends and fellow professors have also shared their insights, ideas, and reading suggestions. Ata Moharreri, of Lim College, former managing editor of the *Massachusetts Review*, continues to be a wellspring of intellectual curiosity and inspiration. Jaime Pensado, professor of history at Notre Dame University, has maintained a steady interest in the project, and our periodic exchanges have included discussions about our respective areas of research. Additionally, Alexey Golubev's insightful theoretical work in his book, *The Things of Life: Materiality in Late Soviet Russia* (2020), left an intellectual impact on me. Our occasional discussions—often accompanied by tacos, wine, and coffee—provided me with fresh insights into the realm of material history.

One of the most profound sources of motivation and intellectual curiosity about my research stemmed from my close friendship with Romina Robles Ruvalcalba, PhD (1983–2022). Romina's untimely and deeply disheartening passing left me with such profound feelings of anger and sorrow that I have been unable to find solace in tears since her death. Beyond her role as an exceptional intellectual and human being, she was a devoted mother, daughter, sister, and friend. Romina's presence graced our lives with joy, warmth, and a uniquely humorous sardonic wit. Romina's enthusiasm for my research not only kept me honest but also kindled my continued pursuit of this project.

In conclusion, I extend my sincere appreciation to several organizations and individuals who generously contributed to this work. The Hemeroteca Nacional at UNAM deserves special acknowledgment for granting me permission to publish several images from *El Colono*. Ana Krahmer, director of the Digital Newspaper Program at the University of North Texas Libraries, promptly granted me permission to use two images from the Portal to Texas History. Additionally, I express my deep gratitude to Carlos Uzcanga Gaona of the Museo Andrés Blaisten for his efficient assistance and for granting permission to feature Saturnino Herrán's masterpiece, "La Cosecha" (1909), on the cover of this book.

Lastly, I wish to convey my heartfelt thanks to my extended family in San Antonio, Texas, for their unwavering emotional support and understanding throughout the arduous journey of writing an academic book. I am aware that my relentless inquisitiveness may be challenging to put up with at times, so I am grateful for their patience and sense of humor, especially from my daughter Jessi Ylani Hernández. I love you, Mija, and thank you for always making me laugh. Warm embraces go out to my beloved sisters, Lucia Gabriela Hernández and María Guadalupe Hernández Tovar, whose boundless sense of humor, sarcasm, and zest for life have no limits. Their children have also inherited these qualities, and I am delighted by the moments we share as a family. "My special boy," Caesar Mendez, always brings laughter into my life and keeps me updated on all things related to jazz in Japan. Susanna and Luciano Tovar's intelligence and independence inspire confidence in their generation, and I cherish the time we spend together during the holidays. My brother, César Daniel Hernández, holds me accountable and continually challenges my political opinions. He has been my best friend since childhood and it is always fun to reminisce about growing up in San Antonio and having *huevos rancheros* every other Friday at Piedras Negras Cafe. His children, Zsofia and Zsolt Hernández, are following in their parents' footsteps and reaffirming my belief in their generation, particularly in their rejection of cellphones and all forms of social media. My parents, José Gabriel Hernández and Martha Antonia Hernández, who recently celebrated their fifty-sixth wedding anniversary, continue to motivate me, test my limits, make me laugh, and encourage me to embrace a positive outlook on life . . . to be a yes-sayer!

INTRODUCTION

Colonizing Ourselves examines the case of Luis Siliceo of San Antonio, Texas, from the 1890s up to the turn of the twentieth century. In 1895, the administration of Porfirio Díaz awarded Siliceo a colonization contract totaling one million hectares (2.47 million acres) to resettle "Mexico-Texano" families in several states of the republic.[1] In the same year Siliceo started a biweekly newspaper called *El Colono* that was subsidized by the Díaz administration. This partnership corroborates the Mexican government's direct involvement in the protection and resettlement of diasporic Mexicans to consolidate the country's northern frontier as well as to thwart increased Mexican migration to the United States.

A couple of years into Siliceo's colonization enterprise, the staff of *El Colono* assessed the "favorable probabilities" of their labors with a historical autocritique in an 1897 editorial.[2] What had started as a "first repatriation meeting in Texas on 12 April in front of a considerable number of Mexicans" had now become the "Mexican Colonization Enterprise."[3] The resettlement of "Mexico-Texanos" toward several frontier colonies had in turn influenced "simple European workers" to follow the same southward movement, including Germans, Spaniards, Swedes, Norwegians, and "a large number of Chickasaw Indian families." That edition of *El Colono* noted that there were "a total of 692 families willing to arrive at the end of the current year" and that the colony's director had already received "1,200 more petitions from Mexicans who wish to repatriate."[4] This was certainly not the first back-to-Mexico movement, but it did represent a pattern of Tejano resettlement beginning at the end of the Mexican-American War (1848).[5]

With two years of experience under their collective belt, the staff at the Mexican Colonization Enterprise had now explored every facet, procedure, and practice of the colonization process and felt confident in expressing their opinion that ethnic Mexicans were the preferred settler-colonists. Special treatment for these colonists was even ensconced in Article XVI of the 1883 Land and Colonization Law.[6] Siliceo skillfully employed this law, and his newspapers

MEXICAN COLONIZATION ENTERPRISE
LUIS SILIÇEO,
Concessionary.
Authorized by the Mexican Federal and State Governments, under contracts, to carry out properly the colonizAtion of
THOUSANDS OF ACRES OF SUPERIOR LANDS.
Large and small tracts for sale in all desirable sections of the Mexican Republic,
Fit for Coffee, Cocoa, Vanilla, Rubber, Cotton, Sugar-Cane, Cereals, Fruits and Vegetables of every description, at prices rangin from
$3 AGRE MEXICAN CURRENCY
Members of the following Nations are invited to colonize: Germany, Denmark, Norway, Belgium, Sweden, Holland, Spain, Ireland, Switzerland, Italy, Russia, France, Austria, Hungary, England and Scotland.
Excellent climate, plenty of rain, sure crops, near to populated towns, industries in their infancy, best inducements offered, titles guaranted
HEALTH AND MONEY, NO HUMBUG.
Send for a copy of the contract it you wish to be either investors, organizers or colonists.
And if this does not interest you, please send a word to your friends in the country which you may feel desireous to benefit thereby.
P. O. Box 54 Bis, City of Mexico. Mexico.
LUIS SILICEO, Concessionary

Advertisement for the Mexican Colonization Enterprise (1895). Luis Siliceo of San Antonio, Texas, was awarded 2.5 million acres of land in Mexico to resettle Tejano agricultural workers skilled in modern farming techniques. From *El Colono*. *Courtesy of the Hemeroteca Nacional de México, Universidad Nacional Autónoma de México.*

published details of the legislation—and his contract—numerous times during his editorship.

The staff of *El Colono*, though, went one step further in their interpretation of the law by declaring that their colonists were "superior" to all other "races" because of their enlightenment, cultural affinity, and experience living in the more modern United States. As stated in the newspaper's first issue, "The Mexican with whom the Government and our director is concerned is perhaps superior to any other race for the colonization of our soil because he is strong and resists the weather and changes of climate more than the Africans themselves."[7] In the late 1890s, such discussions about the "racial superiority" of particular groups over others were a common trope throughout Mexico, the United States, and the globe.[8] Accordingly, a capacity to thrive in harsh and inhospitable climates was filtered through a frontier social Darwinism that had become part and parcel of the daily discourse in the nineteenth-century borderlands public sphere.[9] This hierarchy of preferred colonists included not just ethnic Mexicans but Mexico's indigenous populations as well, in a practice commonly referred to as *autocolonización*, or autocolonization.[10]

Siliceo notably amplified this concept of self-colonization to include diasporic populations in the United States, particularly in his home state of Texas. In an April 1897 issue of *El Colono*, the staff noted the progress of two colonies that had already been resettled: Colonia Patria in the state of Tamaulipas and Colonia Zacapú in Michoacán. The latter report, subtitled "The Colonization of the Indians," recounted the recent "return of twenty families to the homeland." Here, the writers took the opportunity to criticize supporters of foreign colonization by republishing a proposed policy that neatly summarized their worldview: "Colonizing with repatriated families and with Indians should be the preferred work of the Secretary of this branch. If we are not constituted ourselves, we can hardly constitute the others"—others meaning everyone else.[11]

This opinion was not expressed in *El Colono* alone. Several newspapers throughout the country published similar views, showcasing the impressive capability and spread of new printing technologies.[12] "These ideas," the *Colono* staff went so far as to suggest, were "dominant within us" and "expanded by our director in some lines of collaboration that were published in *El Domingo* of Toluca in the previous week's issue." Here, the two papers were in agreement concerning the "persistently increasing tendency" of the "men of the government" to "bring to this Mexican land men of different races and from other populations, provided that these men are industrious and hardworking." However, noted the rebuttal in *El Colono*, "We have in the heart of the republic numerous tribes, the primitive settlers of this territory, who live as if they had no homeland and as if they were not capable of reaching the degrees of civility and culture that distinguish others, without a doubt, less fortunate."[13] Those behind the Mexican Colonization Enterprise believed that it would be more "humane" and "patriotic" to begin colonization efforts with the millions of "indígenas" who "live without bread and without a home" instead of relying on foreign immigration.

The genesis of *El Colono*'s line of thinking harkened back to earlier nineteenth-century debates between liberals, puros, and conservatives about whether the country should open its doors to foreign immigrants from Europe and Asia or should instead redistribute its citizens toward sparsely settled areas of the Mexican Republic.[14] In these earlier debates, permitting non-Catholic foreign immigration was rejected because of religious differences, but as the technological underpinning of the industrial revolution gave way to conventional provincialisms, these attitudes also shifted to align with the more authoritative language of the day; namely, "science."[15] It is notable that not only were discussions about the supposed superiority of one ethnic group over another given scientific authority, but even an activity as ancient as human colonization would be systematized and considered to have a scientific basis by the close of the century.[16]

Although an early supporter of foreign colonization, "Siliceo believed that the Mexican government's first duty was to create Indian colonies" and to imitate the colonization projects undertaken by José Vicente Villada, the governor of the state of Mexico.[17] Siliceo and his staff believed that in due time foreigners would settle in the country, but "let us at least do something for a race that some have tried to underestimate, to make their traditions of heroism, art, and civilization disappear." From their point of view, one need look no further than the archaeological sites of the "Tarascan," "Otomi," "Zapotec," and "Maya" peoples for evidence of their "supreme abnegation for the most difficult tasks." "Saving this race through stimulus and school education should be the desire of other governments as is already the case in the State of Mexico," they contended.[18] Believing that Mexican mestizaje was uniquely positive, many in the public sphere argued that the country was setting an example for the rest of the world to follow.[19] Here, Siliceo's Mexico-Texano colonists would serve the dual role of simultaneously improving the land as well as—by osmosis, the thinking went—the indigenous populations located in the vicinity.

In an era when settlers were proxies for potential economic growth, diasporic migrants were transformed into the very agents of "order and progress" in nineteenth-century Mexico. I argue that Mexico, like its northern neighbor, is a settler colonial state but the colonization process evolved in a unique way because of the country's growing diasporic population following the Mexican-American War (1846–48). Specifically, contemporaries described the Mexican colonization policies that were adopted and implemented as autocolonization. Unlike settler colonial states that relied on attracting millions of settlers from abroad, especially from Europe, Mexico received less than 1 percent of these nineteenth-century immigrants. This fact, coupled with the growing migration of farmers and laborers northward toward the United States, compelled various Mexican administrations to address labor emigration in numerous ways, culminating in the passage of the 1883 Land and Colonization Law. Part of its logic was to stymie migration across the international boundary by giving preferential treatment to any Mexican in the United States who was willing to return and resettle in the republic.

My historiographical approach to the concept of colonization from prehuman times up to the 1890s, when Siliceo negotiated his contract, unfolds broadly by narrating various global, national, and regional histories of colonization. From a planetary perspective, it becomes easier to appreciate Mexico's nineteenth-century consolidation of its autocolonization policy. Siliceo's back-to-Mexico movement opens a window into how politicians, bureaucrats, and Tejanos of that era argued for and against the benefits of settler colonization in Mexico.

Historiographical Approach

Autocolonization remained Mexico's colonization policy for the entirety of the nineteenth century, especially after the secessionist revolt of Texas in the late 1820s.[20] From 1846 to 1940, a period when as many as 160 million humans migrated across the planet, politicians and colonization "experts" debated how best to attract the multitudes arriving in the Western Hemisphere.[21] These migrations affected the social and political borders of every immigrant-receiving nation, including Mexico and the United States. However, after the proverbial dust settled, the various debates over colonization policy and practice overwhelmingly converged to autocolonization, even after the Mexican Revolution that began in 1911.[22] Autocolonization is exactly what it sounds like and was neatly summarized by Severiano Galicia in his 1893 presentation to the National Congress on Agriculture titled "Auto-Colonization in Mexico. Speech by Engineer Severiano Galicia, in Support of His Bill on the Colonization of the Unpopulated Lands of the Republic by the Mexicans Themselves."[23]

At the end of the nineteenth century, engineer José Covarrubias, the head of the First Section on Colonization in the Department of Development and Colonization, concluded his extensive study of global immigration and comparative settlements by highlighting autocolonization as follows: "It must always be borne in mind that *the nationals* will be the main element in the colonization of the new lands."[24] He termed these individuals *hijos del país*; that is, "sons of the nation." Building on decades of comparative study and historicizing the concept of colonization to the moment of Iberian-Mexican contact, he effectively confirmed the well-established Porfirian position on autocolonization in 1906. In the final paragraph of his study, Covarrubias defined the term in the following manner: "Colonization is the act of dividing land of positive agricultural and commercial value into lots and distributing those lots to capable settlers who come on their own initiative." In conclusion, he opined that the "idea of colonizing barren deserts with foreigners [should] be dispensed with; an idea that has been the obsession of governments and colonizing companies; notwithstanding the failures to which it has invariably led."[25] Where did this idea about colonizing deserted lands with foreigners come from? And why did Covarrubias, as the head of the First Section on Colonization, feel compelled to end his extensive study by emphasizing that "sons of the nation" were the most suitable colonists? How did diasporic Mexicans come to occupy preferential status among settlers in the text of the 1883 Land and Colonization Law? I believe that the autocolonization of Luis Siliceo's Mexico-Texano colonists provides us with some historical insights into these questions.

The notion of autocolonization may seem uncharacteristic in the world of settler colonial studies, yet it was predicated on all the basic assumptions of comparable settler colonial states.[26] Discussions of colonization in Mexico tend to immediately evoke the so-called colonial period (1521–1821), even though each of the major interpretations of this period often tells you more about the teller than the tale.[27] Lamentably, these interpretations of the past are frequently plotted alongside contemporary political positions that find it difficult to imagine collaboration, cooperation, and consolidation.[28] For instance, current historiographies of colonial Mexico question the periodization of the colonial period and even the notion that there was a conquest at all.[29] These diverging perspectives partly explain why some Chicano historians have described Mexican American history as one in which mestizos acted as the colonizer, the collaborator, and the colonized.[30] As Beth Saler has proposed for the United States, I too want to suggest that post-independence Mexico should be considered, first, as a "postcolonial republic, and second, concomitantly," as a "settler empire."[31]

As competing settler colonial nations throughout the nineteenth century, the United States and Mexico adopted a multiplicity of colonization-cum-settlement methods in an effort to control, direct, and ultimately capitalize on the migration of fifty-seven to sixty million Europeans to all parts of the Western Hemisphere.[32] By the end of the first period of mass immigration to the Western Hemisphere in 1930, Mexico had received less than 1 percent of all European immigrants and was more a "nation of emigrants" than what most settler colonial societies tend to be: a "nation of immigrants."[33] Many of these settlers were from the most industrialized nations of the period, and Mexican Científicos (Scientists) reasoned that such immigrants' expertise in agriculture, business, and modern industries offered the most desirable aspects of western modernity.[34] However, the existence of long-established Hispano families in the US Southwest, coupled with the increasing northward migration of Mexicans from the 1830s onward, narrowed the colonization debate toward the challenge of how to stem the departure of the Mexican population. In seeking to reverse this trend, various administrations sought to direct mass movements of humans toward Mexico's sparsely populated northern frontiers, which for generations had been natural targets for raiding by "indios bárbaros."[35] Prior to 1885, a substantial portion of what is today the US Southwest was actually contested and controlled by Amerindian empires, a fact that empirically contradicts binational interpretations focused exclusively on Mexico versus the United States.[36]

By 1880, Mexican politicians could no longer ignore the mass emigration of Mexican nationals to the United States.[37] The growing flight of young men and workers to another country undermined the Científicos' efforts to industrialize and modernize Mexico. For every foreigner who arrived in Mexico between 1821 and 1876, two Mexicans emigrated to the United States. This disparity continued to increase and, by 1880, the foreign population numbered between 25,000 and 35,000 while the number of Mexican migrants in the United States totaled 68,399. According to the 1910 US census, there were 221,915 Mexicans residing in the US Southwest; at the same time, a mere 116,527 foreign immigrants resided in Mexico, leaving a population deficit of 105,388. The fallout of the Mexican Revolution that began in 1911 increased the northward migration of Mexicans so considerably that by 1930 there were 1,422,533 Mexicans residing in the US Southwest. In other words, upward of 5.2 Mexicans left for the United States for every foreigner who came to Mexico.[38]

The fact that laborers were migrating northward while the administration was experimenting with foreign colonization struck both inside and outside observers in the late nineteenth century as a paradoxical policy. This is why a mere two years after Siliceo's contract with the Díaz administration, *El Colono* could state, "In our humble opinion, as we have already clearly expressed, the colonization of Mexicans who are returning to reclaim their homeland and that of those who inhabit it as nomadic tribes, without organization or incentive for work, as is the case with the unfortunate indigenous race, should be given preference over foreign colonization. This is what convenience dictates and what reclaims national identity. Asian or European colonists may come later, but first, we need to colonize ourselves."[39]

To legally complement what was taking place in the economic realm, the 1894 Law on Alienation and Occupation of Vacant Lands allowed foreigners and citizens of the republic to solicit lands for the purposes of colonization with no limits on "extensions."[40] This law slightly amended a few of the provisions in the 1883 Land and Colonization Law and opened colonization to a broader group of recruits, but it also expanded opportunities for abuse, which led to its repeal at the end of 1902.[41] Indirectly, the arrival of a handful of foreign colonists was enough to spur nationalist competition within the country and across the international boundary. The jurist and "intellectual precursor of the Mexican Revolution" Wistano Luis Orozco observed of the 1894 legislation, "With more reason, Mexicans residing abroad can ascertain and acquire such lands, especially if they keep their Mexican nationality in accordance with the law."[42] It was within this larger context that Siliceo negotiated an extensive contract to organize and relocate settler-colonists on some 2.5 million acres of land (about the area of Connecticut) in seven Mexican states.[43] *El Colono* regularly published big announcements and served as the mechanism for Siliceo and his staff to propound their theories on the "Art of Colonization."[44] Unsurprisingly for the era, and granted legitimacy by Siliceo's contract with the Díaz administration, these "theories of colonization" were given a scientific authentication that naturally veered toward the nationalistic and chauvinistic.

Historiographies of Settler Colonialism and Autocolonization

Settler colonialism can be defined as a "specific mode of domination where a community of exogenous settlers permanently displace to a new locale, eliminate or displace indigenous populations and sovereignties, and constitute an autonomous political body."[45] Unlike in countries like Australia, in Mexico "elimination" was not encoded in policy, since the cyclic battles between "indios bárbaros" versus "indios civilizados" and "indios bravos" continued throughout the nineteenth century. Even when the state could have eliminated rebellious indigenous groups, captives were usually shipped off to labor camps of one sort or another because their toil and submission was preferable to summary liquidation. Generally speaking, acculturation and assimilation remained the modus operandi of Mexican regimes, but efforts to Mexicanize indigenous populations would later come to include diasporic populations in the United States.[46]

When the Dirección de Colonización, or Department of Colonization, was established in 1846, its executive actions in the service of state formation were essentially the same as directives that had been outlined and published in previous decrees, circulars, regulations, and laws.[47] Article 45 of the Regulation of 4 December 1846 for the Department of Colonization set forth the establishment of military colonies of Mexicans, foreigners, or both, on government-designated borders to prevent "barbarian invasions." The Department of Colonization was to grant these settlers land at no cost in exchange for this service.[48] In both the extensive annals of Australian settler colonialism and the early history of Mexico, even prisoners and vagabonds were regarded as potential settler-colonists—a strategic way for the state to transform a "social problem" into a valuable asset for nation building.[49] For example, the Projects of Colonization of 5 July 1848 suggested that colonies should "advantageously substitute for the correction system in the best prisons, and in our circumstances a great problem is solved, thus providing for the integrity of the territory." This defense against the "barbarian Indians" would in turn "purge the devouring woodworm from the heart of the republic that tears it apart."[50] In both of these examples, the deployment of settler-colonists along the northern frontier was intended to make legible those populations that had refused to accept colonial domination and preferred nomadic to sedentary lifeways.[51] It was the land of these "nomadic tribes" that the staff of *El Colono* sought to possess when they suggested "the colonization of Mexicans who return to recover the soil of the homeland" be given preference over foreigners and all other settler-colonists.[52]

By colonizing the deserts and frontiers, and in many cases, rancherias and traditional nomadic hunting grounds, the state's impulse toward civilization attempted a variable "logic of elimination" that sought to assimilate these populations into the larger body politic through force, coercion, or tribute.[53] Although an official state ideology of mestizaje may seem to contradict Patrick Wolfe's theoretical architecture, a generation before the writings of settler colonialism became commonplace, the anthropologist Guillermo Bonfil Batalla had articulated something quite similar when he referred to these "logics of elimination" as "ethnocide" or "de-Indianization." In his words, "De-Indianization has been achieved when, ideologically, the population stops considering itself Indian, even though the lifeway may continue much as before. Such communities are non-Indian without knowing that they are Indian."[54] Bonfil Batalla was effectively criticizing the state's ideology of mestizaje while recognizing that a profound Mesoamerican culture and civilization lay at the core of contemporary Mexican identity.[55]

While the Mexican government's ultimate goal—territoriality and the consolidation of the state—was political, assimilation into a more disciplined mestizo identity, a social outcome, was a hoped-for by-product of this forced colonization.[56] "When settlers claim land," the historian Lorenzo Veracini points out, "it is recurrently in the context of a language that refers to 'higher use,' and assimilation policies are recurrently designed to 'uplift,' 'elevate,' and 'raise' indigenous communities."[57] It was these uplifting tropes of "salvation" and "higher civilization" that masked the logic of corporate colonization companies pursuing "order and progress"—the mantra of the Científico classes. That said, settler colonialism, as scholars in the field have noted, is a complex process that does not unfold in exactly the same manner in every settler society.[58] While the case of Mexico is comparable to those of like-minded settler societies, it is unique in its practice of recruiting its diasporic populations abroad, including those ethnic populations fully acculturated into a competing settler society. The impulse to reincorporate diasporic populations into the larger body politic is reminiscent of earlier Mesoamerican, and then Iberian, efforts at absorbing indigenous populations from the sixteenth through nineteenth centuries.[59]

The issue of colonialism, and therefore colonization in general, has been the subject of much historiographical dispute for centuries.[60] Within this historiography, the investigation of settler colonialism is a recent development, yet it has an extensive pedigree derived from well-worn concepts. Given the similarity of settler colonialism to previous theoretical models such as internal colonialism or the internal colony model, some readers may be familiar with the arguments if not with the Mexican government's extensive efforts at colonizing its diasporic populations in the United States.[61] For instance, Mexico's Department of Colonization is never discussed or referenced in the literature on internal colonialism or the internal colonial model, a fact that strikes me as important to consider empirically.[62] Throughout its many manifestations until 1911, the Department of Colonization actively encouraged, recruited, and subsidized the relocation—and yes, colonization—of thousands of diasporic Mexicans who had resided in the United States since at least the 1830s.[63]

Today, settler colonial theory is considered a phenomenon not restricted to the "colonial period" but rather extending well into the modern era in a multitude of different forms, including contemporary gentrification and attempts to colonize exoplanets.[64] One of the best-known proponents of the theory is the anthropologist Patrick Wolfe, whose 2006 article "Settler Colonialism and the Elimination of the Native" set forth a particular and comparative outline of the elementary features of settler colonialism.[65] His work is today considered foundational to the field of settler colonial studies and also has a growing share of critics.[66] Wolfe argues that "settler colonialism was foundational to modernity" and not merely an "event" of the bygone colonial era. To his way of thinking, there are both negative and positive aspects of Australian settler colonialism, but the ultimate "logic of settler colonization" is to *eliminate* the so-called natives. The logic of the Australian case is obviously not applicable to most of Mexican history, but geographical considerations are important to consider before drawing any concrete conclusions, particularly in terms of the periodization of colonization.[67]

But what does "elimination" mean in a society that has embraced its indigenous and whose population shares significant amounts of Amerindian DNA?[68] The nation-state of Mexico was named after one of the Mesoamerican hegemons of the Central Valley, and mestizaje has been the official state ideology for two centuries. By contrast, the name "Australia" comes from the Latin *Terra Australis* (Southern Land), and the nation still maintains a symbolic relationship with the British monarchy while the nature of Mexico's relations with various Iberian royals depends on the political party in power.[69] For Wolfe, "elimination refers to more than the summary liquidation of indigenous people, though it includes that. In its positive aspect, the logic of elimination marks a return whereby the native repressed continues to structure settler colonial society. It is both as complex social formation and as continuity through time that I term settler colonization *a structure rather than an event*, and it is on this basis that I shall consider its relationship to genocide."[70] Responding to ongoing criticism, Wolfe would later clarify that what he was particularly interested in were "the multifarious procedures whereby settler-colonial societies have sought to eliminate the problem of indigenous heteronomy through the biocultural assimilation of indigenous peoples."[71]

Although Wolfe does not mention Mexico in his publications, his framework resembles the analysis and historical conjectures of much of eighteenth- and nineteenth-century Mexican frontier history, particularly as various indigenous, European, Catholic, and later Mexican officials sought to settle and pacify the northern deserts through a variety of colonization schemes. As Wolfe observes about other case studies, settler-colonists will usually adopt indigenous identities to make a stronger claim to the land, but routine tendencies to "go native" are also well recorded in the historiography.[72]

The cooperation and collaboration between states and their frontier settlers share a similar trajectory in several global contexts when they are analyzed in the context of settler colonial societies. Even so, the various forms of settler colonization that evolved in the northern frontiers of the Mexican Republic coincide more closely with Wolfe's theories than do the varied forms of settlement that developed in the central or southern regions of the country.[73] *Indigenismo* took root in the latter regions and metamorphosed into what Mauricio Tenorio Trillo has referred to as "Porfirian indigenism."[74] In this sense, the regional comparisons between southern, central, and northern Mexico can be best appreciated through Wolfe's observation that "frontier individuals' endless appeals for state protection . . . presupposed a commonality between the private and official realms."[75] In light of the distance between Mexico City and far-flung desert provinces such as Chihuahua, Sonora, or Coahuila, the coordination necessary for logistical, material, and administrative support was paramount for state consolidation. And, of course, both settler-colonists and state bureaucrats actively sought to build upon these commonalities via laws, decrees, and contracts.[76] Frontier resettlement is usually a shambolic process, but eventually it benefits the colonizer, the colonization contractor, and the autocolonized.[77]

In contrast to Tasmania or Australia, the mestizo state that emerged over the centuries melded western European economic and legal structures with Mesoamerican political and sociocultural modalities. Borrowing a phrase from the French sociologist Pierre Bourdieu, I suggest that the eventful meeting between Iberians and Mexicans in 1521 and their collaboration in subsequent invasions and colonizations of the territory constituted a *structure structured upon a pre-existing structure.*[78] Colonization for the following three centuries was essentially an assemblage of the two preexisting human traditions that gradually metamorphosed into a synthesis of conflict, cooperation, and reconciliation.

After independence in 1821, the evolving mestizo consensus converted, as Guillermo Prieto famously said, the "Mexicans into the *gachupines* of the Indians."[79] This trope was repeated a century later by the sociologist and jurist Pablo González Casanova when he made the radical claim that "with direct disappearance of the domination of the natives by the foreigner appears the notion of the domination and exploitation of the natives by the natives." Casanova went even further in his critique, suggesting that "the 'indigenista' and liberal literature of the nineteenth century indicates the replacement of the domination of the Spanish with that of the 'Creoles,' and in fact, the exploitation of indigenous people continues having the same characteristics as in the era prior to independence."[80] Given the historicity of these ideas, such observations are tantamount to presentist virtue signaling, particularly considering the fact that contemporary historians continue to question the idea, periodization, and nomenclature of a "colonial period."[81] As the state monopolized "the legitimate use of physical force" over its territory during the Porfiriato, a more romantic view of the post-independence era was literally grounded in the nationalist retellings of state-sponsored historiography as enshrined in national monuments.[82] As General Díaz was about to start his second term as president, the publication of *México a través de los siglos* (1883–90) highlighted a new species of "Porfirian indigenism" by building a "conciliatory bridge between the conflicted present and the several pasts of the nation for the first time."[83]

Following the Mexican-American War, a particularly fierce episode in the continual struggle for continental supremacy, Mexicans who now found themselves on the US side of the international boundary became the ideal, modern, and loyal settler-colonists to collaborate in this nationalist colonization project.[84] By the dawn of the Porfiriato, the idea that "Mexico-Texanos" were the "ideal colonists" to pacify the northern frontiers had become a common theme in the "Greater Mexico" press and hence a constituent factor in the longer history of frontier colonization.[85]

Summary of Chapters

To organize this narrative from the global to the granular, I have divided this book into five sections—totaling fourteen chapters—that appreciate the historicity of colonization but also its evolution into a species of corporate colonization in the late nineteenth century. My chronological methodology is akin to a set of Matryoshka nesting dolls whereby the largest dolls represent the global perspective while the smaller dolls variously signify the national, regional, and local points of view. I endeavor to historicize and thus contextualize how colonization evolved and changed over time as the nation-state closed its grip upon the frontiers and peoples of the republic. The nineteenth-century consolidation of the US and Mexican nation-states are always in the process of becoming, and the expansion and retraction of frontiers betwixt and between Comanche and Apache empires was not a foregone conclusion.[86] By historicizing colonization from macro to micro points of view, I hope to show how colonization evolved in hominid history first, then in national history, then in regional history, and finally in a particular case of autocolonization at the close of the nineteenth century sponsored by Luis Siliceo—one of dozens of back-to-Mexico movements that materialized throughout the nineteenth century.[87]

Such an extensive corpus of historical material requires an approach to historical interpretation that consistently engages with historiographical analysis, as suggested by Ranajit Guha—that is, to write history historiographically.[88] Methodologically, the periodization influences the source base as the narrative moves from studies on archaeogenetics to statistical data built from Mexican declaration forms at the close of the nineteenth century. Given the lengthy literature on the subject, the sections are necessarily succinct and representative of larger patterns that reveal the insights of simple historicizing. Since I am a historian by training, the narrative is chronological but also thematic. As someone that teaches historiography and philosophies of history, I understand and teach that historical narratives are evolving, but there is still consensus, and future research is both expected and necessary.[89] The epilogue will bring all these scripts, ideas, and historical observations together to summarize my main thesis that Mexico is a settler colonial state whose principal characteristic is its policy of autocolonization. While most settler colonial states attracted foreign immigrants from Europe or Asia, the competition for labor and settler-colonists along the Mexico-US international boundary initiated and modified Mexican colonization policy to attract its growing diaspora in the United States.[90] All contemporary nation-states are effectively settler colonial states, and this monograph is my individual take on the subject, based largely on my own research interests and observations as a Mexicanist.[91]

In keeping with my organization scheme, the first part ponders the history of human settlement from a global perspective through a general approach to the issue of colonization.[92] Chapter 1 necessarily paints world history with broad strokes because I historicize the concept of colonization as simple human settlements that "move into and live in (a place) as a new type of plant or animal."[93] The "out of Africa" theory of human migration maintains that our hominin ancestors were migrating, settling, and effectively colonizing the entire planet beginning at least 300,000 years ago.[94] Given the rather extensive periodization of this narrative, the chapters are general in nature and mostly follow the prevailing assimilationist model of human emergence.[95] In that vein, I summarize some recent studies in archaeogenetics to illustrate how colonization, constituted simply as human settlement, has been a feature of Hominidae evolution since time immemorial and is more ancient than tool making.[96]

Recent studies of ancient DNA (deoxyribonucleic acid) have also confirmed that there were so many sexual encounters between various hominin relatives that modern-day *Homo sapiens* carry significant percentages of Neanderthal, Denisovan, and several other unidentified hominins whose genomes have yet to be sequenced.[97] Seemingly every month another academic paper is published revealing new ghost populations, new fossils, and even new species of hominins, so that I am led to suggest that our own species is more akin to a *Homo colonus mixticius* (mixed settler man). All *Homo sapiens* are in essence colonizers, the products of colonization, or at least the offspring of "settler-colonists" long passed. In the memorable words of Friedrich Nietzsche, "for since we happen to be the results of earlier generations we are also the results of their aberrations, passions and errors, even crimes; it is not possible quite to free oneself from this chain."[98]

To bring the argument closer to a continental perspective, I then analyze the variations of human mixture on the Iberian Peninsula before 1492 along with recent studies on population history in Mesoamerica for the same period. Several recent studies of ancient DNA help illuminate how deep-seated these ethnic mixtures were before European and Mesoamerican peoples discovered each other's worlds in the sixteenth century. When Old World and New World civilizations encountered each other, their shared history of mestizaje created the "Mesoamerican conquistador," a new figure in world history.[99] This is the figure in colonial Mexican history who eventually broke through the ancient Mesoamerican geographies with horses and firearms and began to pacify and colonize the northern frontiers of the new global empire.[100] Mexican independence in 1821 meant that formerly Spanish territorial claims across the continent required the presence and protection of a new settler colonial state, placing Mexico on a collision course with its growing neighbor to the north. These historical processes and contingencies culminated in the Mexican-American War in 1846 and the formation of a federal-level colonization agency charged solely with organizing, settling, and militarizing the frontiers of the fractured Mexican nation.

Chapters 3 through 5 in part 2 compile more than two decades of research on the various manifestations of the Dirección de Colonización (Department of Colonization) through analysis of a series of colonization laws, decrees, and studies between 1846 and 1911 as the department evolved to target ethnic Mexicans in the United States. The "colonization" of Mexico, I suggest, did not necessarily end with independence in 1821, but continued intermittently for the remainder of the nineteenth and into the twentieth centuries.[101] Colonization would take on even more urgency after 1836, when Tejano and Euro-American colonists in Texas rebelled against central rule and petitioned the US Congress for annexation, which was granted in 1845. The formation of the Department of Colonization during a foreign war a year later in 1846 underscored the importance to the Mexican government of having a single agency charged with this important task.[102]

Due to a variety of circumstances, including civil wars, Amerindian raiding, administrative disorder, foreign debts, unsurveyed lands, and industries that could provide employment, most Asian and European immigrants opted to settle in countries with relatively stable and robust economies such as Argentina, Cuba, Australia, Uruguay, South Africa, New Zealand, and especially the United States. By offering grants of land, these emerging former colonies converted immigrants into settler-colonists, thus displacing and diminishing the indigenous populations.[103] In the absence of immigrants from abroad, the most viable options for the burgeoning Mexican state were its diasporic populations now located in territories ceded to the United States and a handful of Amerindian groups considered to be "civilized tribes." Settler colonial–style colonization emerged during the latter half of the nineteenth century and culminated in more than sixty official colonies, yet Siliceo's enterprise is notably absent from the government's official statistics.[104] In this way, autocolonización was the ultimate consensus throughout the century, and I characterize the repatriation of these diasporic populations as a species of "resettler colonization."

After a survey of the national context, I begin part 3 by examining the story of Luis Siliceo of San Antonio, Texas, and his colonization contract with the administration of General Porfirio Díaz, signed in 1895. Chapters 6–8 deal with various aspects of Siliceo's contract with the Díaz administration and provide some background to the many diasporic debates in various Mexican and Mexican American newspapers. I examine the process of negotiating a colonization contract, the debates in the Greater Mexico public sphere over repatriation and resettlement, and the formation of what I call "folk sociology," a set of unscientific popular beliefs based on personal bias, hearsay, gossip, rumor, and generalizations.[105] Historical research is contingent upon the archival record, but oftentimes the latter modifies the initial research question. In this case, the location of several drafts of Siliceo's colonization contract open a rare window into the hard-nosed negotiation tactics of the Científico bureaucracy. Although all government contracts were published in many venues and newspapers, it is rare to find series of handwritten drafts of proposed colonization contracts during this era—and unpacking these primary documents reveals much about the morality (i.e., hierarchy of values) of the colonizer and contracting agent.[106]

While the historical record is never comprehensive, the Siliceo contract file holds at least three separate handwritten drafts of the contract, with renegotiations and rewording of legalese continuing well into 1898. Siliceo and the Díaz administration engaged in an ongoing struggle for the upper hand in each round of the negotiations. Siliceo's successful negotiation of this contract enabled him to potentially resettle colonists on upwards of one million hectares in several states throughout the Mexican Republic. This amount of land, then as today, is a staggering expanse of terrain. Siliceo parlayed this contract into multiple business opportunities related to resettlement. The views of his resettlement project ran the gamut from positive to negative on both sides of the international boundary, but Siliceo was not without his victories. Always the propagandist, he took the opportunity to meet with some newspapermen, persuading them to report that his high-quality settlers of "hard-working, moralized families, educated in the hard school of ostracism" would bring great benefits to any community that received them.[107]

Part 4 (chapters 9–11) deals with the history and content of Siliceo's main weapon of propaganda, his newspaper *El Colono.* An almost complete set of issues is held at the Universidad Nacional Autónoma de México (UNAM), providing ample primary and secondary material to analyze the goals of this paper and how its staff sought to realize them. Unlike any other colonization agent of this era, Siliceo was able to negotiate a subsidy of five hundred pesos per month from the Díaz administration to publish this bimonthly newspaper, which he did consistently until the end of his contract in May 1900. *El Colono* looked to project a positive image of Mexico to appeal to the broader audience of "immigrating races" who were settling across the globe. A minor part of Siliceo's logic was that if Mexico-Texanos were to resettle in Mexico proper, this would in turn stimulate the immigration to Mexico of German colonists, who were considered to be industrious, morally upright, and easily assimilated. To combat some of the negative press circulating in other outlets, *El Colono* ran a monthly feature titled "La repatriación," which gave a nationalist spin to resettlement and supplied updates on the groups of families who had returned to Mexico under Siliceo's direction. The final section of part 4 examines the formation, structure, and mutual-aid aspects of forty Uniones Fraternales de Repatriación.

Finally, part 5, "Meeting Siliceo's Settler-Colonists," focuses on the granular details of declaration forms archived in Siliceo's file and condenses my global approach to a very particular case study. Although these documents cannot recover the intimate biography of each settler-colonist, in chapters 12 through 14 I summarize statistical findings based on them. The discovery, transcription, translation, and quantification of such a rich set of documentation have never been presented in any historiography of Mexican colonization. The records provide a glimpse into the occupational status, age, gender, and place of birth of each settler who returned under Siliceo's resettlement project. The 239 separate declaration forms record, in both Spanish and English, the name, age, civil status, sex, place of birth, and level of literacy of 877 individuals. The many possibilities for analysis have compelled me to limit my discussion to a few trends and tendencies: (1) typical characteristics of the declarations; (2) characteristics of a typical settler-colonist; and (3) material possessions, livestock, tools, and machinery.

Most of the declarants were born in Mexico, but their spouses and children generally were not. Many of these adult male declarants were from northern and central Mexico, regions that have a prominent history of outmigration. All settlers in the sample were "agricultores" who owned their animals, tools, machinery, and equipment. This finding empirically contradicts one of the main disputes in the Greater Mexico press, which disparaged the kind and quality of settlers returning to Mexico and questioned whether they should be allowed into the country. Most of these settlers were married with children, and from the declarations, they returned with their household possessions and animals. Joining these families were hundreds of companion species, especially fowl, equines, and bovines. Trains were the major form of human transportation in the nineteenth century, so not unexpectedly, almost five hundred equines and bovines traveled with these migrants as they resettled southward. These companion species were important sources of protein and raw materials but were also needed to pull cars, carriages, carts, plows, farming implements, and other agricultural machines. The last chapter of this section examines this material history in light of the literature on technology transfer during the Porfiriato while also supplying the most granular data on these Mexico-Texano settler-colonists.

In the epilogue I summarize the book and share a few conclusions about Mexico's political project of mestizaje. Mexico has historically imagined itself as a mestizo nation, but nations are not static for all time and all of history. It seems that early in the nineteenth century, at least some Mexican liberals argued that the newly independent nation should become a "nation of immigrants" in the mold of its neighbors to the north and south.[108] As might be expected, the events of 1836 and the subsequent Mexican-American War effectively destroyed that political trajectory and forever shifted the diplomatic relations between the two settler colonial states.[109] The mass migration of laborers to the United States during the Mexican-American War and the gold rush in California the following year initiated a human flow that continues unabated to this day.[110] From then on, Mexico would evolve into a "nation of emigrants."[111] The multiplicity of narratives has obscured the long history of migration to the United States and the Mexican government's concerted efforts to modify its land policies in order to attract these migrant workers and expatriates back to their home country. The history of resettlement in Mexico not only helps us to understand these interwoven processes, but it also highlights the role of the state in managing mass movements of people.

Mostly for political reasons, contemporary Eurocentric and liberal perspectives continue to focus on the emigration of Mexicans and Central Americans to the United States without considering basic structural circular migration patterns that have existed for almost two centuries. The 1883 Land and Colonization Law was one effort to direct the tide of northward population movements toward sparsely settled areas of the republic, thus converting a "social problem" into a useful tool for state formation.[112] Modern-day nations have shown that with appropriate standards and guidelines, the effective relocation of once-diasporic populations can produce geopolitical results with planetary implications.[113] My findings highlight historical lessons to be learned for the contemporary conundrums of global mass migrations, expulsions, deportations, and resettlements.

PART I

COLONIZATION IN HUMAN, CONTINENTAL, AND MEXICAN HISTORY

CHAPTER 1

MESOAMERICAN AND IBERIAN COLONIZATIONS

The migration of *Homo erectus* from Africa to Europe, the Middle East, and Asia occurred about 1.7 million years ago, and in light of this fact, I propose that colonization is older than the modern-day human species.[1] Hominid migrations and settlement are as old as bipedalism. Colonization, meaning the spread, migration, and development of an organism into inhabited or uninhabited settlements, has been a feature of human evolution from time immemorial.[2]

Homo colonus mixticius

Because our bipedal human ancestors could walk long distances, they migrated and settled all over the planet, an activity that continues unabated today.[3] Early hominid colonization resulted in contact among various Hominidae and eventually contributed genetic material to our own species.[4] *Homo sapiens* are akin to a species of "mestizo hominin," one that has clearly inherited the genetic material of several now-extinct ancestors.[5] Physical anthropologist Chris Stringer of the Natural History Museum, London, agrees when he states:

> I think that what we call *Homo sapiens* today is a kind of an amalgamation of different lineages in different parts of Africa that at times were evolving separately, and other times when the climates allowed it, they spread and they met and mixed and they exchange genes and ideas. So, we get a kind of complex web of interactions in Africa. . . . Some of these populations become extinct when the climate turns against them, others carry on. And so, we finally get a merging of these groups in the last 100,000 years to become *Homo sapiens* as we know it today.[6]

That we humans are here today is due to the steady migration, settlement, and colonization of the planet by our ancestors.[7]

Given that *Homo sapiens* has been mixing and remixing for millennia before the existence of anything resembling a nation-state, it should come as no surprise that current studies of contemporary human populations reveal similar patterns of mixing.[8] Hominidae relations with other species of hominids, like migration and colonization itself, are a central feature of human history.[9] We will probably never know why our ancient hominin ancestors became extinct or why many of us share such significant amounts of our own DNA with them. I suspect the process was complicated, as it still is today. Are the archaeological sites that we see today, strewn with stone tools and bone shards, the locations of hominin habitation and settlement or the remnants of some prehistoric crime scene, the site where hominids butchered and ate each other?

A millennium before 1492, the Christian colonization of the Iberian Peninsula came about as an accident of empire building in which ethnic mixtures created an Iberian mestizaje.[10] But centuries before the arrival of Roman soldiers in Hispania, several Greek colonies had already been established on the peninsula.[11] Preceding the Greek colonies were those of the Phoenicians, and before that there were Celtic colonists.[12] These studies, moreover, reveal "that by the Roman period, Southern Iberia had experienced a major influx of North African ancestry, probably related to the well-known mobility patterns during the Roman Empire, or to the earlier Phoenician-Punic presences."[13] One could be forgiven for assuming that much of this admixture was due to the eighth-century colonizations by North African Berbers who had recently converted to Islam. But genome-wide data from 271 ancient Iberians "reveal sporadic contacts between Iberia and North Africa by ~2500 BCE, and by ~2000 BCE, the replacement of 40% of Iberia's ancestry and nearly 100% of its Y-chromosomes by people with Steppe ancestry."[14] In sum, the Iberian Peninsula has a long multiethnic history, and recent studies in archaeogenetics suggest that Iberians share higher levels of admixture with North Africans than do their European cousins.[15]

The varied forms of what I am calling "ancient mestizaje" are the norm, and as David Reich reminds us, "present-day populations are blends of past populations, which were blends themselves."[16] Similar processes took place across the globe in the Western Hemisphere. The peopling of the Western Hemisphere thirty-three thousand years ago was an act of human settlement and therefore colonization.[17] Ancient Siberians "traveled onto a land bridge" that linked Asia and North America, then "mated with East Asians" and created "another genetically distinct group" whom researchers have named "Ancient Paleo-Siberians."[18] David Reich observes that at least four prehistoric migrations to Latin America from Asia have been confirmed, and recent DNA research among Amazonian peoples suggests that there were other migrations and peoples yet to be discovered.[19] In other words, there are "ghost populations" of now-extinct hominids.[20] "The Suruí and some of their neighbors in Amazonia," argues Reich, "harbor some ancestry from a different founding population of the Americas, whose ancestors arrived at a time and along a route we still do not understand."[21] What is undeniable is that the *Homo sapiens* who migrated from Siberia to the Americas were of mixed ancestry before, during, and after their initial migrations.

In due course, the various waves of migration into the Western Hemisphere created an array of ethnic groups, hundreds of languages, and perhaps thousands of tribal groups.[22] The genetic, cultural, and linguistic mixing, unmixing, and remixing of these assemblages produced empires and writing systems that emerged and reconstituted themselves in accordance with their own historical traditions.[23] Although Mexico retains sixty-eight distinct indigenous languages, the "rise and demise" of the Maya, Zapotec, Nahuatl, Mixtec, and Toltec Empires are still frequent areas of study among Mexicanists.[24] In 1428, the expanding Mexica-Aztec Empire forged a "triple alliance" with competing rivals, which reinforced a structure where each new monarch expanded their territory in order to extract more tribute and cement their own imperial legacy through conquest and colonization.[25] Frances F. Berdán and Michael E. Smith maintain that "these processes were neither new nor unusual in Mesoamerican prehistory; however, the Aztecs did develop the imperial scheme on an unprecedented scale."[26] Numerous Chichimec tribes presented barriers to Mexica-Aztec expansion for centuries, but Chichimec migrations also replenished the population of the expanding empire.[27] As political scientist James C. Scott observes, "recognition of the barbarians as an earlier, but not irremediably different people led, in principle, to the assumption that they were capable of eventually becoming fully civilized."[28] Thus, the fact that the Chichimec were historically portrayed as barbarians appears to be an Iberian imposition, a holdover from their own colonial experiences under Roman rule and, before that, Hellenic hegemony.[29]

These Mesoamerican and western civilizations had more in common with each other than previously thought, including similar understandings of blood, expansion, and colonization.[30] The arrival and subsequent alliance of Iberian and Nahuatl conquistadors, however, began a century-long process of colonization into northern deserts that had historically shielded the Chichimec distant cousins of the Nahua peoples.[31] Mesoamerican traditions of colonization and incorporation merged with Iberian colonization practices during the sixteenth century, and this deadly assemblage would persist with some modifications until the early twentieth century under the pretext of legibility in the service of state formation.[32] Although these two civilizations developed in distinct parts of the globe, with different views of the world and understandings of human history, they had more in common than not. The resemblances are further demonstrated in their shared understandings of military colonization and expansion, as the following pages will make clear.[33]

From Conquistadors to Chicanos: Conflict and Confluence in Colonization Historiographies

Histories of colonization and colonialism in Mexico have traditionally been told from the perspective of an Iberian imposition that began with the arrival of Hernán Cortés in 1519 and lasted approximately three centuries until 1821.[34] The usual, and now state-sponsored, history of "Mexican Independence" in 1821 can be described as postcolonial "history from below"—one which challenged an empire for its liberation from *gachupin* tyranny and oppression.[35] The reasons for this Manichaean perspective of the past are Mexico's nationalist historiography coupled with antiquarian Eurocentric binaries that cast bygone epochs as struggles between civilization and barbarism.[36] Nonetheless, Jaime Rodríguez reminds us that "many erroneously believe that the Spanish monarchy was highly centralized, confuse absolute with autocratic rule, and equate the modern concept of colony with pre-nineteenth-century governing practices."[37] The years that follow that singularly significant event are then divided into historical episodes in which the newly independent nation is invaded anew and civil wars threaten to dissolve the republic into a dialectical chaos.[38] But when these historical narratives are filtered through the prism of Matt S. Meier and Feliciano Ribera's "Chicano perspective," the population in the ceded territories of Mexico is transformed from "conquistadors to Chicanos"; that is, from the colonizer to the colonized.[39] This interpretation of Mexican history obscures while simultaneously revealing past colonizations as instances of active collaboration in a long and complicated historical process. Certainly, these shifting interpretations constitute one of many challenges to state-sponsored historiographies.

Christian Duverger, chair of social and cultural anthropology of Mesoamerica at the Ecole des Hautes Etudes en Sciences Sociales, has recently chimed in on similar historiographical debates by claiming that Hernán Cortés was a proponent of Mexican mestizaje.[40] Criticizing Mexico's state-sponsored historical narratives, he suggests that "the idea of an official history is a monolithic history . . . more than an official history there was an ideology."[41] This point of view, according to Duverger, has ignored how Cortés came to embrace an indigenous view of mestizaje when he purportedly stated, "I am in favor of mestizaje and I want to have mestizo offspring."[42] Duverger's biographies of Cortés, and especially his *El primer mestizaje: la clave para entender el pasado Mesoamericano* (2007), essentially plot the narrative of Mexican history as a mutual mestizaje. Duverger suggests that contemporary Mexicans should embrace a mutual (Mesoamerican and Iberian) mestizo identity in place of the contemporary tropes of the "Black Legend," which occasionally rear their head during state-sponsored historical commemorations.[43]

The historiographical debates concerning conquest and colonization in Mexico shift over time and have come to include diasporic arguments that challenge state-sponsored periodizations. Gregory Rodriguez notes correctly that the initiation of Spanish contact should be dated to 1511 rather than 1519 because the former date is both more historically accurate and changes the dynamics of the event.[44] Based on historical documentation, Rodriguez suggests that the Iberians first encountered the Maya, which is more sensitive to the historical temporalities of that era than the monumental meeting between the Iberians and Mexica-Aztecs in Tenochtitlan eight years later.[45] It is worth remembering that Iberians had explored the Caribbean for twenty-seven years (1492–1519) before Cortés and his men reconnoitered the Yucatán Peninsula and met heavy resistance from the Maya. Some of these initial contacts, as Christopher Columbus discovered on his fourth and final voyage in 1502, did not turn out well for the European explorers and certainly did not make for a "monumental history" of chivalry, bravado, and glorious conquest.[46] In the case of 1511, Spanish contact with the Maya led to a shipwreck and the subsequent capture, enslavement, fattening, sacrifice, and some cannibalization of the survivors.[47] The "ambivalent conquest" of this Maya region continued sporadically for four centuries, and the initial dilemma of two shipwrecked Spaniards from an earlier 1511 expedition provides Rodriguez with an interesting microcosm with which to craft his counternarrative of early Iberian experiences with Yucatec Maya groups.[48]

Challenging the periodization of Mexico's national narrative necessarily also entails questioning the usual tropes of contact, conflict, and confluence in the history of colonization.[49] The "official story" is well known to every school-age child in Mexico today, and a version of it is included in most textbooks assigned in US colleges and universities as well.[50] When Cortés sailed west from Cuba in February 1519, his voyage was the third expedition to reach Yucatán and he knew of at least two surviving Spaniards who had escaped the obsidian blade: Gonzalo Guerrero and Jerónimo de Aguilar, OFM. The latter was a slave of the Maya chief Zamanzana while the former was now married to the "daughter of Na Chan Can, a Mayan nobleman."[51] Although a common sailor, Guerrero had acculturated and consequently "married up" into the Maya nobility, had "tattooed his face and body," and had pierced his ears. In other words, he had "gone native."[52] When Guerrero was asked to return with the Iberians, he refused and conveyed in brotherly terms, "I am married and have three children, and they look at me as Cacique here, and a captain in time of war." Pointing to his children, he lovingly declared, "now look at my three children, how beautiful they are!" These precious children are the first mestizos of Mexico, and it is this narrative and periodization a few years before the fall of Tenochtitlan that Rodriguez believes historians should reconsider. In light of this obvious oversight, Rodriguez suggests that historians should reorient their periodization to appreciate the historical temporality while simultaneously reimagining a more positive historical narrative that is life-affirming in place of the selective periodicity of the state.[53]

Yet whatever periodization one opts to privilege, this five hundred–year admixture "among Amerindians, Europeans, and Africans, principally, has come to shape the present-day gene pool of Mexicans, particularly Mestizos." This ethnic group currently represents about 93% of the total Mexican population, and regional differences among these communities are correlated with some elements of regional settler colonization.[54] As David Reich explains, mixing "defines national identity" in Mexico.[55] Historiographical debates over contact, conflict, and subsequent colonization should take into account the multiplicity of conflicting narratives, including the struggles fought between Iberians themselves, the competition for souls amongst Catholic orders, rivalries between monarchs and explorers, fights among members of ships' crews, and all combinations thereof.[56] The "failed" Iberian explorations throughout the Western Hemisphere are only a microcosm of the many battles these early explorers endured, to say nothing of the indigenous resistance they met with.[57] Ongoing studies within the field of archaeogenetics promise to complexify and enrich our perspectives on the past, and any historiography of this period should at least attempt to acknowledge these nuances.[58] One need not agree with all of these varying interpretations, but to acknowledge them is the first step in understanding the historical context in which they emerged.

Founding Colonies: The Mesoamerican Conquistador

Certainly, among the many similarities Mexicans and Iberians shared was their common experience with collaboration, conquest, and colonization.[59] The mestizo state that emerged from these instances of cooperation and conflict combined two governmentalities, Western European economic and legal structures with Mesoamerican political and sociocultural modalities of the Western Hemisphere.[60] Both civilizations shared several practices and particularities that Mexicanists have attributed to the urbanization of sophisticated civilizations, even suggesting that "in many ways, the Europeans and indigenous peoples of the central areas had more in common than either did with the other peoples of the hemisphere."[61] Thus, one can reason that the history of colonization in Mexico is a "structure rather than an event"; however, this "logic of elimination" adopted more of a "logic of coerced Mexicanization" with the aim to acculturate a majority indigenous population following the battle of Tenochtitlan in 1521.[62]

I agree that this encounter created the "Mesoamerican conquistador," a new figure in world history.[63] The primary reason Iberian conquistadors and their ecclesiastical companions survived and thrived was due to alliances with various indigenous groups, in particular the Tlaxcalans, who fought together with the Iberians to settle and colonize vast swaths of the northern frontier.[64] Doctor José Eleuterio González, physician, botanist, politician, philanthropist, and author of numerous monographs, noted that the "first conquistadors of the New Kingdom of Nuevo León . . . were both Spaniard and Tlaxcalan."[65] Appropriating the title of conquistador for themselves, native Mesoamericans constituted the vast majority of participants in the *entradas*, which metamorphosed into a political structure "grafted together from Iberian and Indigenous ones. . . . [Hence] Tlaxcalans were both cultural intermediaries between Europeans and other Indians and the authors of their own political systems."[66]

Following the military collapse of Tenochtitlan, indigenous and Iberian conquistadors set off to pacify and colonize Guatemala from 1524 to 1542 and "there [were] reports of native groups traveling as far south as El Salvador and as far north as Santa Fe, New Mexico," as well as by sea to Cuba, Honduras, Peru, the Philippines, and the Dominican Republic.[67] Laura Matthew's research leads her to argue that a "conservative estimate, then, would be that 10,000–12,000 warriors from central and southern Mexico participated in various invasions of Central America, oftentimes accompanied or followed by their families and friends."[68] These expansionist impulses did not end after 1821, but rather continued throughout the nineteenth century, only this time implemented by the new mestizo rulers.[69]

While the number of towns established by Tlaxcalans remains a topic of considerable debate, five original colonies are officially commemorated.[70] Tlaxcalans were vital allies in the initial subjugation of peoples outside the core of Nahuatl civilization; their access to Iberian military technology and horses enabled them to establish colonies in Guatemala, El Salvador, and several mining regions in New Spain, including Texas and as far north as Alta California.[71] These settlements combined the functions of garrison, mission, town, and presidio and were soon widely distributed throughout the northern frontiers.[72] In the words of Andrea Martínez Baracs, the Tlaxcalans, unlike other indigenous nations, "considered themselves conquerors as opposed to conquered."[73] So, when the Tlaxcalans celebrated their founding in Nuevo León of a colony upon the lands of the Guachichil Indians in 1768, the descendants of these colonizers justified their actions as a civilizing mission that would instruct the "indios bárbaros" to "be industrious and live in order and Christianity in the way of life of the Tlaxcalans."[74]

These patterns, argues Martínez Baracs and most ethnohistorians studying the indigenous colonies, were merely "a pre-Hispanic expansionist practice, promoted by the colonial power as a strategy of conquest after the fall of Tenochtitlan."[75] As these Tlaxcalan conquistadors expanded their range, they were joined by Cholulteca, Mexica-Azteca, Tarasco, Huejotzinga, and Otomí peoples, who also migrated north and expanded outside their original provinces.[76] These northward entradas had their counterparts in a southern direction as well, and scholars are now concluding that these moments of alliance were not instances of subjugation but a "gathering of two military forces who both sought advancement."[77] Given the demographic history of that era, the fact that much of this colonization process was accomplished with indigenous colonists and militias should come as little surprise. Indeed, settlement via colonization would come to include "immigrant Indians" from the United States in the decades following independence and throughout the twentieth century.[78]

Colonization of the northern desert regions with indigenous allies and migrant Indians followed a similar pattern of consolidation that aligned with an administrative solidification in other parts of the Spanish Empire, including possessions across the Pacific Ocean. Just three years before the Tlaxcalans celebrated their monumental founding of five colonies, 336 Mexican convicts sailed for Manila in what Eva Maria Mehl has described as a "process of convict transportation and military recruitment" in the "Spanish Pacific World." This little-known but significant history, according to Mehl, saw colonial Mexican authorities transport upwards of four thousand veterans, soldiers, criminals, deserters, and undesirables to garrisons in the Philippines in order to settle the most distant boundary of Spain's empire.[79] Whereas in the histories of the Tlaxcalan and indigenous colonizations of the northern frontiers of Mexico, the indios bárbaros were colonized so that they could learn from the Tlaxcalans to be industrious Christians, in the Philippines, Mexican soldiers, veterans, convicts, and undesirables were sent to fight "indios bravos," and thus further the "Mexicanization—or New Hispanization—of the Philippines." In both cases, these forced migrations and subsequent colonizations "suggest . . . that metropolitan and colonial officials conceived of the remote Philippines as an extension of the Mexican world."[80]

In this chapter I propose that human settlement, and therefore colonization, is a common feature of our humanity and is older than our modern-day species. Hominid migrations are as old as bipedalism. These movements produced contact with other hominids and a mestizo *Homo sapiens* who—depending on each human's own individual ancestry—carries DNA from long-lost ancestors like Denisovans and Neanderthals, to name only the species that we have been able to identify and whose genome has been sequenced. Every fruitful civilization on the planet has engaged in some form of military, religious, or economic expansion that invariably led to a species of colonization. To illustrate this observation, I described how colonization took place in Mesoamerica and on the Iberian Peninsula independently before 1492. These two civilizations had more in common with each other than previously thought, with similar understandings of blood, expansion, and colonization being just a few of their shared concepts. The resemblances are further proven in their shared understandings of military colonization and expansion.

This was followed by an analysis of the colonization of the geographical space of New Spain during the colonial period, first by questioning the periodization and narrative of the "conquest" of Mexico. Both Mexican and Mexican American historians have questioned the "conquest narrative" and offered different periodizations and interpretations of a past that have been coopted by state-sponsored narratives. The meeting between Maya, Nahuatl, and Iberian peoples in the early sixteenth century opened a global opportunity for a process that had been taking place since time immemorial—the making of mestizaje. The contact, conflict, and later confluence of two large empires—Iberian and Mesoamerican—created a formidable assemblage that together made significant advances into geographical areas that until then had successfully resisted Mexica-Aztec expansion. In short, I want to suggest that the assemblage of Iberian traditions of colonization combined with Mesoamerican modalities during the sixteenth century to form a deadly "war machine" in the service of the new state.[81] This encounter created the "Mesoamerican conquistador." Tlaxcalan conquistadors were joined by Cholulteca, Mexica-Aztec, Tarasco, Huejotzinga, Chichimeca, and Otomí peoples, to name only a few. Historicizing the formation of the first Tlaxcalan and Iberian colonies along the northern frontiers of the empire demonstrates how cooperation between Mesoamericans and Iberians and adoption of Iberian technologies and equines led to establishment of the first permanent colonies of the new empire. From 1550 to 1848, approximately two hundred presidios emerged along the frontiers of "New Spain" and later Mexico. These outposts evolved from modest garrisons into a distinctive form of military colonization, consistently supported by mestizo and indigenous allies. The next chapter springboards from these observations to examine colonization as it developed after 1821 in the newly formed Mexican Empire.

CHAPTER 2

MEXICAN COLONIZATION

Assembling and Disassembling the Nation

When Mexico gained independence from Spain in 1821, several significant issues remained unresolved with the conclusion of hostilities, including pending cases with respect to ongoing colonization efforts along the northern frontiers.[1] Recognizing the potential threats posed by competing American, French, Russian, Comanche, Yaqui, and Apache empires, Spanish and Mexican officials responded with strategic plans to fortify the realm's frontiers.[2] Efforts to grant lands for colonization were well under way for generations before independence, efforts which can be measured in the number of concessions made to potential colonizers.[3] Each grant to a settler-colonist came with instructions regarding the surveying and allocating of the land and recording of the transaction. Hence, in 1767 when "settlers in the colonies founded by José de Escandón in South Texas" were granted a "Spanish royal commission," the appointed commissioners "were instructed to survey the various settlements and jurisdictions, to distribute the land to individual settlers, and record all transactions." Furthermore, the crown asked that the division of land be based on "merit and seniority" so that the colonists would be divided into "three categories: original, old, and recent settlers."[4]

Mexican Colonization after Independence—A Settler Colonial Empire

Before independence in 1821 the Spanish government had awarded colonization contracts in the Texas, New Mexico, and California territories.[5] However, the number of land grants during the Mexican period (1821–48) greatly surpassed these previous efforts, reflecting the urgency of the moment.[6] Tomás Almaguer notes that in California "more than seven hundred such grants, each of up to eleven square leagues (approximately 49,000 acres), were issued by the Mexican government between 1833 and the American occupation in 1846."[7] From 1821 until 1835, "forty-one empresario grants were made" in Texas, with the majority going to "emigrants from the United States."[8] In New Mexico, thirty-nine empresario land contracts were awarded between 1821 and 1853, and they were much larger than those in Texas—in a few cases measuring a million acres.[9] The difference between New Mexico and California on the one hand, and Texas on the other, was that during the 1820s and early 1830s no colonization contracts were given to foreigners in the former whereas in the latter foreigners received a majority of the empresario grants.[10] This preceding tally does not include the grants awarded by state officials, such as those in Tamaulipas, who "also sought to encourage colonization of its vacant lands through the colonization law of 1825"—a signal of the continuing tension between states and Mexico City.[11] The constitutional and legislative struggles between federalists and centralists was even more pronounced in mid-nineteenth-century Mexico than in the present, as these two camps often further subdivided along the lines of political persuasion: in this case, liberals, moderates, and conservatives.[12]

Liberals, conservatives, and moderates also did not see eye to eye in their approach to the question of immigration-cum-colonization.[13] In contrast to the sporadic, chaotic landings of millions of Europeans in large cities such as New York City or Buenos Aires, the process of immigration was better managed in Mexico, due primarily to the rather insignificant number of foreigners who made their way to the country after 1821. Hence, one could argue that colonization was logistically more sophisticated in Mexico and usually entailed heavy state surveillance in the form of inspectors' reports.[14] Mexican liberals (federalists) wanted to attract more European immigration because some believed that acculturation and contact with industralized nations would "uplift" the indigenes and infuse "new blood" into the body politic.[15] Catholic-minded conservatives (centralists), on the other hand, believed that the "national interest required that population growth come from within by protecting the Indian, not further alienating him."[16] The ultimate goal of both camps was that European immigrants-cum-settler-colonists would eventually be assimilated into the larger mass of Mexican society as Mesoamericans had been previously.[17] So, irrespective of political party or masonic lodge, all seemingly agreed that the end goal was comprehensive Mexicanization via the colonization of all immigrants, both foreign and domestic. The only question that remained was what kind of settler-colonists each of the growing factions preferred. Autocolonization was the one policy that every faction universally agreed upon because it entailed resettling ethnic Mexicans and so-called indios in strategic locations along the frontiers, thereby lessening the threat of secessionist movements.[18]

Histories and legal documents concerning what constituted a "Mexican" usually began and ended with an acknowledgment of "El Indio" as the foundation of the Mexican Empire, particularly in the context of debates over European immigration following independence.[19] Historian Jorge Chávez Chávez suggests that to transform Mexico into a westernized democracy, government officials undertook a series of measures that he summarizes as follows:

> To achieve these goals, they had to implement a series of political actions, among which the following stood out: imposing a new type of education on them, where they would be taught new cultural values and forget their own; promoting foreign colonization to achieve biological and cultural mestizaje; subjecting them and even exterminating them through armed repression if they resisted in a drastic manner (such as rebellion or insurrection) to the new colonization. All of this with the sole purpose of making the indigenous people abandon their various cultural identities, created and re-created during the colonial period, and incorporating them into another, the Mexican one.[20]

The "new" Mexican identity that Chávez outlines should be modified to include an analysis of autocolonization from below—one that considers indigenous peoples, native sons, and eventually ethnic Mexicans abroad.[21] Foreign colonists, for instance, were subject to the same process of Mexicanization throughout the entirety of the century. The handful of European immigrants who arrived in Mexico were contractually compelled to adopt the cultural values of the new nation and were given special privileges if they agreed to "mix with Mexican families" and marry "Mexican women," a practice dating back to the early sixteenth century.[22] In light of some of these factors, compounded by the establishment and multiple restructurings of the Department of Colonization, it seems more practical to propose that post-independence Mexico "was a postcolonial republic, and second, concomitantly, that it was a settler empire."[23]

Autocolonization as Colonization Policy: Amerindian Diasporas in Mexico

Settler colonization policy and practice throughout this period (1821–46) expanded to incorporate a number of Amerindian groups from the United States such as the "Five Civilized Tribes," who were being relocated by a series of Indian removal acts.[24] While European immigrants were arriving daily on the eastern seaboard of the United States, the sons and daughters of earlier settlers were moving westward onto the traditional lands of numerous indigenous communities.[25] A number of these displaced groups eventually made their way southward to Mexico and petitioned that government for lands.[26] Early on, various Mexican administrations seized on opportunities presented by the movements of "migrant Indians"—a practice that continued until the turn of the next century.[27] In the words of Gilles Deleuze and Félix Guattari, "the constitution of a military institution or an army necessarily implies a territorialisation of the war machine, in other words, the granting of land ("colonial" or domestic), which can take very diverse forms."[28] One of the many forms that colonization policy acquired in the aftermath of the Texas rebellion was the incorporation of displaced groups ("immigrant Indians") from outside Mexico into the "war machine" through an expanded version of autocolonization.

An extended survey of Cherokee history is beyond the scope of this chapter, but in many ways, their chronicle is reminiscent of Florescano's diaspora model, where a larger group is "destroyed by internal conflict," which in turn leads to "another migration cycle."[29] The Cherokees had occupied parts of Pennsylvania, Alabama, Georgia, Tennessee, Virginia, and the Carolinas in the sixteenth century until internal and external processes forced them westward across the Mississippi River by the early nineteenth century.[30] In 1811, the Chickamauga Cherokees, along with other Cherokee, Delaware, Creek, and Choctaw groups, were living in Arkansas in an area known as Lost Prairie; this group migrated to Texas by 1819, drawn by the "hunting sojourns to the buffalo prairie of the Brazos River region."[31] Archaeologist Christopher Rodning observes that after two centuries of this migration cycle, a "linguistic blending" coupled with an "overlapping of social structures" created "an identifiable Cherokee identity" that was composed of "multiethnic congeries."[32] In time, the settlement of Cherokees would come to incorporate other "refugee Indians, including Shawnees, Delawares, Kickapoos, Choctaws, Biloxis, Alabamas, Coushattas," and other Cherokee bands.[33]

Several of these different factions were being swayed by an "increasingly influential generation of 'mixed-blood' Western-educated Cherokee leaders" who would shape the "future of Cherokee politics."[34] Chief John Bowles (Duwali, or Bold Hunter) was the leader of one such faction.[35] "The Bowl," as he was known, was born in North Carolina around 1756, the son of a Scottish-Irish trader and a Cherokee mother.[36] Chief Bowles succeeded Dragging Canoe as the town chief in 1792 and eventually became the leader of the Chickamauga Cherokees. When Bowles and the Chickamauga Cherokees arrived in what is today Dallas in 1819–20, the "prairie Indians . . . forced them to settle near Nacogdoches" in East Texas.[37] To formally secure these lands, Bowles and the newly elected Chief Richard Fields traveled to San Antonio in the fall of 1822 to meet with José Félix Trespalacios, governor of the Province of Texas. With the transition from an imperial to an independent Mexican nation under way, Trespalacios signed a provisional treaty with the Chickamauga Cherokees that would allow the leaders to make their case "before His Imperial Majesty." About half a dozen Cherokee warriors accompanied Fields and Bowles to Saltillo, where Governor Trespalacios had enthusiastically "dispatched an officer with the original copy of the agreement" to give to the "Commandant of the Eastern Internal Provinces."[38]

Once in Mexico City, the Chickamauga Cherokee delegation (along with several other empresarios) witnessed the overthrow of Agustín de Iturbide and, later, the installment of a triumvirate of generals. The coup against Iturbide less than in a year into his reign placed colonization concessions in question for the Cherokees. The Mexican government would eventually pass the National Colonization Law on 18 August 1824, while Texas and Coahuila passed a colonization law on 25 March 1825, but neither of these laws included the Cherokees.[39] This state of legal limbo continued until 1833, when Chief Bowles and his coterie were offered lands farther north in an area "selected strategically to defend Texas against the Comanches."[40] The offer was rejected, and two years later the region would be embroiled in a war with Santa Anna and his mostly conscripted Mexican army.

The military alliance with the Chickamauga Cherokees was so important during the wars between Texas and Mexico that the fifty-four delegates who met at San Felipe de Austin in November 1835 unanimously adopted a "solemn declaration" at the core of which was "their just claims to lands" for which they had petitioned the Mexican government. These lands were to be protected and the Cherokees were declared "just owners of the soil."[41] The agreement kept the peace between the various factions until the treaty was sent to the Texas senate the following year and relegated to a committee for further study. At year's end, the agreement was declared "null and void," even as rumors swirled that Mexican agents had visited the Cherokees promising lands, arms, and ammunition "if the Americans were driven out."[42] The Texas senate reasoned that "the provisional government had exceeded its powers in negotiating the Treaty, which was not only detrimental to the Republic of Texas, but also violated the legal rights of many citizens."[43]

In a period when loyalties could shift by the month, much of the angst can be attributed to rumors that Cherokees were plotting with Mexicans to overthrow the nascent Texas government.[44] These allegations were confirmed in July 1838 when an intercepted letter from Vicente Córdova to Manuel Flores, a Mexican Indian agent, was found to "[hold] a commission from General Vicente Filosola to raise the Indians as auxiliaries to the National Army."[45] With Sam Houston out of the Texas presidency, the Cherokees no longer had their main supporter, and the new executive wasted little time in sending troops to their territory and forcing their expulsion from the state. These events led to the final Cherokee war in Texas and the death of Chief Bowles on 16 July 1839; at the age of eighty-three he was killed with a gunshot to the head. Bowles's wife and children were taken hostage and "the captured Cherokees were eventually sent to Indian Territory, while others fled to Louisiana and Mexico."[46] The remaining Cherokees who made it to Mexico "settled in a village near the small town of San Fernando" in the state of Coahuila.[47]

The history of the Chickamauga Cherokees in Mexico proper (yet to be written) is connected to national and state efforts to settle the country's frontiers in the interest of military security. In August 1840, General Manuel Arista "heard rumors that Cherokees and other tribes were massing at the headwaters of the Brazos" and sent messages promising "arms and ammunition to assist in the recovery of their lands." It was later recounted that "eighty Cherokee warriors were reportedly traveling" with Córdova between San Antonio and Matamoros, perhaps in response to Arista's promises.[48] The number of Cherokees who settled in the town of San Fernando de Rosas is unknown, and it is likely that some also could have settled in the colonies of Muzquiz or El Remolino in Coahuila.[49] All of these locations continued to receive a number of Amerindian groups until the close of the century, as numerous requests for resettlement testify.[50]

Historicizing Texas Colonization: Primary Discourses of Settler Colonization

The history of colonization in Mexico is essentially the history of state formation, or to use the words of Prussian philosopher G. W. F. Hegel, a "record of its own development."[51] This is to say that the "production and circulation" of these "first histories" generated by Mexican officials were "both necessarily contingent on reasons of State" and for the dissemination of its accomplishments.[52] Because government officials charged with the task of "development, colonization, industry, and commerce" used nationalist historiography to justify frontier settlement, this effectively became the narrative that subsequent historians reproduced and reinterpreted.[53] Interpretations of the past regularly shift, and historiographies surrounding the colonization of Texas are controversial because of contemporary culture wars partly generated by state efforts to impose particular narratives of the past.[54] Some in the Secretaría de Fomento believed that a failure to effectively colonize Texas had led to the current debacle and that more aggressive settler colonization was required to forestall claims to land by competing settler colonial empires. Thus, the interpretations and debates over colonization among the highest-ranking representatives of the state were also historiographical in nature, affecting both contemporaneous colonization policy and secondary and tertiary historiographical interpretations thereafter.[55]

Writing a decade after the Mexican-American War, the minister of the Secretaría de Estado y del Despacho de Relaciones Interiores y Esteriores José María Lafragua attributed the "Texas fiasco" to a lack of settler-colonists and to larger structural forces beyond the control of any nation-state. In the decrees establishing the Department of Colonization, Lafragua historicized the reasons why colonization was "fundamental for the enlargement and prosperity of the Republic." Lamenting that poorly written colonization laws had enabled colonists in Texas to take advantage of a misguided Mexican policy, Lafragua wrote,

> Laws have been enacted one after another regarding this matter, and contracts for the establishment of colonies have been made, but to no effect or results. The only one that was established and thrived is the one that revolted in Texas because the intent behind its establishment was not an economic or commercial enterprise, but the usurpation of our territory, taking advantage of the youthful innocence with which the Republic welcomed all foreign nations in the early days of its independent existence. This fact demonstrates that the colonization laws were inadequate.[56]

Lafragua's experience during the war with the United States served as a real-time demonstration of the inadequacy of earlier colonization laws in terms of population growth and prevention of usurpation. Over time, all versions of a nation's history, even those preserved within the "primary discourse" of state archives, evolve based on the prevailing political, economic, and social conditions. Historical narratology emerged as a discursive tool to rationalize the implementation of new colonization laws aimed at avoiding the errors of the past.[57] The war with the United States, as Luis G. Cuevas sardonically observed, "did little more than draw back the veil that covered the eyes of those who hoped that the disorderly public administration and the corrupt organization of our army would not hinder a defense made according to the rules of the art [of war] nor inspire despair in the good servants of the nation."[58] In this clash between two settler colonial states, the events of Texas marked a watershed for shifting colonization policy inwards.

After the Mexican-American War, agency officials charged with colonization of the republic recast the events in Texas in terms of realpolitik, which necessarily meant portraying earlier colonization laws and achievements as failures. Thus, in his report to the Mexican Congress a decade later, the first minister of development, colonization, industry, and commerce, Manuel Siliceo, cites the example of Texas (in the 1830s) as a rationale for excluding foreign immigrants (in the 1850s) until Mexico's borders were secured and well fortified.[59] Considering these past precedents, Siliceo's historical exercise and explanation of logistically practical military planning is worth considering:

> In view of these disastrous results, there will be no shortage of those who believe that the introduction of foreigners to populate our vacant lands jeopardizes the security of the nation, and indeed, this will always be the case if the same lack of foresight that characterized the colonization of that Department is followed. At that time, the immense distance separating it from the center of the Republic was not taken into account, nor its proximity to a major power that had previously expressed its desire to incorporate it into its territory, for which it only had to reach out, while the Mexican government, to prevent it, had to traverse hundreds of leagues, many of them desolate, and lacked the resources to sustain an army.[60]

According to Siliceo's practical analysis, the cession of Texas was due primarily to logistical difficulties related to demographics and ongoing struggles between rival settler colonial states. The lengthy distance of this colonization project from the center of the republic inadvertently facilitated the settlement the territory by a neighboring competitor that had merely to "extend its hand" to the colonists while Mexico "had to cross a few hundred leagues, largely deserted, and without resources to sustain an army." Colonization policy is thus narrated in terms of concrete details such as military strategy in place of Lafragua's anthropomorphic characterization of "youthful innocence."[61]

"How Not to Colonize": Correcting the Mistakes of Past Colonization Policy

Manuel Siliceo's suggestion that inviting Anglos to settle and colonize Texas merely facilitated the imperial ambitions of the United States is illuminating as military history. Siliceo's historical interpretation in 1857 is much more sophisticated than the nationalist trope of manifest destiny that emanates from twenty-first century history departments.[62] Instead of a straightforward narrative, Siliceo provides a thought-provoking perspective on US westward settler colonization. According to Siliceo, this expansion was intricately tied to and, perhaps unintentionally, aided by Mexican colonization policy. In essence, Mexico's colonization strategy found itself subverted by its northern neighbor, which sought to assert ownership over the very settler colonies that were once part of Mexico. The minister of development noted that due to the impracticality of Mexico's colonization policy,

> As a result of this, when citizens of the United States were admitted as settlers in Texas, nothing more was done than to extend their territory, lacking only an express declaration that it rightfully belonged to them, as they already possessed it in fact. Their nationals occupied it while retaining their customs, language, and relationships without any modification, due to the absence of a Mexican population that could have neutralized the tendencies to unite the colonies with the country from which they had originated, and from which they were only separated by a river.[63]

Thus, in Siliceo's opinion, Mexican colonization policy inadvertently facilitated US westward settlement, which led to Mexican land loss instead of fortification of the nation's northern boundaries. Viewed from this historical perspective, the settlement of Texas and today's American Southwest was more contingent than manifest, particularly when hindered by neighboring indigenous empires in the regions then known as Apachería and Comanchería.[64]

Most modern interpretations of the Mexican-American War continue to be nationalist in the sense that Mexico and the United States are the only nation-states discussed while the Amerindian empires and nations are ignored, even though they continued to stand betwixt and between the two hegemons throughout the nineteenth century.[65] These empires influenced the future of the neighboring nation-states and continually disrupted their consolidation. As both the United States and Mexico looked to fortify their frontiers with settler-colonists, the former nation incorporated what was a Tejano "runaway republic" in 1845—nine years after rebelling against Mexican centralization, including botched efforts to reconquer the territory.[66] Most historians today would agree with Siliceo's assessment that "the consequences of this lack of foresight were known too late."[67]

Although retracing some well-trodden chronologies, Siliceo's *memoria* does offer public policy measures grounded in historical analysis. Siliceo notes three particularities that should have been considered and which accurately predict the line of argumentation that would continue into the 1890s. First, the concession of uncultivated lands without having previously demarcated and measured them. Second, the lack of government resources to assist with the first steps of establishing the colonies. Third, the state of perpetual revolution in which, with short intervals, the Mexican Republic found itself in.[68] Earlier reports on colonization in Mexico had deliberated upon these observations, including in the commentaries offered by the early Department of Colonization (1846–52), which can be summarized as another request for surveys, subsidies, and stability.[69]

In a nutshell, Siliceo articulated not only the problems of previous colonization attempts, but also the obstacles to effective colonization in the present and for the next generation.[70] Not only were his recommendations incorporated into future colonization law, but his critique of the ongoing power struggles foretold the social conflict that would eventually consume him and the nation for another decade. Governmental instability and political factionalism were so commonplace after independence that Siliceo's own annual report fell victim to a civil war just a few months later. On 17 December 1857, only two months after the publication of the memoria, General Félix María Zuloaga launched a successful coup against the liberal government of Ignacio Comonfort, setting off the so-called Wars of Reform, which would last several years.[71]

In this chapter, I examine colonization policy and law spanning from the post-independence era to the eve of the Mexican-American War. The tumultuous wars of independence in Mexico exacted a heavy human toll, surpassing that of any other region in Latin America. During this period, colonization emerged as the principal strategy for fortifying the frontiers of the nascent republic against both the expanding United States and indigenous empires. To populate the sparsely inhabited northern frontier regions, policies were enacted to encourage settlement by Mexican nationals, settlers from the country's interior, and foreign immigrants, including those from the United States. A number of these concessions eventually led to a revolt of Texas colonists in 1836 and to the annexation of that territory by the US Congress a mere nine years later. Mexican colonization policy accommodated itself to the shifting borders and boundaries of the 1830s to the 1850s, contracting colonization arrangements with several expelled Amerindian groups. A number of these diasporic groups were escaping the inhospitable social climate created by Democratic President Andrew Jackson's Indian Removal Acts.[72] These realities, coupled with the war a few years later, radically shifted colonization policy in Mexico and led to the creation of the Department of Colonization, charged with organizing, implementing, and expanding the national territory with settler-colonists. The creation, amalgamation, and reorganization of that agency from initial discussions in the 1830s up to 1911 will be the focus of part 2.

PART II

DEPARTMENT OF COLONIZATION, 1846–1911

CHAPTER 3

AUTOCATALYTIC COLONIZATION AS STATE FORMATION

Some Legal and Material Structures

Attempts to reconquer Texas from 1837 until it was annexed by the US Congress in 1845 only fueled antagonisms between the two settler colonial states of Mexico and the United States. Fears of *reconquista* stoked violence and a number of expulsions from Texas.[1] The ominous clouds of territorial loss were looming on the horizon, obliging the Mexican government to implement a coherent colonization policy to prevent additional encroachment on the country's claimed lands.[2]

Colonization as Collateral: Prewar State Formation

Following the series of events leading to the Texas Revolt of 1836, Mexico used the territories now comprising the US states of Texas, New Mexico, Utah, Arizona, California, and Nevada as collateral to obtain loans from British investors. These funds were sought to settle foreign debts accumulated since achieving independence. Concerned about potential annexation by the United States through coercive or deceptive means, the Mexican government issued bonds against the worth of the northern frontier. Simultaneously, a third party was incorporated into the geopolitical maneuverings. As the economist Richard Salvucci has observed about this particular stratagem, "If British bondholders took legal possession of lands in Texas, then the British government would be placed, in one way or another, in the position of guaranteeing Mexican sovereignty over Texas in the course of safeguarding its national claims to land title."[3]

General Juan Almonte, who was sent to Texas two years before the revolt, in 1834, to conduct an inspection and prepare a "secret report" on the territory, seemingly agreed with these later arrangements, stating "the consequences of this measure will be immense: with it we prevent Texas from carrying out its independence because we will have created an interest against it."[4] Thus, Mexico effectively placed a lien on all of its "vacant lands." In Salvucci's succinct assessment, "the 'tract' of land under consideration as security for the bondholders would become the 'disputed' boundary between Mexico and the United States, the ostensible casus belli in 1846."[5]

Almost a year after the US Congress annexed Texas as the twenty-eighth state, the Department of Colonization was established in Mexico by the Decree of 27 November 1846.[6] The noted Mexican historian Moisés González Navarro points out that two months prior to the implementation of this decree, a commission had been formed to discuss the formation of a colonization agency.[7] This commission convened on 18 August 1846 but for "various reasons" nothing came of it. Perhaps the outbreak of war precluded any policy recommendations from being issued by the commission, yet the report of the inaugural minister of the Department of Colonization also highlighted importance of attracting young immigrant soldiers who could easily be turned to military advantage.[8] As in the case of the Chickamauga Cherokees, the minister proposed that promises of land and concessions could be offered as compensation to potential citizen-soldiers in the service of state formation.

Later juntas charged with colonization looked to recruit European immigrants to fight alongside Mexican nationals during the war in order to "dismember the invading army." General Mariano Arista proposed giving 320 acres of "good lands" to any soldier willing to desert the US military, especially Irish Catholics.[9] Religious differences between Protestants and Catholics continued to permeate public debates over colonization policy, and a religious kinship with Irish immigrants was understandable.[10] The idea was to simultaneously recruit soldiers among Europeans who would "populate the invaded territory with people who are generally dedicated to work."[11] Other colonization instructions and memoranda appeared in the coming months, but it was the first colonization junta, composed of Antonio Garay, Mariano Macedo, and Mariano Gálvez, that formed the Department of Colonization and Industry.[12]

The Decree of 27 November 1846 establishing the Department of Colonization borrows much of the same structure, format, and language as previous colonization laws that promoted settlement of the northern frontiers of the republic, but the genealogical justification has some interesting caveats that require elaboration.[13] The first article of this decree grounds its legality not only in the current wartime circumstances, but also in the agreements of a law passed on 1 June 1839,

"Ley—aprobando el convenio celebrado en Londres el 17 de Septiembre de 1837, con los tenedores de bonos mexicanos" (Law—Approving the agreement signed in London on 17 September 1837, with Mexican bondholders), citing Article 16 specifically.[14] This article is worth probing because it details a number of fiscal obligations that constrained the governmentality of various administrations at a time when they were facing the geopolitical challenges of forestalling an expanding settler colonial society to the north.[15]

Presumably, British bondholders and past Mexican administrations had collateralized government lands in an attempt to consolidate foreign debts and guard against the probability that the United States would take control of Mexico's northern territories.[16] Article 16 states that the government "will proceed to appoint as soon as possible, through the respective ministry, a board of directors of colonization at the immediate orders of the supreme government, composed of three persons instructed in the branches that it comprises." This junta was to have technical expertise "in the measurement of the land, designation of lands, and rules to make effective the colonization and other operations that must be practiced."[17] Given the fiscal uncertainties, the Decree of 27 November 1846 was legally bound to follow the precedents outlined in the 1839 law. Several Amerindian empires and many indigenous communities were settled on the collateralized lands—or were in complete control of them—but their presence has never been acknowledged.[18] Thus, the decree setting up the Department of Colonization had been pondered prior to 1846, but the war with the United States and binding legal obligations hastened its creation.[19]

The Decree of 27 November 1846 followed on the heels of three major battles, in a context where the chaos of war was compounded by an unsettled domestic policy.[20] Engagements with US forces took place even as the Mexican army battled growing resistance from its own citizens.[21] The creation of the Department of Colonization was intended to directly address what many had come to believe was one of the primary causes of the Mexican-American War: the inability to settle the northern frontiers with a military and civilian presence.[22] The importance of the decree lies in the fact that the colonization department it established came to give preferential treatment to diasporic populations including migrant Indians and Mexicans residing in the United States.[23] However, military and civilian authorities continued to disagree concerning the colonization issue well into the Porfiriato, and misunderstandings eventually arose between municipal, state, and federal agencies.[24] At the center of these policy differences was which level of government (local, regional, or national) had direct authority over the so-called *terrenos baldíos* (vacant government lands).

Establishing a Department of Colonization: An Autocatalytic Perspective

The Decree of 27 November 1846 was amplified only a week later by a series of *reglamentos* ("regulations" or "bylaws") and *circulares*, which included the Reglamento de 4 de Diciembre de 1846 para la Dirección de Colonización (Regulation of 4 December 1846 for the Department of Colonization) and Circular de 4 de Diciembre de 1846: Recomendando la exacta observancia de las medidas que contiene el decreto expedido para el establecimiento de la Dirección de Colonización (Recommending the exact observance of the measures contained in the decree issued for the establishment of the Department of Colonization).[25] In essence, the first decree established the Department of Colonization, the subsequent reglamento outlined the mandate for the department, and the circular clarified and contextualized additional instructions.

But how was the notion of colonization translated into a governmental agency, and how did that agency's actions acquire the force of law and, at times, actual implementation? The reglamento was full of bureaucratic justifications. Note the overbearing legalese of the text and the warning that other amendments were to come:

> José Mariano de Salas, General of the Brigade in charge of the supreme executive power of the United Mexican States, to the inhabitants of the Republic, be informed: That, steadfast in the desire to make effective the benefits that the colonization system should produce in the Republic, and considering that the decree issued on the 27th of the previous month, which established the Directorate of this branch, will not yield all the results that should be expected unless its powers are detailed from the outset: bearing in mind the project in which these powers are outlined, presented by the same Directorate, which has been diligently and effectively engaged in its preparation since its installation, in compliance with what was stipulated in Article 3 of the aforementioned decree of the 27th of the previous month, and while the Congress, taking into account the initiative that the Government has decided to undertake, establishes the main foundations upon which the success of colonization will depend, I have deemed it appropriate to decree the following.[26]

Even by today's standards, the publication of this legislation calling for the formation of an agency and the supporting documents precisely outlining its mandate is quite rapid and testifies to the urgency of the moment.

The Reglamento de 4 de Diciembre de 1846 contains an extensive set of directives comprising fifty-seven articles with numerous addenda that sketch the most comprehensive outline of colonization policy at that time. Unlike later colonization laws that focus almost exclusively on the settlement of colonists and the allotment of lands, this reglamento seemingly collapses all previous theoretical and actual attempts at colonization under a single agency spanning military, ecclesiastic, agricultural, financial, and cultural concerns. For this reason, the formation of the Department of Colonization can be described as *autocatalytic:* "each advance made other advances more likely."[27]

The Reglamento de 4 de Diciembre de 1846 is the Department of Colonization's "first history," scripting the historical narrative that would be repeated in subsequent historiographies.[28] The reglamento was conjoined with the Circular de 4 de Diciembre de 1846, signed by José María Lafragua and issued on the same date. I segue to these two documents because they are intended to complement each other; the circular is a short essay summarizing the fifty-seven articles in the reglamento. Hence, the reglamento and associated documents become the "first history" of the Department of Colonization and the primary source for later historiographies of Mexican colonization employed in the service of state formation.

As "first histories" these primary sources can also be interpreted as "liberal historiography" because they reveal the class interests of the legislators who sought to marginalize nomadic peoples and indios bárbaros.[29] Once more, Ranajit Guha's insights prove illuminating. Legislative policies serve as intertwined narratives, reflecting the perspectives of those in positions of authority. These policies also mark the initial stride toward acknowledging that frontier society is often perceived as both barbaric and desolate. Guha notes that historiographical exercises that seek "to change the world and to maintain it in its current state have indeed been the dual functions of liberal historiography performed on behalf of the class for which it speaks."[30] The decrees and policies outlined here can be analyzed in this light. In the face of war, chaos, and territorial dismemberment, these colonization laws are intimate utopian projections of a well-ordered, peaceful, and progressive society.

The Reglamento of 4 de Diciembre de 1846 recapitulates earlier colonization policies into a modern assemblage that incorporates military, industrial, and religious concerns from centuries past. Taking the example of military colonization, Article 45 states, "Military colonies, made up of Mexicans or foreigners, or of each other, will also be founded on the coasts and borders where the Government designates, especially to prevent the barbarians from breaking into the country, and in them the settlers will be granted, free of charge, land assigned by the Department of Colonization, with the approval of the Government."[31] Alongside the clear references to the military objectives of the Department of Colonization is the understanding that the new agency's role is to prevent the entry of "barbarians," understood as indios bárbaros. The agency is charged with either effecting their eventual assimilation or preventing their attacks and raids. Traditionally, military, ecclesiastical, or state actors with similar goals had undertaken separate efforts at colonizing the northern frontiers. The new strategy was to unite these three groups of agents under one department to coordinate their approaches to settler colonization. This novel Department of Colonization is reminiscent of Patrick Wolfe's description of an "all-inclusive land centered project(s) that coordinates a comprehensive range of agencies, from the metropolitan centre to the frontier encampment, with a view to eliminating nomadic Indigenous societies."[32] As such, the manifestation of colonization policy embedded in the Reglamento of 4 de Diciembre de 1846 evokes an earlier effort at state consolidation but reinscribes it as colonization policy.

First Repatriation Commissions: The Case of Coahuila

Because the outbreak of the Mexican-American War directly precipitated the creation of the Department of Colonization, a military approach was applied to domestic policy.[33] Specifically, the northern frontier was divided into the three regions—Nuevo México–Chihuahua, Tamaulipas-Coahuila-Texas, and Sonora-California—and a repatriation commission was assigned to each one.[34] The primary function of these repatriation commissions, like that of the Department of Colonization, was to identify and provide administrative and financial support to Mexican citizens who elected to resettle across the new international boundary established by the Treaty of Guadalupe Hidalgo (1848).[35] Because the New Mexico Territory was the most populated, it was deemed the most crucial of the three areas and thus the First Repatriation Commission was promptly established to administer it.[36]

Legislation implemented to encourage Mexican citizens to resettle under the auspices of the Department of Colonization and the repatriation commissions provided both the abstract and the material (in the form of agents) governmental

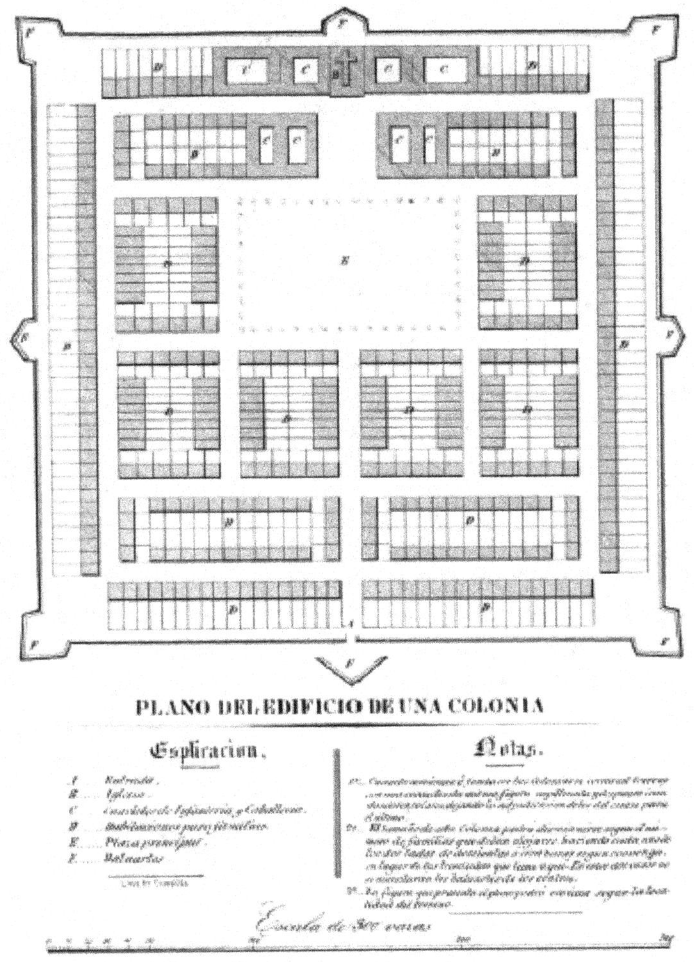

“Construction Plan of a Military Colony” (1848). This plan represents one of many architectural designs that usually accompanied proposals for the establishment of military colonies along the northern frontiers of the Mexican Republic.

authority needed to station dozens of settlements along the newly established frontiers.[37] Postwar instability, limited financial resources, shifting geopolitical boundaries, resistance from US authorities, and internal accusations of financial mismanagement all hindered the operation of the initial repatriation commissions. Still, half a dozen resettlement colonies emerged along the northern frontier from Baja California to Tamaulipas. Here, I focus on those in Coahuila and Texas, which were once a single state.[38]

The 1850 resettlement of 618 individuals from Nacogdoches, Texas, to El Remolino, Coahuila, presents a useful case for evaluating the Mexican government's efficacy in efforts at repatriation and resettlement.[39] Through his research in regional archives, the architectural historian Alejandro González Milea has revealed a wealth of information about the years of engineering and urban planning necessary for a new settlement to be conceived, organized, and executed.[40] The fact that both Mexicans and Amerindians were resettled from Texas to Coahuila can be understood as an example of civilian and military cooperation for the benefit of resettlement. It was state officials who first awarded Antonio Menchaca lands in El Remolino on which to form a civilian colony with a "total of two hundred Mexican families."[41] Federal officials had already identified the location as a promising site for resettlement by 1850, thanks in large part to the work of the Primera Compañía de la Guardia Nacional. González Milea suggests that "the new population of El Remolino had its origin in two interrelated circumstances; on the one hand, it should be seen as part of the natural movement of civilians who were gradually becoming involved in the broad plan for the military colonies." But on the other hand, he continues, "it is feasible to grant it autonomy of aims and purposes, considering the project as an example of a new generation of efforts corresponding to colonies of repatriates and civilian colonies."[42]

While the formation of El Remolino involved a range of actors, none shouldered a greater load than Antonio Menchaca. In 1849, Menchaca appears as "ensign, second rate, attached to the military colony of Laredo"; he was given a colonization concession the following year by state officials in Coahuila.[43] Menchaca compiled a list of people from Nacogdoches, Texas, who were willing to relocate to El Remolino.[44] Of the 618 settler-colonists, 146 were children; that is, under the age of fourteen. In his correspondence with numerous government officials, Menchaca listed only three female heads of household.[45] Thirty-eight months later, in October 1853, Menchaca billed the federal government 20,632 pesos, later adding 7,080 pesos in unforeseen expenses as he led the settlers from

East Texas toward the state of Coahuila.[46] The Ministry of Foreign Relations responded to Menchaca's request by saying that due to the "scantiness of the treasury" the government was currently not in a position to "make the proposed expenditure."[47] Nonetheless, the settlement advanced and served as a base for other resettlement efforts in subsequent years—a pattern that can observed when analyzing the historicity of these relocations. In light of the number of foreign loans that the government was bound to repay with interest, exchanges denying settlers' requests for funds were typical. Yet there was no shortage of legislation inviting Mexicans in the United States to resettle along the newly formed frontier.[48]

Although little government aid was forthcoming and conditions on the ground were difficult, the establishment of the settler colony of El Remolino, Coahuila, slowly progressed over the next few decades.[49] As part of this effort, the governor of Nuevo León–Coahuila, Santiago Vidaurri, published a notice in 1858 encouraging Mexican families in Bexar County, Texas, to resettle in El Remolino.[50] That year a San Antonio newspaper also published an impassioned "announcement" from Manuel Leal inviting residents in Texas to resettle across the border in Coahuila:

> United by bonds of friendship and kinship with the Mexicans residing in the state of Texas, my home country, and especially those in the County of Bexar, convinced that it is not in their best interest to continue living in a country where they have no security for their lives or their property, as evidenced by many recent events that have led to almost daily emigration, I am pleased to inform you that I have requested from the higher authorities of the State of Nuevo León and Coahuila sufficient and even more fertile lands than those in Texas, in the Rio Grande area, so that all who wish to can come to colonize, assured that among their brethren, if not all the necessary security, at least what we ourselves enjoy, will be found.[51]

The sporadic resettlement of El Remolino continued after Menchaca's project. And as was typical, the appeals for colonists regularly channeled nationalist sentiment to serve the practical interest of maintaining territorial hegemony and a military presence along the frontier.[52] As González Milea observed, the colonists of El Remolino "reported that Lipan Indians had already been settled as early as 1868" and this was "considered a resounding success under the idea that their 'reduction' was beneficial for the pacification of the entire state."[53]

Although the first repatriation commissions disbanded by the 1860s, the practice of resettlement did not fade, remaining either in public memory or in numerous state and federal calls for the resettlement of "hijos del país." Today, El Remolino is a town of about four hundred individuals, with a majority (71 percent) being considered indigenous and about 24 percent speaking an indigenous language.[54] As the town's history demonstrates, "the new population of El Remolino had its origin in two interrelated circumstances" that brought together state and military officials, as the federal government took the lead in the early planning of the settlement using the National Guard. At the same time, the settlement can be appreciated as "an example of a new generation of efforts" toward populating the northern frontiers with repatriates and civilian colonies.[55] In addition, the colony apparently became part of the historical memory for Amerindian refugees, in that long after its founding, it continued to be a resettlement location for a number of other indigenous peoples. In sum, the collaborative establishment of El Remolino reflects a case of local, state, federal, and military cooperation in the service of colonization.

This chapter outlined the establishment of the Department of Colonization in 1846 as directed in legislation addressing the resettlement of Mexican Americans from the United States following the end of hostilities. I highlighted both its existence as a government agency charged with settler colonization and what its creation reveals about the Mexican nation's astute project of state formation in the face of external and internal challenges including foreign debt and foreign forays. Through an analysis of this agency's first report to the congress, I historicized earlier colonization efforts and examined the implementation of the first repatriation commissions following the end of the war in 1848. State-sponsored resettlement efforts along the northern frontier set a tradition of repatriation in motion, reinforcing a folk belief that Mexico was a refuge for relocation. A case study of the settlement of El Remolino, Coahuila, in 1850 with colonists from neighboring Nacogdoches, Texas, illustrates the process of repatriation during a tumultuous period and underscores the cooperation of regional and military officials in the complicated process of military colonization in the postwar period.

CHAPTER 4

COLONIZATION AT MIDCENTURY

Wars of Reform and the Reforms of War

On 16 September 1857, the Ministerio de Fomento published "La primera memoria del Ministerio de Fomento," authored by Manuel Siliceo.[1] Appearing only two months prior to the Plan de Tacubaya on 17 December 1857, which initiated the bloody Wars of Reform, the document mirrors identical narratives of previous colonization efforts against a backdrop of constant uprisings and political coups.[2] The publication of this first memoria was either the calm before the storm or merely one more opportunity to historicize the nation's colonization efforts for the current administration. What started as the Dirección de Colonización was soon renamed the Dirección de Colonización e Industria and then reorganized as the Secretaría de Fomento, Colonización, Industria y Comercio (Department of Development, Colonization, Industry, and Commerce; Secretaría de Fomento for short). Thereafter, colonization was in the hands of an agency charged with development, industry, and commerce, each of which was seen as complementary to the other branches. Befitting a modern government agency, the professionalization of history also figures prominently in Siliceo's narrative, and as the late Mexican historian Enrique Florescano notes, "the interpretation of the past is one of the most deeply engrained habits of nations."[3]

In his *Lectures on the Philosophy of World History*, G. W. F. Hegel suggests that there are three varieties of historical writing: original, reflective, and philosophical. Original history is based on the viewing of historical events "being made," with the works of Herodotus and Thucydides being examples. The authors were present at the time they were writing and their "descriptions are for the most part limited to deeds, events, and states of society, which they had before their eyes, and whose spirit they shared." Today we might describe these historians as ancient eyewitnesses, but Hegel also believes that these authors "simply transferred what was passing in the world around them, to the realm of representative intellect. An external phenomenon is thus translated into an internal conception." In this way, Siliceo's "original history" of colonization in Mexico is but a description of "deeds, events, and states of society, which they had before their eyes, and whose spirit they shared." Siliceo noticeably projected the political world around him onto the historical narrative he provided, and while his opinions on colonization do represent a "first history" in the Hegelian sense, they are also reflective, philosophical, and even practical in a number of areas.[4]

Correct though Siliceo may have been, he effectively rehashes many of the historical narratives from earlier memorias in his new interpretation. Simultaneously, he charts the historiographical future: his re-inscription of the trope of "failure to adequately colonize" will be repeated by historians a century later.[5] Siliceo writes, "If a detailed reason could be given about the work that the Ministry has carried out in these two branches, it would be easy to fill out a few hundred sheets, and that nevertheless, one needs to give an idea of the work of the Ministry so that it is known and to see the results."[6] Because Siliceo consulted the first memorias of the Dirección de Colonización, he largely retraces the main arguments about the difficulty of colonization amid war, administrative disorder, and a lack of peace and stability. From a careful reading of the government's colonization reports, it becomes clear they simply reproduced the primary documentation of that era without any critical examination of the broader political context in which those "original histories" were written.

Siliceo's first report as minister follows the narrative tropes of earlier annual reports, decrees, reglamentos, and other publications related to colonization law and policy. After acknowledging that many pages could be dedicated to reciting the nation's efforts at colonization, Siliceo proceeds to repeat that the country's lands need to be surveyed before they can be populated with settlers:

> Because of this, it has seemed appropriate to me to first present the observations that naturally arise from the examination of the multitude of records related to colonization, and then to explain what has been done since the creation of this Secretariat. In order to effectively carry out the colonization efforts, it was essential to have knowledge of the lands where they were to be established and those which the government could make available. Therefore, I believed it necessary to begin by examining what has been practiced in the investigation and demarcation of public lands, as they not

> only form the foundation of colonization but also constitute an important aspect of public wealth.[7]

Siliceo enumerates a previously unmentioned benefit of surveying, one that is equally important from a state perspective. Surveying the land paves the way for the division and allocation of these vast expanses and thus enables the state to build a system for collecting taxes. As James C. Scott has suggested, "Living within a state [means], virtually by definition, taxes, conscription, corvée labor, and, for most, a condition of servitude; these conditions [are] at the core of the state's strategic and military advantages."[8] Siliceo had the right idea, but at this historical moment, colonization as state formation would be hindered by another human fiction; namely, tolerance for cultural and religious differences.[9]

In his first report, Siliceo once again employed history, law, and public policy in the service of state formation, but internal conflicts thwarted the realization of a practical colonization program for several more years. The Constitution of 1857 had been ratified just months before the publication of Siliceo's report.[10] The fallout from the Mexican-American War triggered a series of military coups, with political instability continuing for another generation thereafter. Due to the "administrative disorder" of the era, the minister spent considerable ink relitigating the post-independence years, including the history of colonization in Mexico. The "Texas episode" was prominently invoked throughout this report, emphasizing the state's perspective that the confrontation with its northern neighbor was a battle over land and settler loyalties. Siliceo thus demarcates the colonization of Texas as a historic watershed, going so far as to criticize land concessions granted by General Terán in 1823.[11] Siliceo thus judges and condemns earlier administrations—to paraphrase Hegel—in the *court of world history*.[12]

Siliceo historicizes the process of land grants to the so-called colonial period by noting that the concentration of large estates is in part due to a system going back three centuries. As he sees it, the problem began with the granting of large parcels of land to the first generation of Iberian conquistadors. Some of the minister's excursions into Mexican history are worth analyzing, while keeping in mind that the report forms a record of the work carried out under his leadership. Siliceo suggests,

> Since the number of conquerors was limited in relation to the vast expanse of the country they had brought under their dominion, it happened that even when they took as much land as they wanted without restriction, there were always significant gaps that they gradually added to their possessions

> as they either sold part of them or the activities they allocated to them expanded. This led to the concentration of territorial ownership in a few hands, the incredible size of some rural estates that encompassed more land than several European sovereignties combined, and ultimately, what was originally thought to be five or six leagues in size turned out to be thirty or forty.[13]

The civil war in 1857 would in part be fought over indigenous and ecclesiastical corporations with substantial landholdings and privileges. In Siliceo's narrative, the historic concentration of lands in the hands of a few elites becomes entangled with contemporaneous efforts to colonize and rationalize the nation. Siliceo's narrative can be corroborated with other contemporary sources, but given that only a generation had passed since independence from Spain, such an explanation is to be expected.[14] Siliceo writes his exposition of the acquisition of landed estates by Mexican *hacendados* and the Catholic Church at a moment when laws are being passed aimed at inhibiting the accumulation of large corporate landholdings, underscoring how the contemporary political context influenced this first memoria.[15]

Colonization amid French Occupation

The violence and disruption of the Wars of Reform beginning immediately after the publication of the 1857 memoria guaranteed that the federal government would make little progress in its efforts to colonize and settle the vast expanses of the nation.[16] To institutionalize the reforms that had been fought for, "in 1857 the Congress drafted a liberal federalist constitution. The new constitution ended special authority for clergy; limited the power of the Church, placed the army under civilian control, abolished hereditary titles and imprisonment for debt, and gave Mexicans their first genuine bill of rights."[17] This victory of the liberals in 1860 was deemed unacceptable by the clergy, conservative intellectuals, landowners, and substantial segments of the military elite. In time, the divisions paved the way for an unlikely French intervention in 1861 and for a competition between two governments for domestic hegemony and international recognition.

After the second French intervention in 1861, the Mexican government had become divided into two distinct factions, with President Benito Juárez governing from the northern region while the conservatives, alongside their monarchical collaborator, acted as if they were the rightful rulers of the fragmented republic.[18] This unique situation in Mexican history found its parallel across the international border during the same era. In the United States, Northerners regarded Abraham Lincoln as their rightful president, while the Southern states acknowledged Jefferson Davis in the same capacity. In both nations, the presence of two rival administrations resulted in the creation of dual archives containing documents originating from analogous federal and administrative bodies, all established to secure the support of the populace and attain international recognition for their respective governments.[19] In Mexico between 1862 and 1864, the Ministro Imperial de Fomento, Colonización, Industria, y Comercio issued a more detailed and nuanced report that effectively restated common knowledge about colonization but with several policy recommendations. By contrast, the government of Benito Juárez re-created Fomento and renamed it the Ministro de Justicia, Fomento e Instrucción Pública.[20] Both factions agreed on the need to protect the country's northern frontiers, and in one of those rare historical ironies, the new emperor—invited to Mexico by the conservative faction—promptly adopted the liberal position on colonization!

Ferdinand Maximilian Joseph was born in Vienna, Austria on 6 July 1832 and died in Querétaro, Mexico on 19 June 1867 at the age of thirty-four. He had accepted the offer to occupy the Mexican throne when he was only thirty years old, believing that the Mexican people had elected him as their monarch.[21] The *Encyclopaedia Britannica* entry on Maximilian summarizes this well-known historical narrative by noting that he was "archduke of Austria and Emperor of Mexico, a man whose *naïve Liberalism* proved unequal to the international intrigues that had put him on the throne and to the brutal struggles within Mexico that led to his execution."[22] Indeed, on entering Mexico, Maximilian was greeted by fierce opposition that ended tragically for everyone involved, including the conservative generals who supported his administration. Maximilian's execution on 19 June 1867 marked an end not only to the Wars of Reform, but also to any future European efforts to interfere in Mexico's affairs and rule it as an imperial possession. In the words of anthropologist and historian Claudio Lomnitz, "the bullet that killed Maximilian effectively ended the possibility of ever establishing a European-backed monarchy, while making a highly visible international statement about the sovereignty of Mexico and its laws."[23] And, indeed, the legitimate president of Mexico, Benito Juárez, who had previously been president of the Supreme Court, conducted the public execution according to the letter of the law.[24]

Under the direction of the Archduke Maximilian and despite the questionable legal basis of his authority, Mexican conservatives published an annual report that details some particularities of colonization history during that tumultuous period. This report, submitted to "His Majesty" rather than the congress, reveals an interesting amalgamation of liberal and conservative thought that influenced colonization policy thereafter.[25] In several ways, the history of the Ministro Imperial de Fomento and its accomplishments reads very much like the conclusions of Mexican historian Erika Pani regarding this period: "the traditional version of the story tells us that the empire was the 'feeble, puny, rickety' creature of the French monarch's ambition; of Maximilian's gullibility; and of the misguided dreams of monarchy of a minuscule, senile, and impotent Conservative party." In fact, however, the imperial memoria was solid in its argumentation, was published by a competent cabinet, and documented progress made in the realm of colonization in Mexico during these tempestuous years. To quote Pani once more, "A quick survey of the empire's political personnel yields an impressive list of Mexicans of diverse social and ideological or partisan backgrounds, distinguished in the fields of law and culture, with experience in high-level politics since the 1840s. . . . These men were anything but political lightweights." Thus, while these years were consumed by the conflict between two competing governments, the issuing of a report recounting numerous accomplishments underscores Pani's observations about the effectiveness of this administration.[26] Given that there were two agencies jockeying for legitimacy to colonize *terrenos baldíos*, this era could also be interpreted as one when there was too much governmentality.[27]

The author of the only report issued by the Ministro Imperial de Fomento was Luis Robles Pezuela, who documented the agency's efforts from October 1864 to March 1866. Like most of the intelligentsia of the nineteenth century, Robles Pezuela was an engineer and closely linked to the railroad companies of the era.[28] He begins his report in the usual historiographic manner by naming his predecessor, "Since Mr. Siliceo published his interesting Memoria de Fomento of 1857, no similar official document has since seen the light of day."[29] This statement is important for a few reasons, not the least of which is an assessment of the documentary record based on available government documentation. But the observation also reveals the impact of the Wars of Reform on Mexican society and governmentality.

The minister of development's position on European colonization in Mexico reflects a policy shift whereby the conservatives had now assimilated the liberal position.[30] This stance marks a historical watershed because, at least in terms of immigration and colonization policy in Mexico, all sides were collaborating in light of the emperor's efforts at peace and political compromise.[31] Perhaps the now moderate argument for immigration and colonization was more dialectical in its suggestions, because the infusion of "new blood" was the raw material of world powers. Robles Pezuela even went so far as to criticize the provincialism of conservatives of his own party with an imperial twist by plotting the process of colonization as a historical and contemporary truism of successful nations. In contrast to Siliceo's liberal interpretation, Robles Pezuela historicized colonization in the Old World as a way to underscore his argument that "if some, concerned about the spirit of provincialism, doubt this truth, they need only turn to history, and it will tell them that colonization is the lifeblood of nations, to which the Phoenicians owed their prosperity in ancient times, the Greeks, the Carthaginians, and the Romans, and in the modern times, the United States, Brazil, Upper California, and even Australia."[32] Once again, a government official employs nation building and the historical method not only to justify the nation's imperial projects, but to demonstrate its potentiality.

Immigration and Blood Transfusion during the Second Mexican Empire

Within the context of the historical evolution of science and technology, Robles Pezuela's occupation as an engineer assumes significance. It exerts a discernible impact on his administrative methodologies and the scientific discourse he selects for his 1866 report to the emperor. During this period, engineering emerged as a prestigious academic discipline and profession, encompassing various specializations such as mechanical, electrical, and chemical engineering. The prevailing cultural milieu in Mexico, however, retained vestiges of folk beliefs pertaining to human development and the perceived significance of blood and lineage. An example is seen in the advertisements of Californios making their case for resettlement only a decade earlier in 1855: "And what better time for Sonora to take advantage of the circumstances, which under its liberal and protective laws, is the only emigration that is acceptable because of its language, religion, and customs? Right now is the time to populate its frontiers with a Hispanic American population that is useful, energetic, and trained by contact with the Saxon race, the only one that can contain the advances of the barbarous Apache."[33]

Even educated Mexican elites like Robles Pezuela were not immune to folk beliefs about blood and culture that were commonplace at the time. For Europeans of the era, and even for some Mexicans, ideas about race and civilization were still closely tied to notions of blood and lineage.[34] Robles Pezuela's commentary reflects some of that antiquated thinking.[35] He argued colonization was important not only for mapping the territory of the republic and for making legible the landscape, but also because the process offered an opportunity to infuse *new blood* into the body politic:

> I will not cease to recommend the advantages that it [immigration] has produced at all times to the nations that have openly adopted it, because there is no one who can ignore that the introduction of new arms, new capital, and new industries infuse unprecedented vitality into any place they are directed, just as a body that has been reduced to the brink of weakness by illness is revitalized and gains strength through the transfusion of blood.[36]

The use of metaphors about blood transfusion is suggestive. Perhaps Robles Pezuela deliberately employed them in the service of justifying French intervention, implying that the disease of liberalism infecting the body politic needed the transfusion of an archduke duped onto an imperial operating table. Or perhaps Robles Pezuela was alluding to the transfusion research of Benneke, who "attempted to revive an asphyxiated neonate by transfusing with bright red umbilical blood into the umbilical vein."[37] In hindsight, both scenarios seem feasible, but the imperial attempt to infuse Maximilian into Mexican politics ended with an agonizing death for the patient and a lifetime descent into madness for his wife, Carlota.

This chapter examined how colonization became institutionalized during the mid-nineteenth century. This era witnessed a significant rethinking of certain national values, leading to the acceptance of freedom of religion prior to the Wars of Reform (1857–60).[38] This era has been the topic of much research, because it was followed by French occupation from 1861 until June 1867, when the archduke Maximilian was executed by a firing squad. Despite the perception that wars, interventions, and chaos were the order of the day, the activity of the Imperial Department of Development, Colonization, Industry, and Commerce during these years was considerable. Settlement and colonization continued during these turbulent years, and the agency continued to function even during a foreign occupation of sorts. The Texas Episode, the Mexican-American War, filibustering along the northern frontiers, and two French interventions all served to institutionalize a colonization policy that would come to rely on hijos del país, or autocolonization. This process will be the subject of chapter 5.

CHAPTER 5

"HIJOS DEL PAÍS"

Autocolonization, 1876–1911

The Plan de Tuxtepec, initiated in 1876, marked the beginning of the "Tuxtepec Revolution" led by Porfirio Díaz, which aimed to remove President Sebastián Lerdo de Tejada from office. Its main objectives included toppling Lerdo due to his breach of the no re-election principle, restoring the 1857 Constitution, and advocating for liberal ideals. Díaz's leadership propelled him to the presidency, ushering in the era of technocratic governance known today as the Porfiriato. Ironically, Díaz later violated the same no re-election principle, leading to political turmoil and social unrest in Mexico after his departure in 1911.[1] The election of Porfirio Díaz as president changed the nature of Mexican politics for the following generation and offered hope for peace and stability for the first time in half a century.[2] For Díaz, according to one of his most judicious biographers, Paul Garner, internal political peace was "first and foremost." As such, "this was the principal and central task of the first Díaz administration, and it remained a consistent priority throughout the history of the entire regime. Contemporary apologists (and later Porfirista historiography) considered the establishment of the *pax porfiriana* as one of its principal achievements, and it became the main justification for Díaz's successive re-elections after 1884."[3]

Porfirian Pragmatic Political Management

Porfirian political strategy was hatched in the northern regions, a fact that had implications for frontier state politics. As Juan Mora-Torres observes, "Díaz did not take matters lightly. Perhaps for precautionary reasons, he immediately took the first steps in integrating the entire north into his state centralization projects in 1884, which served to undermine the political authority of frontier allies."[4] The new reality and the period of stability were reflected in the report submitted by the new minister of development, Vicente Riva Palacio. Riva Palacio's first report as secretary of fomento in 1877 is pragmatic and uncharacteristically absent of verbosity. On taking the helm of one of the largest government agencies in Mexico, Riva Palacio observed that war had squandered government resources and destroyed the progress (including infrastructure) that had been achieved by earlier administrations. Whatever funds were made available were eventually consumed by the war machine. To the head of an agency responsible for development, colonization, industry, and commerce, it was clear that the civil war was to blame for the lack of progress in public infrastructure:

> The civil war in which the country found itself embroiled, in order to assert its rights, led naturally and inevitably to halting the works initiated on public roads, the destruction of the telegraph network in many areas, and the abandonment of it in others. Even before that, the drainage works in the Valley had been interrupted, despite the urgent need to continue them to improve the sanitary conditions of the capital of the Republic. No steps were taken to promote foreign immigration, nor was there any effort made to enact provisions that would support and encourage agriculture, trade, and industry. The drainage of Mexico City was not initiated, let alone the prospect of its beautification. Science was also not granted the protection it deserves in all civilized nations. In short, the funds allocated by law to this Secretariat were diverted from their intended purpose and used for the exigencies of war.[5]

Given this comprehensive description of civil war and social instability in the country, it is interesting that the author ignores the coup that brought his government to power—the so-called Revolution of Tuxtepec in 1876.[6] At the same time, he minces few words in describing the appalling situation of the country and rejecting past approaches to colonization in favor of the mantra of the era: "order and progress."[7]

Vicente E. Manero, the head of the First Section supervised by Riva Palacio, issued a report that exemplifies the typical approach to historical and public policy considerations concerning colonization initiatives. Manero, who is aligned with the views of Riva Palacio, has earned recognition for his numerous contributions to colonization historiography.[8] He offers a more concise presentation of the subject matter. While recounting the extensive history of colonization endeavors, he astutely notes that "previous attempts have, for the most part, met with failure or yielded unsatisfactory results. This is not necessary to remember, because their history is recent and nobody ignores it; so, keeping them in mind to ensure that colonization will produce the same fruits in the future, you, Citizen Secretary, have walked with the measure and prudence that such precedents advise."[9]

In addition to presenting several of the same concerns voiced by earlier ministers of development, Riva Palacio highlights earlier obstacles to colonization. More reserved and cautious than his predecessors, he notes that the contents of his report "will make our national representatives understand why I do not give an account of the great works on colonization in this chapter, despite the fact that the Secretariat of my position is entrusted with this branch."[10] This plain speaking set the tone for the department's public communications. In many ways, the change of discourse signaled the "more administration and less politics" approach taken by the Díaz administration in 1876.[11] Justo Sierra commented about Díaz that "with this leadership, the country made progress, though not without hitches." Garner describes this style of governance as "pragmatic political management."[12]

Manero also highlights the many colonization laws and similar policies that were already "on the books."[13] This represents a significant shift in the administration's approach to colonization compared to its predecessors, as well as a practical example of placing legal history in the service of the secretary of development. While recognizing past precedent, Manero also musters several laws that potential colonists could take advantage of. The Law of 31 May 1875 (passed the year before) granted the executive the authority to approve colonization contracts and constituted the most relevant legislation prior to the passage of the 1883 Land and Colonization Law.[14] Although Manero admits that more progress could be made, he cites successes with several colonization contracts in Baja California, including the rancherias of La Tía Juana (Tijuana) and Tecate.[15] Tijuana was at the center of several resettlement efforts throughout the nineteenth century.[16] The settler-colonists who came to inhabit those lands, in the words of historian Bibiana Santiago Guerrero, "were Mexicans coming, in significant numbers, from Sonora, Alta California, and the Southern District of Baja California; others were originally from Portugal, France, and the United States. Only those of Mexican descent were authorized to settle in the colony, and the few foreigners took root in the neighboring ranches."[17] Both Tijuana and Tecate developed into colonies and today are major population centers along the northern frontier of Baja California.[18] In fact, Tijuana, a city of more than two million people, is one of the busiest ports of entry between the United States and Mexico.

Turning toward los Hijos del País

After serving as governor of the Distrito Federal in 1880, the newly elected president, General Manuel González, selected the well-known General Carlos Pacheco as his secretario de fomento, colonización, industria, y comercio in mid-1881. González's choice of Pacheco generated some interest among the Mexican press, particularly since both men had lost an arm in service to the nation. Generals González and Pacheco were army veterans with extensive military experience, including in conflicts and war zones. Their shared injury "prompted the uncharitable remark from *El Lunes*" that "having a mutilated arm is becoming fashionable among our politicians."[19] If the details of Pacheco's biography are exact, he served in that position for the next decade, until his premature death in 1891.

In that time, Pacheco's name became synonymous with the Department of Development, and the phrase "Fomento is Pacheco," was said to be a common refrain of the era.[20] General Pacheco came to embody the government agency itself, and under his direction, first under González and later under Díaz, the ministry would see its greatest successes and allocations. Although he took the reins of power in 1881, his first report to the congress covered the period between December 1877 and December 1882, exactly a year before passage of the 1883 Land and Colonization Law. Like his predecessors, Pacheco appears to have studied the previous memorias, but he wastes little time engaging in political banter. In the words of historian Don Coerver, "Pacheco soon proved himself to be a man in whom both Díaz and González could place their trust."[21]

When General González assumed the presidency, he appointed Porfirio Díaz as his first secretary of fomento. However, Díaz resigned within six months and General Pacheco shouldered leadership of the agency, embarking upon a proactive approach to address the issue of settler colonization. Notably, he benefited from a substantial budgetary allocation for this purpose. While a meager sum of 20,000 pesos had been earmarked for colonization expenses in fiscal year 1880–81, a notable transformation occurred in fiscal year 1882–83, with more than one million pesos being allocated for colonization endeavors. Furthermore, despite impending financial challenges, which culminated in the crisis of 1883–84, the colonization initiatives remained relatively insulated; the budget for fiscal year 1883–84 allocated approximately 700,000 pesos to cover colonization-related expenses.[22] These would be the highest amounts allotted to the Secretaría de Fomento in its history, and also the last time the agency would enjoy such a budget.

Under Pacheco's direction, the Secretaría de Fomento, Colonización, Industria, y Comercio established, inspected, and reported on actual colonies. In his report, Pacheco reminded readers that "from the first years of the existence of Mexico as an Independent nation, its government was concerned with the urgent need that such an extensive and depopulated country has to attract to its bosom the arms that are indispensable for the exploitation of its natural resources." Pacheco presumed that "the quick and prodigious example of development that the Republic of the United States of North America had achieved, due to colonization, spurred the desires that Mexican rulers had conceived from the beginning to colonize our vast and fertile regions."[23]

Like earlier heads of the agency, Pacheco had carefully studied the extensive historiography of colonization published in the printed memorias, but he plotted his account according to what he saw as the most attractive destinations of global immigration; namely, the governments of the United States, and to a lesser extent, Argentina. The Homestead Act of 1862, enacted during the US Civil War, was interpreted as the raison d'être of this "prodigious development." Considering peace and stability to be the foundation of good governance, Pacheco presented that as the first stage in his historiographical analysis. The second stage would be a Mexican-style homestead act that would ground settlers to the soil, leading to the next step in this pyramidal logic. Pacheco, like past secretaries of development and colonization, could not overemphasize the primary obstacle to colonization, which was the political instability of the country ever since the wars for independence. He succinctly characterized the situation with an apologia: "Unfortunately, and despite colonization being generally considered as the question of vital importance for the future of Mexico, the deplorable political and economic state that the Republic has maintained for more than half a century was an insurmountable obstacle to the realization of the best intentions."[24] Yet, by the time Pacheco's memoria was published in 1885, the country had experienced what was perhaps the longest period of stability and peace since the turn of the last century. Pacheco later elaborated as follows:

> Constant civil war, accompanied by its inseparable retinue of public insecurity, industrial and commercial paralysis, disequilibrium in the administration, and scarcity in the treasury reduced with each passing day the hope of setting up a system of colonies. Even when the different governments

> that have succeeded each other since the era of Independence were able to command sufficient pecuniary resources to undertake the great task of colonizing the country, European colonists avoided settling in Mexican territory due to the lack of security that reigned in it. The industrious emigrant who leaves his native country for fortune seeks first a country that will grant him sufficient guarantees to work in peace, and without being exposed to losing the fruit of his efforts in a revolution or armed robbery. Peace is the greatest attraction to colonization, and unfortunately that has been lacking in the Republic for a long time.[25]

Once more, the issue of "administrative disorder" is invoked to explain the problems and pitfalls of colonization during past administrations.

Like earlier ministers of development, Pacheco believed the lack of peace and the constant political and economic instability of the country made immigration to Mexico very unattractive. Immigrants simply chose to migrate to other countries, thus generating waves of spontaneous settlement in areas outside Mexico. In Pacheco's words, "the beautiful ideal to be aspired to is spontaneous colonization. But since the emigration currents had been directed toward other countries, due to the well-earned reputation of insecurity that the constant state of internal wars caused in Mexico, it was necessary to make an effort to dispel that reputation, attracting to the country, by means of a generous welcome, the first immigrants who set the example of establishing themselves in our homeland."[26] This notion of the "first colonists" setting the example for future migrants is indicative of the perspective of incremental colonization shared by the Mexican intelligentsia of that era.

The successful establishment of colonists in strategic locales, it was believed, would in turn spur the spontaneous migration of millions of Europeans to Mexican ports of entry. Mexico did not experience any sort of spontaneous immigration from Europe during the nineteenth century, and one could argue, for much of the twentieth century.[27] But at least Pacheco could include some good news in the report to the Mexican Congress: European immigration to Mexico was on the right path.

The report authored by the head of the First Section on Colonization in the Department of Development and Colonization, Antonio García Cubas, enumerated a total of eighteen colonization contracts that were granted during the period from 1877 to 1882. However, it is worth emphasizing that the mere existence of contracts does not invariably culminate in the establishment of functioning

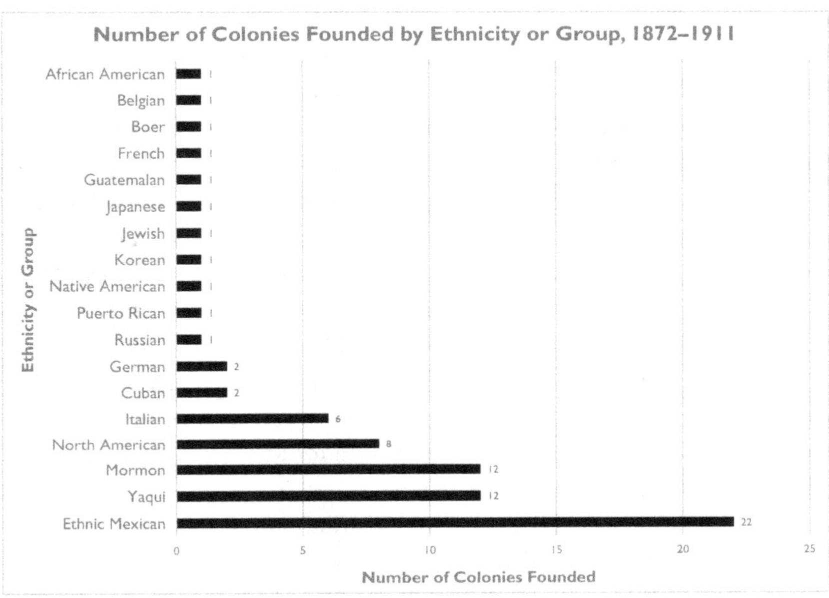

The number of colonies founded during the Porfiriato (1876–1911) is regularly cited at sixty, founded by ethnic groups from around the world. Ethnic Mexicans from the United States or other parts of Mexico constituted the majority of the colonists during this period.
Graph by author.

colonies. García Cubas, in his comprehensive assessment, proceeded to furnish an intricate analysis of the colonies that had been successfully established or were in the process of being instituted throughout the nation. Notably, his report highlighted the acquisition of approximately twelve properties from hacendados, while the remaining six contracts adhered to the provisions delineated within the framework of the Law of 31 May 1857.[28] The largest plot, located in Coahuila, totaled 1,355,330 hectares and was "conceded to C. Emeterio de la Garza" on 23 June 1881. There is some debate as to whether the amounts the Secretaría de Fomento paid may have constituted another layer of graft for the landowners and the government agents, but the report specifies that the Secretaría de Fomento y Colonización paid $169,988.50 for these properties, which apparently totaled 1,636,423 hectares.[29]

Colonization during the Pax Porfiriana

Beginning at the end of November 1883, the chamber of deputies, followed by the senate, debated and eventually passed the Ley de 15 de Diciembre de 1883, known as the Land and Colonization Law of 1883.[30] It mandated that Mexican, European, and American land and colonization firms would receive compensation in the form of one-third of the surveyed land. Furthermore, they were obliged to populate their acquired territories with settler-colonists from around the globe.[31] The law provided the legal framework for surveying the vast expanses of the nation's frontier regions and a system for populating and colonizing those areas with settler-colonists, especially with ethnic Mexicans residing north of the country, in order to render the land productive.[32] It was assumed in the legislation and in the ongoing popular debate that citizens who had migrated to the United States would return and "modernize and civilize" the desert landscapes still inhabited and raided by so-called "uncivilized barbarous Indians."[33] Consonant with the liberalization of immigration policies in several post-independence Latin American nations, the 1883 law stood in for Mexico's official migration policy until the "great rebellion" of 1911.[35]

Paralleling the state's desire to make the nation's borders and frontiers more legible to the Porfirians of the period, the expectations for the colonization companies and the settler-colonists are clearly demarcated, particularly the preference for "Mexicans residing abroad who wish to settle in the deserts of the Republic's borders." Under Article 16, these modern colonists "shall have the right to free transfer of land, with the conditions of Section III of Article 3 and up to an extension of two hundred hectares with the enjoyment for fifteen years of the exemptions granted by this law."[35] Section III of Article 3 is vital to understanding how the preference for certain colonists was enshrined in immigration and colonization policy during this period—preferences that were regularly articulated, albeit inconsistently, until the close of the century.[36]

Although a significant trope within the post-Porfirian historiography is the myth that "foreigners" were privileged above Mexican citizens during the Porfiriato, this folk belief was continually being contradicted. For instance, historian Mark Wasserman maintains that "the Porfiriato did not favor foreigners to the extent proffered by the official history of the Revolution, nor did the Revolution treat foreigners as badly as some historians have maintained."[37] From my own analysis of colonization, I agree that this seems to have been the case. Returning to Article 3, it granted citizens and foreigners lands that had been "surveyed, measured, fractioned and valued," but those Mexicans abroad who were granted free land qualified for twice the amount and were exempt from taxes for fifteen years. Indeed, Section III of Article 3 states that these colonists can obtain more lands gratis. Accordingly, and "whenever the colonists shall demand it . . . the amount of land shall not exceed one hundred hectares." Ownership of the land was only transferred to colonists who could prove that they had cultivated at least one-tenth of the land "during five consecutive years."[38] From the passage of the 1883 law until its modification eleven years later, millions of hectares were surveyed, allotted, and transferred from the public domain to various private entities, with Mexicans in the United States receiving preferential treatment if they opted to populate northern frontier regions.

Even though several companies saw their contracts rescinded for not following the letter of the law, the fifty private companies that were awarded government contracts "were both the agents and beneficiaries of the greatest single turnover of public lands in the nation's history."[39] According to the most recent estimates, the total amount of public land acquired directly under this law between 1878 and 1908 was in the neighborhood of 21.2 million hectares. Given that the land companies were given a third of the land area they demarcated, it is estimated that they surveyed roughly 63.6 million hectares.[40]

By the conclusion of the two administrations that implemented these colonization policies, a total of sixty colonies had been established: sixteen under the Díaz administration and forty-four by private enterprises. Notably, Mexicans and Mexican Americans were responsible for the establishment of eight out of the sixteen colonies initiated by the government, constituting half of the total. Furthermore, individuals of Mexican descent who had relocated from the United States comprised nearly a quarter of the population within the forty-four colonies established by private companies over the course of this thirty-five-year timeframe.[41] These statistics, compiled from official records spanning the years 1876 to 1911, offer valuable insights. However, it is imperative to acknowledge the potential for revised figures due to the identification and confirmation of colonies that may not have been documented in the official records, particularly those that were never registered with Fomento.[42] It is crucial to recognize that the actual number of ethnic Mexican colonies established during the Porfiriato certainly exceeds the figures presented here. This undercount can be attributed to events occurring after 1911 that led to the dissolution of several foreign colonies. The disbandment resulted from a variety of factors, ranging from epidemic outbreaks—as occurred in the six Italian colonies—to the influence of revolutionary sentiments, particularly observed in the pillaging and ultimate devastation of most of the twelve Mormon colonies. In the aftermath of these events, ethnic Mexican settlers reclaimed and repopulated the abandoned foreign colonies. It is worth emphasizing that the periodization and statistical analysis employed have implications for the conclusions drawn. Thus, a comprehensive evaluation of these colonies is indispensable, because it has the potential to significantly modify the overarching statistical landscape, especially if we incorporate the twelve Yaqui colonies in Sonora within the same periodization.[43]

The formation of the Mexican state in the nineteenth century shares similarities with state-building efforts in analogous nations endeavoring to establish governance over diverse nomadic populations residing within their territorial boundaries. The state initiative aimed at rendering these populations legible, or comprehensible, to the governing authorities, became conspicuous due to the concurrent phenomenon of mass migration of Mexican laborers and agriculturalists northward. Simultaneously, instances of "Indian raiding and plundering" persisted. Consequently, Chihuahua emerged as the primary recipient of the 50 percent of colonization projects allocated to the northern frontier, with twenty colonies being located in that state. The remaining ten colonies were situated in central regions, the southern Pacific, and the Gulf of Mexico.[44] "As a practical matter," James C. Scott astutely observes, "most nation-states have tried, insofar as they had the means, to give substance to this vision, establishing armed border posts, moving loyal populations to the frontier and relocating or driving away 'disloyal' populations, clearing frontier lands for sedentary agriculture, building roads to the borders, and registering hitherto fugitive peoples."[45] The historical evolution of settler colonization in both Mexico and other nation-states was driven by a shared objective of solidifying and regulating national borders. This endeavor was implemented through the establishment of governmental agencies and legislative frameworks designed to facilitate the inclusion of specific population groups while deterring others. Aside from debates over exact numbers and demographic compositions, what sets Mexico's approach apart is the marked scarcity of European settlers and the deliberate preference in the 1883 colonization law accorded to Mexican communities as the primary participants in the settler-colonist initiative.[46]

More colonies, official and unofficial, were set up between the early 1870s and the close of the century than during any other period in Mexican history. The administration of General Díaz is rightly given much credit for these *colonias*; however, resettlement was well under way before that time and had seen an uptick beginning in 1870 during the administration of Benito Juárez. Moisés González Navarro's classic three-volume monograph concluded that around sixty colonies were founded from 1876 to 1911, when revolution upended Mexican politics and

Siliceo's agreement with the Ministerio de Fomento relies on much of the same logic as earlier colonization contracts that had been published in the agency's annual reports, bulletins, journals, government publications, and public news sources.[6] However, the contract stands out for its sheer geographical scope and, later, for the newspaper subsidy. Consider the opening paragraph of the contract, which sets forth that "the government is obligated to sell to Mr. Luis Siliceo, or to the companies that he may organize, and to his legitimate successors, up to one million hectares of uncultivated and national lands that may be available for sale, in the states of Chihuahua, Coahuila, Guerrero, México, Michoacán, Puebla, and Veracruz, with the exclusive purpose of colonizing them."[7] Given that Siliceo never specified the amount of land he wished to colonize or where in Mexico the colonies would be founded, the awarding of such an extensive contract may have something to do with Siliceo's cultural capital and his ability to propagandize his project throughout Greater Mexico. The final version of the contract, in fact, gives Siliceo access to the entire country as long as he negotiates with the appropriate state and municipal authorities.

Given past precedent, though, it seems likely that in its negotiations with Siliceo the Díaz administration followed the typical playbook of appropriating local repatriation agents and societies—as had taken place in California and Texas during the 1850s.[8] Siliceo was not the first diasporic Mexican to appeal for a back-to-Mexico exodus, and as a state apparatus with a long historical memory, Científicos knew all too well how to absorb and influence human activities. The awarding of what amounted to 2.47 million acres of land (about half the area of New Jersey) in several states was both carrot and stick, as Siliceo soon discovered, compelling him to study the Land and Colonization Law of 1883 in detail.[9] The first version of the contract contains forty-five articles, each with copious sections and amendments; in fact, the constant modifications made by the Científicos warrant a chapter of their own. These amendments were always to the benefit of the colonists and the administration. What distinguishes Siliceo's colonization contract is that it would come to include a five-year subsidy for publishing a newspaper encouraging the resettlement of ethnic Mexicans from the United States. This in essence makes Siliceo a proxy for the Mexican government and, by extension, an arm of Científico propaganda efforts.

Many exploratory paths are made when analyzing primary documentation, each of which can cause the researcher to veer off into many different historical plots. Evelyne Sánchez, of the Centre National de la Recherche Scientifique, argues that Siliceo's success was due in part to the reassuring familiarity of his

CHAPTER 6

CONTRACTING COLONIZATION

Luis Siliceo and El Colono

On 5 July 1895, Luis Siliceo wrote to the Ministro de Fomento, Colonización, e Industria requesting to "celebrate a contract" with the government of Mexico "for the repatriation of Mexicans now residing in the United States *ahead of* recruiting Americans and foreign colonists for the Mexican Republic." With his letter he enclosed a description of his project and a plea that the "citizen minister" consider the project, because it "preferentially benefits individuals of Mexican nationality, without neglecting European colonization."[1] In this petition and in subsequent correspondence, Siliceo encapsulated a mantra that he rehearsed well into the 1920s: he preferred members of his own "raza." Though the response from the ministry was decisively positive, the contract went through at least half a dozen modifications before being finalized that fall.[2] Mixing profits with patriotism, all parties endeavored to renegotiate the contract to their own benefit well into the 1900s. Even though the administration terminated the contract at the close of the nineteenth century, the business relationship seemingly continued for another two decades.[3] The correspondence between Siliceo and the Científicos who staffed the Ministerio de Fomento, Colonización, e Industria provides an interesting window into the contentious contractual process of settler colonization a decade prior to the "great rebellion."[4] In Siliceo's file at the Archivo Histórico de Terrenos Nacionales, there are at least three handwritten contracts—with corrections, entire articles crossed through, sarcastic margin notes, modifications, and adjustments always benefiting the administration—that illuminate the strategic thinking of the government and its relationship with the growing ethnic Mexican populations in the US Southwest.[5] In the end, both Siliceo and the Ministerio de Fomento negotiated their best outcome based on their nineteenth-century version of a cost-benefit analysis.

Mexican society, including (as one would expect) the country's administrative apparatus. For the entirety of the Porfirian era, all these settlements had to have a certain percentage of ethnic Mexicans among the colonists; the proportions ranged from 25 to 100 percent, depending on the contract. In expanding the periodization, moreover, it is reasonable to maintain that most colonists during the entire Porfiriato were ethnic Mexicans from either the United States or Mexico itself. As I will argue, the number of Mexican-origin resettlers via colonization was much higher than has previously been proposed and should change our historiographical perspective.[47] In the following chapter, I seek to show why the process of changing the government's original tally requires empirical examples of colonization that include not only actions but also primary data in the form of legal contracts between the colonizer and the colonization company manager.

PART III

THE FOLK SOCIOLOGY OF CONTRACTING COLONIZATION IN GREATER MEXICO

ideas, which were "widely shared among the country's political and intellectual elites."[10] I agree. Some of his ideas in the initial contract did not harmonize with the Científico agenda, so the agency revised them, and Siliceo accepted all suggestions without protest. One of the more interesting substitutions concerns the term "raza," which can be translated as "race," "ethnicity," or "nationality."[11] Article 3 of the first draft of the contract reads that "Mr. Siliceo is hereby authorized to establish agricultural, mining, or industrial colonies on the lands he may designate and acquire for repatriated Mexicans, individuals of the same race [raza], or Europeans accepted by the government, on the lands he may acquire from the same government or from private individuals, subject to the provisions of the law of 15 December 1883 and the stipulations of this contract."[12]

"Raza" appeared several times in the first draft of the contract, and the staff at Fomento crossed it out on at least three occasions. There is no doubt that the bureaucrats at Fomento replaced "raza" with "nationality" or "origin" due to the public nature of these legal documents. While Siliceo employed the term on at least eight occasions in his first draft, "raza" appeared in the final published contracts only in reference to purebred animals.[13] The Mexican state effectively removed all caste categories after 1821 and, as this example shows, continued to do so in the 1890s, only this time with "raza." It appears that Siliceo's usage of the term was influenced in part by his residency in the US South, where Jim Crow laws were still in effect.[14] Whatever the case, both parties renegotiated the contract whenever obstacles presented themselves, particularly when the demands were consonant with the interests of the administration and its objectives, and they ultimately came to an accord. Fomento had particularly good negotiators, who were also competing with their peers for attention and promotion, a dynamic that always placed contractual agents at a disadvantage.

Family Connections Related to Colonization

Luis Siliceo's colonization project has generated some interest among historians in the United States, Mexico, and Europe, but his biographical details are sparse and seem to draw from one another. What is certain is that there was a familial relationship between Manuel and Luis Siliceo.[15] Based on family records they were uncle and nephew.[16] Biographical details on Manuel Siliceo are quite abundant due to his role as the ministro de fomento, colonización, industria, y comercio in the administration of Ignacio Comonfort from 1855 to 1857. He had the misfortune of heading the agency in a historical moment that witnessed civil war, coups, and at least one filibustering expedition.[17] On 16 September 1857, near the end of his tenure, the ministry published its first annual report as presented by D. Manuel Siliceo.[18] Manuel's writings and actions concerning the repatriation of Mexicans from the United States during the Comonfort administration aligned with those of Luis Siliceo four decades later.[19]

Manuel Siliceo was one of the more vocal proponents of Mexican American resettlement, especially after war with the United States generated an increase in Sonoran outmigration to the goldfields of California.[20] This northward migration left the frontiers open to more raiding by indios bárbaros. Although a few miners returned quite wealthy, many others were subject to maltreatment under the "new order of things" in the gold placers of California.[21] Minister Siliceo maintained that there were "great advantages" to welcoming these Sonoran settlers home because "they do not mix with the Anglo-Saxon race" with whom they lack a common culture, and they would fare much better as colonists in Sonora.[22] In the context of nation-state formation, Siliceo emphasized that the government could manage these extraterritorial movements by incorporating them into the nation's larger colonization designs.

Secretary Siliceo's role in appointing Jesús Islas as repatriation commissioner for California in 1856 is perhaps the most obvious example of his position on the resettlement of Mexicans from the United States. Commenting on the self-funded and independent back-to-Mexico movement of Jesús Islas's Junta para Promover la Emigración de Todos los Hispanos-Americanos Residentes en California (Junta to Promote the Emigration of All Hispanic-Americans Residing in California), Siliceo suggested,

> If the supreme government decides to provide its protection to the project initiated by Mr. Jesús Islas, it seems that it would be convenient to appoint this individual as a colonization agent in accordance with the law of 16 February 1854, in order to facilitate the relocation of the Hispanic-American population to Sonora. This should be done in coordination with the government of the new state and in agreement with the agent in Hermosillo regarding the lands to be granted based on the number of individuals who immigrate, the location where the colonies will be established, and the assistance to be provided to those who cannot relocate on their own.[23]

Thus, officials in Mexico City coopted the most visible leader of a local, California mutual-aid society and appointed him the repatriation commissioner for the northwestern area.[24]

This appointment would later become ensconced in law, but an interesting overlap appears here between the two Siliceos, Manuel (the minister) and Luis (the editor of *El Colono*).

After the Mexican-American War, various Mexican administrations successfully co-opted a number of back-to-Mexico movements and their leaders. One notable example can be read in the Disposición de 13 de Febrero de 1856 promulgated in order to "promote the emigration of the Hispanic American race residing in California, in order to take advantage of it for the colonization of the state of Sonora." The document that conveyed this mandate took the form of a personal letter referencing the resettlement of Californios coupled with policy recommendations about how to collaborate with Jesús Islas in California. Manuel Siliceo noted that the knowledgeable "inhabitants of Sonora, well aware of this project, have joyfully embraced it, recognizing not only the benefits it promises in terms of cultivating their vast deserts and defending against barbarians but also the potential for reuniting a portion of Sonorans in California who, due to limited resources, have been unable to return to their homeland."[25] The exchange between government officials and frontier settlers is reminiscent of Wolfe's observation regarding "frontier individuals' endless appeals for state protection" and the close collaboration needed for proper resettlement.[26] Both parties evidently aimed to curtail Indian raids and till the soil of the homeland.

What the older Siliceo saw in the colonization of the northern frontiers was a product of the historicity of the postwar period. The Texas revolt in 1836 and the diplomatic fallout from the Mexican-American War altered the trajectory of Mexico's settler colonial imaginaries toward loyal and culturally amicable resettlers living in the United States, including several Amerindian groups. Indeed, the military dimension of colonization policy being vital to national security is made plain when he writes about "the significant benefits that this emigration will bring forth if the Supreme government provides assistance, as it does not raise concerns for public safety, given that the inhabitants, due to their language, customs, religion, and their past [negative] experiences in California, will not be able to harmonize their sentiments with those of the Northern Republic."[27] Siliceo was perspicacious and prescient in his observations that anti-American sentiment was the best loyalty test for potential frontier settlers along the international border with an enemy nation. Negative experiences as manifested in a species of "reactive ethnicity" was the ideal ideology of *ressentiment* for fortifying the northern frontiers of the Mexican state.[28]

Colonization was always the centerpiece of nineteenth-century frontier defense, and the Disposición de 13 de Febrero de 1856 is an example of this thinking. Clearly, colonization was the primary concern of frontier governance at this time in Sonora, but so were the threats of filibusters and continued Indian raiding.[29] Siliceo pointed out that Californios were "the only migrants who [could] immediately make the lands of the State of Sonora productive and contain the depredations of the Barbarians." This colonization of Hispanic Americans from California was especially important for frontier states like Sonora, which "[was] very exposed to be invaded by greedy adventurers due to its scant population."[30] Siliceo was not only an astute politician and head of the Ministerio de Fomento, but apparently also a prophet. Islas and his colonization project would later be disbanded amid allegations of filibusterism and conspiracy against the government.[31] Mexican officials quickly discovered that the filibustering expedition of Henry A. Crabb had attempted to blend in among the resettlers, and the expedition members were eventually captured and executed.[32] According to at least one newspaper account, the Californio colonists proceeded with resettling in Ures, Sonora, after they participated in thwarting Crabb's expedition.[33]

The resettlement of Mexicans in the United States, it would thus appear, was part of the Siliceo family's history, and it certainly is now.[34] Manuel is never mentioned in any of the correspondence among the Díaz administration, the bureaucrats in Fomento, and Luis Siliceo, yet the two relatives seem passionate about the resettlement of Mexicans from the United States. The coincidence seemed too apparent not to indulge with a brief historical digression into Luis Siliceo's family background as it relates to the idea of autocolonization.[35]

Luis Siliceo's Various Businesses and Interests

Luis Gonzaga Homobano Siliceo Chousal (1855–1928) was born in León, Guanajuato, Mexico, to José María Siliceo and Doña Elena Chousal. On 16 February 1855 he was baptized in the Santa Iglesia Parroquial de la Ciudad de León.[36] For most of his life, Siliceo used just his first name and middle initial, and rarely is Gonzaga, Homobano, or Chousal mentioned in the available documentation. Siliceo's childhood was spent primarily in the city of León, which, as historians of Mexican migration to the United States will attest, is one of the traditional centers of migrant laborers.[37] The early social phenomenon of northward migration made an impression on Siliceo, who by the age of thirty-one had migrated to the southern United States. In the city of New Orleans on 6 January 1887, Siliceo married Marie Camelia Debat, whom the 1880 US census lists as being from Spain.[38] In 1907 Siliceo married a second time, this time to a younger woman, Sunny Mendoza, a "Mexico-Texana," in Mexico City. Sunny was the daughter of Nicanor Mendoza, Siliceo's trusted colleague during the resettlement project and one of the many who migrated south from San Antonio, Texas, to Michoacán at the close of the nineteenth century.

The handful of historiographical characterizations of Siliceo commonly begin and end with his editorship of *El Colono* and his well-publicized resettlement projects, probably because a few repositories have three of the five volumes of the newspaper (from 1895 to late 1898).[39] His propagandizing of colonization overshadowed the many businesses he operated before, during, and after his proprietorship of *El Colono* in 1900.[40] Siliceo claimed to have been studying the question of colonization for at least three years before embarking on this endeavor, but once he was able to capitalize on it, his interests spread into numerous areas beyond resettlement and real estate.[41] Articles in *El Colono* mention the newspaper *La Repatriación* on several occasions, which suggests that Siliceo also owned this periodical.[42] Evelyne Sánchez observes that Siliceo was an astute opportunist who saw a business prospect when he purchased a local paper, *El Cronista Mexicano*, and later transformed it into *El Colono* to publish state-sponsored propaganda. He was also the principal stakeholder in the colonization contract that effectively gave him access to 2.5 million acres. In addition to running three newspapers, he owned a photography studio and later expanded into the sale of livestock, seeds, agricultural equipment, machines, everyday farming implements, metals, and subscriptions, along with engaging in mining, advising/consulting, teaching English, and serving as an intermediary for several foreign business interests.

Siliceo's long-term interest in colonization and other businesses appears to have continued for at least two more decades after the end of this contract in 1900.[43] During the 1920s, he ran a photography business out of 317½ West Commerce in downtown San Antonio while continuing to advertise his resettlement business (at the same address) as the "Only Repatriation Agency; Luis G. Siliceo, General Manager."[44] Given that Siliceo continued to do business for years after the conclusion of his first contract with the Departamento de Fomento, Colonización, e Industria, it stands to reason that he managed to retain important business connections with subsequent administrations in Mexico City, particularly after the events of 1910. Thus, once he returned to San Antonio from Mexico City, it was natural that he would fall back into profitable and secure types of businesses.

Unica Agencia de

REPATRIACION

LUIS G. SILICEO

Director General.

317½ W. Commerce St. San Antonio, Tex.

Nota.—Es indispensable la instalación de Juntas Especiales en donde quiera que haya mexicanos que deseen regresar a la Patria. Para mayores informes, dirigirse por escrito al Agente Director.

One of many ads in *La Prensa* of San Antonio advertising the Repatriation Agency of Luis Siliceo well after the completion of his contract with the Díaz administration in 1900. This example is from Wednesday, September 29, 1920.

Courtesy of The Portal to Texas History, University of North Texas Libraries. Lozano, Ignacio E., La Prensa (San Antonio, TX), vol. 7, no. 2,001, ed. 1, Wednesday, September 29, 1920.

For Siliceo, the resettlement of Mexico-Texanos in Mexico was a source of income that he could tap beginning in 1895 and continuing well into the 1920s, thanks to the considerable experience he acquired over that quarter century. However, colonization activities represent just a handful of the enterprises identifiable through an analysis of *El Colono* and select records housed at the Archivo General de la Nación in Mexico City. Even as Siliceo diligently managed the affairs of *El Colono* and orchestrated the relocation of countless fellow countrymen, he demonstrated remarkable versatility by concurrently engaging in a multitude of other endeavors, often partnering with foreign investors. Among the formal requests for concessions Siliceo initiated were at least two contracts in which he and C. W. Wampler sought to negotiate the construction of a calcium carbide factory, illustrating a few of his excursions into "new industries."[45] These contracts were standard in their language, but more research is required to determine the extent and influence of these investments and whether they translated into profits. Siliceo also entered into contracts with the government in areas quite different from photography or colonization, such as for the manufacturing of enamel artifacts and the galvanizing of metal.[46]

Siliceo appears to have enjoyed cordial relations with Mexico City's elite and continued to live in that city after the end of his contract in 1900. The following year he entered into contractual agreements with other government agencies. On 25 September 1901, Siliceo wrote to the director of the National Conservatory of Music in Mexico City to offer free English lessons to twenty students, saying, "[I am] persuaded that the study of languages is useful in any place or time and [am] wishing to make known the special system I employ to teach English." The director of the National Conservatory was quite enthusiastic about the prospect of language classes and wrote directly to the Secretary of Justice and Public Education that very day asking that Siliceo be taken up on his offer.[47] Siliceo was apparently charismatic and very convincing, and regular references to "systems" were one of several calling cards he used in marketing his services.

This chapter delves into the historical context, reception, and critique of Luis Siliceo's endeavors to negotiate a colonization contract with the administration of Porfirio Díaz in 1895. The original contract, handwritten and preserved, encapsulates the intricate negotiations and includes illuminating correspondence with prominent members of the Científico classes. The extensive documentation of these negotiations vividly illustrates the pervasive skepticism surrounding colonization contracts, shedding light on why the authorities ultimately annulled a significant number of them. Minister of Fomento Manuel Fernández Leal, in his candid 1897 annual report, disclosed that an astonishing 55 percent of the colonization contracts signed between 1892 and 1896 had been rendered null and void. The historiographical implications of these voided contracts are substantial, as they are often cited as one of the key structural factors contributing to the eruption of the 1910 revolution, making them a topic deserving of their own study.[48] All colonies established in Mexico during the Porfiriato were by contract; what makes Siliceo's file unusual is that it contains a series of amended contracts, illustrating the extensive negotiation and cooperation between the state and potential *contratistas*.

As it turned out, resettler colonization was far from Siliceo's only interest, and resettlement activities generated a wide variety of partnerships. Not every colonist came fully prepared for such a life-changing endeavor, so Siliceo sold seeds, machinery, farming equipment, livestock, and consultation services. Biographical details about him are not as abundant as those of his relative,

SILICEO,S ADVISING BUREAU.

Best business chances in Mexico, introduced to foreing capitalists and investors in order to facilitate abroad the organization of Companies or corporations.

Colonization enterprises, Concessions, Contracts, Patents, Lands sold, titles examined, reports on mines, indnstries investigated and general information about Mexico's resourses promptly and acuratedly furnished.

BUSINESS WITH THE DEPARTMENTS A SPECIALITY

MAPS AND DRAWINGS OF EVERY DESCRIPTION EXECUTED

Translations, Typewriting and Interpreting

TERMS MODERATE, CORRESPONDENCE SOLICITED.

LUIS SILICEO,
MANAGER AND CONCESSIONARY.

SILICEO'S ADVISING BUREAU.

P. O. BOX 54 BIS. OFFICE 45. STA ISABEL ST

MEXICO CITY, MEX. REP.

Office hours, from 9 A. M. to 1 P. M. and from 3 to 6 P. M.

SUBSCRIBE FOR "EL COLONO"

✳ $1,25 por year ✳

This paper contains important information for those intending to buy lands in Mexico, and is edited by Mr. Luis Siliceo, concessionary from the General and State Governments to colonize, lands in the Republic under liberal contrats.

Office, 45, Santa Isabel St., or P. O. Box 54 Bis.

City of Mexico

Correspondence solicited.

One of many ads in *El Colono* for one of the businesses that Siliceo parleyed from his colonization contract with the Díaz administration.
Courtesy of the Hemeroteca Nacional de México, Universidad Nacional Autónoma de México.

Manuel Siliceo. Still, several policy measures his uncle enacted as ministro de fomento, colonización, industria y comercio from 1855 to 1857 were incorporated into Luis Siliceo's approach to resettlement four decades later. I suggest that there does seem to be a convenient coincidence between these two relatives and their interest in the resettlement of Mexicans from the United States.

CHAPTER 7

DIASPORIC DEBATES AND THE VARIETIES OF SETTLER-COLONISTS

Historically speaking, when Mexican federal and state officials passed colonization laws, the new laws were promptly publicized in government and private publications, including those circulating in Texas and Greater Mexico. The Land and Colonization Law of 1883 generated its share of debate in the senate and the chamber of deputies prior to its passage, and afterwards in the Mexico City public sphere as well. The law granted Mexicans in the United States preferential treatment if they opted to return and populate the northern frontier regions of the republic, but it also allowed for the settlement of select western Europeans considered "industrious."[1]

Early Diasporic Debates over Colonization: "Foot on the Neck of Our Brothers"

"Diasporic debates" can be described as historical disagreements surrounding the possibilities and liabilities of returning to one's country of origin or ethnic homeland. In the case of resettling to Mexico, there was no numerical consistency or ideological slant to these diasporic debates; they seemingly waxed when word got out that another group of compatriots was organizing to resettle and waned with the end of media coverage.

One example of what I would describe as a diasporic debate took place three years prior to Siliceo negotiating his colonization contract. The four-part debate was serialized in *El Correo de Laredo* over a week in April 1892, in response to an editorial entitled, "Why Don't They Come?" which had been reprinted in a Guadalajara newspaper named *El Heraldo*.[2] The back-and-forth that was generated between *El Heraldo* and *El Correo* began by reminding the reader that on the northern side of the Río Bravo, the process of Americanization had material as well as psychological consequences for those who did not resettle in Mexico proper. The vituperative editorial read as follows:

> In the opulent territories that were taken from us in the year 1847, there are over a million Mexicans who, as foreigners in their own land, will eventually have to renounce their ideals, customs, beliefs, and the language of their ancestors and assimilate with their oppressors. Alternatively, they will lead a melancholic existence, consumed by the bitterness of seeing their possessions in foreign hands and never being able to exercise the political rights inherent to their status as members of the human family, all to avoid losing forever the noble title of children of Mexico.[3]

This was just the opening paragraph! The writer suggested that part of the impulse for writing the editorial was to respond to various sensationalized newspaper stories reporting that "a Mexican was hanged or lynched"; "the virtue of two young Mexican girls was abused"; "there was an encounter between so many Yankees and Mexicans"; and that a US state had allegedly "declared that Mexicans, like negroes, have not the rights of whites."[4] The writer projected on this negative newspaper coverage his own "reactive ethnicity," which was partly fueled by new printing technologies driven by the growing influence of advertising.[5] Here, it is important to keep in mind that this epoch also gave rise to the term "yellow journalism." Much like today, "if it bleeds, it leads."[6]

Based simply on the references to Greek and Roman history in the text, the author of the piece was well educated and striving for impartiality, but from a particular point of view. The editorial opens with a critique of US core principles, going so far as to suggest that the country has betrayed its founding ideals, the spirit of Édouard René Lefèbvre de Laboulaye, and thus the liberatory symbolism of the Statue of Liberty (a gift from Laboulaye).[7] "And that nation that boasts the nickname of being great is the one that puts its foot on the neck of our brothers," the author noted sarcastically. The situation has left Mexicans in the United States with "no other shield than their memories and . . . like the Israelites, . . . waiting for a redeeming messiah and liberator." At the same time, "There is certainly no lack of Mexicans, rotten members of our race, who are Germanized and forget their own language." But these are only a handful, the author observes, "who if they inspire any feeling, it is certainly not that of the hatred they deserve for their felony, but that of contempt, for their poor judgment." Most of these Mexicans "retain the love of their homeland, crystallized by misfortune and despair."[8] The core question becomes, given that newspapers are constantly publishing articles about how violent and horrible it is to be Mexican in the United States, "Why Don't They Come?"

Considering the Mexican government's generous offers of land and free importation of animals, the author's question is perhaps also rhetorical, as if to lament the lack of ethnic Mexicans returning to the country. The article ends with a frequently voiced warning about the dangers of Americanization and cultural ethnocide: "The future of your children also demands it; if you want to prevent them from becoming Americanized, raise them in Mexican territory, so that they will be taught to love the tricolor flag, to respect our heroes and to abhor our enemies." The sales pitch ends with the point that the Mexican federal government magnanimously offers at least "four hectares of land free of charge" and the right to bring "animals or implements" without having to pay any taxes for their importation. The question is answered rhetorically with the usual cost-benefit analysis of migration: "Why don't they come?"[9]

The Varieties of Mexican Settler-Colonists

This set of diasporic debates printed only a few years prior to Siliceo's back-to-Mexico movement was indicative of the many concerns and critiques of the Greater Mexico public sphere. Hence, the editor of *El Correo de Laredo*, printed north of the border in Texas, responds to the editorial from *El Heraldo* of Guadalajara with a three-part rejoinder in serialized form—a common feature of nineteenth-century newspapers. The first article essentially agrees with *El Heraldo's* broader and more ideological critiques concerning the hypocrisy of American democracy and the bigotry against "all individuals who have black hair." The second part of the response to *El Heraldo* can be described as a political homage to President Porfirio Díaz, being essentially a "puff piece" that defends his tireless efforts to protect Mexicans in the United States.[10] The final installment ventures into what can be described as "folk sociology," an unscientific set of popular beliefs based on personal bias, hearsay, gossip, rumor, and generalizations.[11] Here, the authors sketch out the three classes of potential colonists they perceive among the Mexico-Texanos: (1) the conquered population, (2) commercial or labor migrants, and (3) fugitives from justice and army deserters.[12] An analysis of these articles offers a window into some of the rhetorical headwinds that Luis Siliceo confronted when he initiated his colonization project three years later.

While articulating a variety of diasporic debates, these critiques also took advantage of the space to analyze nineteenth-century US social norms and customs, including those around "racial" and partisan differences. *El Correo de Laredo*'s first response to the "brilliant article" from *El Heraldo* spends several pages agreeing with the overall critiques of US (lack of) democracy, the horrendous political environment, and the partisan media that typically propagandizes on behalf of one political party over another. During the late nineteenth century, it was well understood that newspapers were partisan in nature, even as they all strove to be impartial and to correct the record when necessary. The United States "has no principles in politics, nor in religion, nor in economics, nor in anything," argued the staff of *El Correo*. The laws of the country are bent or influenced depending on which political party is elected. Worse still is the segregation between "blacks" and "whites" and the ill treatment of Mexicans, who are not seen favorably because they "are considered as descendants of negros, and moreover, as spoils of conquest." Even so, the article also notes that Mexican migrants are regularly involved in local party politics. The staff calculates that as "proof of what we say is the existence of some fifty newspapers that claim to be Mexican," of which only half a dozen are not in the service of some political party.[13] Political participation by Mexicans citizens in US elections was seen by many as an automatic forfeiture of citizenship and a violation of national sovereignty.[14]

The second part of the response came only in late April 1892. Like most historical narratives that discuss the diplomatic histories between the United States and Mexico, *El Correo de Laredo* follows an "authentic historicity" in which the years 1846–48 serve as the obligatory starting point.[15] The difference in the *El Correo* case is its discussion of the election of General Díaz. According to the writers of the second editorial, published only a few days later, on 23 April 1892, Díaz's administration, more so than any before it, is protecting "the interests of the million Mexicans mentioned by our colleague 'El Heraldo' of Guadalajara." After accusing 90 percent of all Mexican newspapers of being partisan mouthpieces, the *El Correo* editorial spends considerable space praising the master politico, Porfirio Díaz. Specifically, President Díaz has "promoted the repatriation of Mexicans by any means at his disposal, offering bonuses to the repatriates, and giving them free lands on Mexican soil." The article laments that the president's good intentions are "sterile," however. Although *El Heraldo* correctly characterizes the oppressive conditions north of the border, in reality Mexicans north of the border frequent consular offices in the United States only when they have some conflict that local authorities cannot resolve. In short, the government is clear about its naturalization laws for "Mexicans in the exterior," but the question remains, if conditions are so negative in the United States, "Why Don't They Go to Mexico"?[16]

For all its biting criticism of US politics, *El Correo de Laredo* leaves no doubt as to where it falls on the Mexican political spectrum: it is a Porfirista publication. The paper's defense of Porfirian colonization policy is worth discussing because it reflects a historiographical trope in the writings on Mexican American colonization. In fact, Mexican historian Lawrence Douglas Taylor Hansen echoes these late-nineteenth-century ideas almost a century later when he argues that the government of Mexico "has not forgotten for a single moment the Mexicans residing in this country, but has provided them with guarantees and even advantages for repatriation, and, disregarding their offers, has circumscribed, by means of appropriate laws, the number of Mexicans entitled to the protection of our flag."[17] There is certainly an argument to be made for such observations, but in concluding their praise for the noble efforts of the Díaz administration to resettle Mexicans from the United States, the authors of *El Colono* end this installment with the same rhetorical question: why don't they seek the legal "protection of our consulates"?[18]

The final installment in the series outlines a species of folk sociology about the various social classes that make up the Mexico-Texano community that could potentially resettle across the international boundary: "Mexicans residing in the United States can be divided into three main classes," suggest the *El Correo* writers: (1) the old conquered population; (2) new economically motivated migrants; and (3) outlaws and deserters. The first group is composed of the natives of Texas, New Mexico, and California who came under the legal jurisdiction of the United States after the end of the Mexican-American War and thus "are not entitled to the protection of the Mexican flag." Writing almost half a century after 1846, the authors state that the population in question has "already formed a new generation" who has "no clear idea of the homeland, or any affection for it." Given their substantial interests and holdings in the United States, these individuals are deemed unlikely to resettle in Mexico, especially since their idea of the country has been so tarnished by "speakers and journalists who describe it as a den of bandits, where disorder, pillage and destruction are a constant threat to all interests."[19] According to the folk sociology, this group of "Mexicanos" were US citizens and therefore unlikely to resettle in Mexico.

The second and third groups in *El Correo*'s folk sociology are, respectively, economic migrants and fugitives from the law. The first group of economic migrants consists of merchants, industrialists, and day laborers who have already "abandoned" and are "abandoning the borders of their homeland in search of fortune, and [are] devoted to increasing their interests." These individuals, not surprisingly, "will certainly not respond to the offers of repatriation if they do not see in them the improvement and expansion of their business."[20] By 1892, the migration of Mexicans northward was flowing like never before, and many of these migrants settled in the cultural enclaves of San Antonio, El Paso, and Laredo, Texas, and began forming a respectable middle class.[21] The difference between the conquered group and this new middle class, argues *El Correo de Laredo*, is "that fraction of the Mexican colony that really represents Mexico in the United States is not persecuted, is not insulted, but rather is well esteemed, because it never ignores its rights and never transgresses the limits of the law."[22] The individuals *El Correo* describes here are what some contemporary scholars might label as "gente decente."[23] Targeting this group for resettlement in Mexico is not viable and, in fact, would "be asking too much of them" because all of them will seemingly echo the identical retort from all corners. "We do not want to go to Mexico to earn fifty cents or one peso, when here we earn two or three pesos." Having presented a basic cost-benefit analysis of contemporary migration, the writers also make sure to point out that this group (to which the staff of *El Correo* belongs) is economically American but Mexican in identity by ending their observations with "if one day the homeland is in danger and needs our blood, we will rush to pour it on its altars, to cleanse the honor of our banners with it."[24] This second group makes up the majority of the ethnic Mexican population in Texas, are the most respectable, and not surprisingly, are also the most patriotic.

The final group of potential repatriates is not only the worst kind of colonist for the Mexican nation, but the stereotype that came to taint Siliceo's later resettlement project. *El Correo de Laredo*'s tripartite folk sociology identifies the most problematic elements of this population as "composed of smugglers, fugitives from justice, deserters from the army, and people of dubious living." The last includes runaway Mexican army conscripts, which from a twenty-first century standpoint, seems like a minor offense. This group is a minority of the population, according to the article writer, but their numbers are growing, and they can easily mix and meld with the other classes of Mexicans. Therefore, their repatriation to Mexico should only be considered after an in-depth study.[25]

In closing and in response to the title of the original *El Heraldo* editorial, "Why Don't They Come," the writers of *El Correo* repeat the common mantra of the labor market: "because under no circumstance is repatriation in their interests."[26] This set of ideas would cause Siliceo difficulty three years later and would become embedded in the diasporic debates circulating in the Greater Mexico public sphere. Economic and material interests were at the center of most decisions to settle or resettle on one or the other side of the international boundary from 1846 on, and this logic dominated most mass movements of people into the late 1890s.

"Proposal to Resettle Mexicans Who Have Evaded the Justice System"

On 24 June 1892, just a few months after *El Correo de Laredo* published its series of editorials on repatriation, an exchange between the heads of the Secretaría de Fomento and the Secretaría de Relaciones Exteriores relayed a colonization proposal from the state of Texas to resettle "Mexicans who have evaded the administration of justice by passing into American territory."[27] This content is worth going over in detail because it represents privately expressed views of concerns that all settler colonial states have confronted.[28] Contrasting a government document produced by the administration with the folk sociology published in the pages of *El Correo* yields a "thick description" of details that illuminate why so much ink and distress was spilled over the occupational status of settler-colonists.[29] Is there some truth to the assessment of the third category of ethnic Mexicans in Texas as being "composed of smugglers, fugitives from justice, deserters from the army, and people of dubious living"?[30] Or are structural conditions like droughts and declining economies more to blame for the criminalization of these "fugitives from justice"?

On 24 March 1892, just one month prior to the publication of the series of editorials in *El Correo de Laredo*, Manuel A. Saldaña of Brownsville, Texas, wrote a letter to Secretary of War and Marine General Pedro Hinojosa in Mexico City. Coincidence? Perhaps. Saldaña begins by claiming that there are as many Mexicans in the states of Texas, New Mexico, Arizona, and California as there are in the Mexican Republic and, with proper guarantees, they could form an ideal group to resettle in Tamaulipas, forming a colony to be named Colonia Hinojosa.[31] The honorific naming of repatriate colonies after an executive, secretary, or some patriotic figure was a not uncommon feature of resettlement; hence, Saldaña's suggested name for the colony was clearly intended to curry favor with the general.[32] In diplomacy, flattery is a useful tool.

Like Luis Siliceo, Saldaña believed that the Mexican "government would be more accepting of the emigration of its nationals who wish to return to their homeland than of the immigration of Chinese or men of color, as has been and is being discussed at present."[33] That "men of color" or Chinese nationals were being privileged over Mexicans is hyperbole, but exaggerations are a common feature of much human correspondence, especially when writers are straining to highlight their viewpoint.[34] The settlement of these foreigners, argued Saldaña, "will bring serious consequences for Mexico" one day, "because the settlers are of foreign nationality." Instead, the Mexican government should look to its people abroad, even if those people did not possess the moral standards as outlined by *El Correo de Laredo.* At least on the question of autocolonization, Saldaña was effectively highlighting the "common sense" ideas of that era's zeitgeist, or at least that of the Científicos.[35]

In his letter to General Hinojosa, Saldaña proposes initially to resettle six hundred families "back into the country at an agreed-upon time, assuring the immigration of 2,000 more families from the state of Texas alone." But unlike Siliceo, whose resettlement project was focused on skilled agriculturalists, Saldaña makes no bones about telling the general that "among these families there are many accused of different crimes before the courts of Mexico." Echoing the words of *El Correo de Laredo,* he stated that a number of these settler-colonists were wanted for "robbery" while "others [were wanted] for murder, others for desertions, and others for violations of the neutrality laws." Although these individuals were citizens of Mexico, many had voted in US elections or were jailed in US state penitentiaries. Saldaña goes so far as to name those involved in criminal cases, including those who had taken up arms against the government of Mexico.[36]

Saldaña echoes the nationalist discourse that calls for the sacrifice of its citizens in the service of the nation by rationalizing his resettlement of "refugees from justice" as a project of patriotic conversion from "bad Mexicans" to "good Mexicans." "There are many nationals who wish to return to Mexico," he writes, "and they hold out hope of being granted their pardon, pledging their word that they will never act against the dignity of the country." If the government approves their eagerly anticipated pardon to return to their cherished homeland, "they will submit to the recognition of all national laws."[37] These heretofore "bad Mexicans"—even those who had taken up arms against the government—could be converted into "good Mexicans" if given the opportunity to resettle in Mexico proper and begin life anew. This is not the type of settler-colonists Siliceo would seek to recruit in the pages of *El Colono*. Siliceo was more of a Tejano Científico and a prophet of "order and progress." In fact, the entire premise of his project was that *his* settler colonists were "soldiers of progress," not "fugitives from justice."[38] But this did not deter the Mexican American press from accusing Siliceo of recruiting "bad Mexicans" as colonists.

In terms of content and style, Saldaña's appeal to General Hinojosa is typical of the written communications between Mexican Americans and government officials in Mexico City; however, it is not the sort of correspondence intended for public consumption. Instead it constitutes what Ranajit Guha refers to as "primary discourse" because of its immediacy, particularly its connection to the centers of power.[39] In other words, "primary discourse" refers not only to the historical authenticity of the "primary source," but also to the communiqué's proximity to those power relations. Moreover, the correspondence provides some interesting secondary sociological background into why some Mexicans were being jailed during this period. These were not criminals by nature, Saldaña argued, but individuals treated unjustly by the US system of justice and who thus held a deep resentment toward it. He reported that "many are the vexations suffered by a multitude of our nationals due to the American authorities, the jails and penitentiaries are full of men who are perhaps innocent, many of them, of the crimes of which they are accused . . . [and] there are also many suffering in the penitentiaries because they, seeing themselves surrounded by innocent and small children asking them for food, have become criminals by taking a sheep, a goat, or holding a horse against the will of its owners."[40]

Extremely difficult economic conditions in South Texas had been compounded four years earlier by a severe drought that ruined many families whose crops were "completely lost" when corn was worth between one and twelve dollars a bushel![41] In light of Saldaña's folk sociology of "bad Mexicans," it would seem *El Correo* could have included four more classes of potential repatriates to complexify their analysis. Saldaña seemed to repeat the suggestions made in the Proyectos de colonización of 5 July 1848 when he suggested that robbers, murderers, army deserters, and former rebels could all be converted from "bad" to "good Mexicans."[42]

The many public debates over resettlement between newspapers based in various states in Mexico and the US Southwest constitute an "imagined community," a print capital network facilitating a Greater Mexico public sphere. The various concerns published by many news sources, particularly as voiced in the debates and discussions surrounding the resettlement of Mexicans from the United States help to situate Siliceo's colonization project (1895 to 1900) in its historical context.[43] These debates were witty, humorous, sarcastic, and replete with historical examples that complexify the historicity of resettlement. As I have tried to show, almost every mass movement of ethnic Mexicans migrating north or returning south throughout the nineteenth century generated various state and local responses. It is not feasible to survey the sentiments of people who lived during that era, so these public debates in the Greater Mexico press offer us one of the few sources of "feeling."[44] Although it is difficult to generalize, debates over colonization policies repeatedly centered on the "kind and quality" of the desired settler-colonists, and this will be the subject of the following chapter.

CHAPTER 8

FOLK SOCIOLOGY IN GREATER MEXICO

It was the summer of 1895 when Siliceo first communicated with Manuel Fernández Leal—the new head of the Ministerio de Fomento, Colonización, e Industria. From that summer through the end of the year, a new series of diasporic debates appeared in a deluge of newspaper articles in Mexico and the United States. The themes resonated with most nineteenth-century arguments concerning the resettlement of Mexican Americans in the northern frontier regions of Mexico, and these sorts of public discussions usually emerged whenever a new repatriation project was being formed.[1] The deliberations took place on both sides of the international boundary, and articles from one newspaper were frequently republished in their entirety elsewhere.[2] For example, *El Fronterizo*, of Tucson, Arizona, came out on Saturday morning and regularly republished articles and commentaries from the neighboring state of Sonora, particularly articles containing any commentary about the diasporic populations in Greater Mexico. Repatriation always concerned populations on both sides of the international boundary, and newspaper debates of the era constitute one of the few sources to gauge this late-nineteenth-century public sentiment.

Folk Sociology in Greater Mexico: Renegades, Migrants, and Ayankados

A week before Siliceo wrote to the Ministerio de Fomento requesting permission to resettle Mexico-Texanos, *El Fronterizo* republished an editorial from *El Imparcial*, based in Hermosillo, Sonora, on the potential resettlement of Mexicans from Texas.[3] As before, the primary issues raised were about the quality of colonists and the economic prospects of resettling in Mexico. *El Imparcial* repeated the common tropes about social class that were circulating in Spanish-language newspapers throughout the Greater Mexico network, including those disparaging the variety of settler-colonists likely to return. Although not supplying an organized taxonomy of social classes per se, the editor of *El Imparcial* came to the same conclusion as *El Correo de Laredo* about Mexican laborers being the most practical colonists for recruitment. Agreeing with his colleagues, the editor wrote approvingly of distinguishing between everyday migrants in search of a better life and outright wrongdoers:

> In this regard, a fair distinction is made between the scoundrels who have gone to the towns of Texas fleeing from the Mexican police or in search of dubious records to make a living, and the laborers who, believing they would find abundant and well-paid work, have left the border towns to settle beyond the dividing line. After many years of harsh hardships, they have become convinced that their future does not lie in that country and are planning to return to their homeland.[4]

Through an examination of the folk sociology of these periodicals, the editor of *El Imparcial* has clearly identified two potential classes of Mexicans considered suitable colonists: disenchanted laborers and the scoundrels who "have gone to the towns of Texas fleeing from the Mexican police." In a more hopeful tone, he later opines that "despite the very bitter truths we have written, work and education can very well regenerate these men and rekindle in them the love for the homeland that, if they have not completely lost, may be slumbering a cataleptic sleep in their renegade hearts."[5] In other words, even these renegades from justice were still potentially good colonists, as Manuel Saldaña had written in his earlier letter. At the same time, the editor mentions a potential third group who could resettle.

The discussion of colonization in Mexico in general, and more narrowly of the best candidates for such an endeavor, provides an interesting window into the Greater Mexico community's overall self-assessment. Moreover, the analysis of late-nineteenth-century intra-ethnic diasporic debates supports an interesting point of view. Specifically, in addition to rehabilitated lawbreakers and disheartened migrants, the editor of *El Imparcial* suggests that the third group who could potentially resettle are individuals "convinced that they can no longer continue living in a country where they do not even enjoy the guarantee of life, and where they are treated with greater contempt than the *chinos y negros*."[6] That Chinese immigrants are mentioned in this Sonoran newspaper speaks volumes about the distance Asian transpacific workers had journeyed. As well, these group comparisons also speak to the self-triangulation of ethnic differences when comparing the lot of Mexicans with that of other groups, including Yankees.[7]

In putting forth the groups of Mexicans who could possibly relocate to Mexico as settler-colonists, the editor identifies another group of people worth discussing: *ayankados*. This term is clearly a Mexicanization of the word "Yankee" signifying something akin to a Yankee-lover or Americanized Mexican. The writers lampooned the "Mexicans who have lived there for many years" and "with few exceptions are more Papist than the Pope; that is to say, they are more *ayankados* than the *yanquis* themselves." Just as "chinos y negros" were disparaged, the comparisons with Yankees were equally biting and sarcastic, especially when applied to that class of Mexicans who had fully assimilated to US culture. Just like recent converts, these Yankee-lovers were more zealous than their coreligionists "to such a degree that they even hate their language, preferring to mumble a detestable English that provokes the laughter of the North Americans themselves."[8] In their reference to the pope in Rome, the writers' ideological point of view was clearly anticlerical, while their disgust of assimilated *ayankados* also underscores their anti-Americanism and cultural chauvinism.

Its location in Sonora certainly provided *El Imparcial* with some distance to insult the Mexican American populations of the US Southwest, especially when it came to *ayankado*-style politics involving Republicans and Democrats. The authors were blunt when naming names, as in the case of O. A. Larrazola, who for many years had swung "the Mexican vote in favor of the Democrat party in that county, by which circumstance he has managed to rise to occupy very important public positions in the courthouse . . . and for those political jobs they have needed nothing more than a few hundred pesos and a few barrels of lager beer paid for by the Democrat Committee."[9] Larrazola's work on behalf of the Democratic Party did eventually pay off: he was elected governor of New Mexico in 1918 and in 1928 became the first Hispanic elected to the US Senate.[10]

Debating Autocolonization in the Greater Mexico Public Sphere

Among the responses to the article in *El Imparcial*, it is interesting to observe several journalistic practices no longer in vogue—one of which is an appreciation of historical context.[11] After reproducing the editorial in its entirety, the writers at *El Fronterizo* proceeded to respectfully disagree with the entirety of the piece, because "from the sense of some of its paragraphs it seems to us that it extends its judgments to others who reside in the United States."[12] Likewise, the paper was one of the few sources that historicized contemporary resettlement efforts with those that took place four decades earlier in the aftermath of the Mexican-American War. It was the lack of historical memory in the *Imparcial* article that animated the response from *El Fronterizo* and the perspective that the latter paper's staff would express throughout the rest of the riposte.

Like the multiple memorias emanating from the Departamento de Fomento, Colonización, e Industria, writers at *El Fronterizo* took a historical approach to the ongoing debate over colonization in Mexico. For them, the first significant episode "was in the year 1856 when the first Mexican repatriates came from California to the border of Sonora, under the protection of the general government, in the number of thirty-something with their families and destined for the old mission of Saric, near the dividing line with the United States, and until then abandoned because of the bloody incursions of the terrible Apaches."[13] Manuel Siliceo was minister of development at that time and authorized the resettlement plan by appointing Jesús Islas the repatriation commissioner for the region; thus, the Californio relocation to Saric took place on his watch.[14] In response to generalizations about the Greater Mexico population, the *Fronterizo* writers sarcastically noted, "[Although] we have not had the opportunity to become closely acquainted with the Mexicans residing in Texas and New Mexico, we are well acquainted with those of Arizona, California, and Colorado, and with respect to these we can say that our learned colleague is in error." Granting the possibility of "corrupt men among them," the writers maintained that "in general, in their immense majority, they are honest, industrious, good Mexicans whose love and veneration for their country has never been dulled by time or distance, as they have well proved, and as we will demonstrate by recalling their patriotic behavior."[15]

As mentioned earlier, the resettlement of Californios to Saric in 1856 has been the subject of historical interest because the episode became mired in so much controversy, suspicion, and filibusterism.[16] In telling the history of this resettlement a decade after the outbreak of the Mexican-American War, the *Fronterizo* writers suggest that "these compatriots had not yet reached the end of their long and painful journey" when their "homeland was invaded by Henry A. Crabb's filibusters" once more. These returning patriots were "good men" who "fought in Caborca among the ranks of the other nationals, some of them succumbing on that journey." After Crabb and his filibustering expedition were massacred in 1857, the colonists "returned in search of their families" and "founded there an agricultural, industrious, and brave colony that lived for many years fighting against the Apaches." According to *El Fronterizo*, the colony was subsequently abandoned by the government, but neither "this abandonment nor the fierce war waged by the Apache to stubbornly contest their former abode made them falter."[17] Just like the settler-colonists of Chihuahua so famously discussed in the prerevolutionary historiography, these individuals were frontier colonists who had endured the harshness of life in the desert and been hardened by war with Apaches.[18] Frontier tropes describing the environmental transformation of European settlers were in vogue during this era, especially among American historians. Such leitmotifs were employed across the Western Hemisphere to project nationalist sentiment coupled with a rugged frontier individualism.[19]

El Fronterizo echoed Ernest Renan's sacrificial analysis in narrating the history of the diaspora as one of resettlement in deserts swarming with "terrible Apaches." When Renan lectured in 1882 about the constitution of nations, he often anthropomorphized the political behavior of a country, making references, for example, to sacrifice, ritual piety, and ancestor worship. For that reason, Renan believed that a nation was a "great solidarity constituted by the feeling of sacrifices made and those that one is still disposed to make. It presupposes a past but is reiterated in the present by a tangible fact: consent, the clearly expressed desire to continue a common life."[20] The first resettlement could have been narrativized as the body politic reassembling itself after a national tragedy, but instead the article pointed out a more concrete example of sacrifice during a foreign invasion. At the time of the French intervention, argued the *Fronterizo* writers, "the Mexicans of California and Arizona gave the world the most eloquent proof of their unshakable affection for the Mexican homeland" when several expatriate fighters came to the country's defense.[21]

To underscore this point, the newspaper reproduced a letter written by President Sebastián Lerdo de Tejada to Francisco Zarco, deputy to the Congress of the Union and celebrated newspaper editor, in June 1864. Historiographically speaking, there were "public documents that accredit their valuable contingent" and "even a good number of those Mexicans went from Arizona to swell the ranks of General Pesqueira in the neighboring state of Sonora." Here, Lerdo requests that Zarco relay his appreciation "to the Mexicans residing in upper California" for their "constant demonstrations" and "worthy sentiments with respect to the war that our country sustains, defending its independence and its institutions."[22] The newspaper's narratological method was a "historicist enterprise," but here an actual primary document is reproduced (and reinscribed) to underscore the historic nature of diasporic patriotism.[23]

El Fronterizo ended its rebuttal to *El Imparcial* by posing the customary rhetorical question in the following form: "Is the repatriation of such a class of Mexicans advisable?" Answering their own query, the staff argued that the resettlement of the diasporic population was a net positive. Like the editors of *La Patria* and several other newspapers, they too stated that the resettlement of Mexicans was a positive development and that "there will be no lack in Texas and New Mexico" of potential colonists.[24] Disagreements were in ample supply among the numerous periodicals throughout Greater Mexico, but there were also cases of conversion to a favorable view of repatriation, as would happen only a few weeks later with at least one newspaper editor who had the occasion to meet Luis Siliceo.

The "Hard School of Ostracism": *El Tiempo* Meets Luis Siliceo

After publishing its rebuttal in favor of repatriation, *El Fronterizo* continued to reprint editorials that both supported and challenged the official position of the newspaper. In the scientific spirit of that era, those commentaries critical of resettlement were regularly republished in their entirety and systematically scrutinized. Themes of repatriation always animated the reading public by stimulating a series of discussions that spoke to questions of national belonging, not to mention the pitfalls and promises of the American dream. If migrants were leaving for "an elsewhere," to use the vocabulary of Lorenzo Veracini, there must be some better place, and in this case that elsewhere was the United States.[25] "The entire press in the capital of the republic and even on the northern border, has been duly concerned with the important matter of the return to their country of thousands of Mexicans," remarked the author of an editorial in *El Fronterizo.* Moreover, it was difficult to determine why these migrants left to begin with; perhaps it was "the vicissitudes of fortune, or the vagaries of our political issues" that "have uprooted" these compatriots "from our homeland and taken [them] to life in the fields and cities of Texas, where they have suffered no small amount of work and humiliation."[26] Hence, when fellow citizens opted to return southward, they provided evidence that life in the United States could manifest itself as a dream or turn into a socioeconomic nightmare.

The articles republished in *El Fronterizo* appeared three weeks after Siliceo initiated his contract with the Departamento de Fomento, suggesting that he was making the rounds of the city's newspapers in search of converts to his cause.[27] As an entrepreneur, Siliceo was familiar with the news business, the importance of propaganda, and the influence of data. With contract in hand, he now had a personal stake in the business of resettlement and made concerted efforts to persuade others of the promise of his enterprise. In narrating his encounter with Siliceo, the editor of *El Tiempo* (Mexico City) wrote, "Among us is Mr. Luis

Siliceo, who has spent many years working on the repatriation project and has not faltered, despite the numerous adversities he has faced. We owe to him accurate information about the enterprise he wishes to undertake and its effectiveness and usefulness." Siliceo shared his own documents, applications, and letters with the staff at *El Tiempo* and convinced them that his project was "well thought out" and that "honest and hardworking men will return to Mexico who will help in the progress of our country."[28]

The concern for this Mexico City newspaper, as for *El Imparcial* of Hermosillo, Sonora, revolved around what class of individuals would be resettling. Due to the general penchant for publishing sensationalist news, there was no shortage of stereotypes about the varied classes of Mexicans in the United States. One of the primary concerns for several outlets was that repatriates should not be "people who have absolutely nothing to live on" and so become an economic burden instead of an obligatory blessing on Mexico. *El Tiempo* wrote approvingly of Siliceo's project because the resettlers that he proposed to bring were "people who have a few small tools, some agricultural implements, and diverse knowledge."[29] In other words, they would not become dependents or wards of the state.

Unlike present-day news outlets, newspapers during this era, including the staff at *El Tiempo*, were not hesitant about admitting mistakes and making public corrections. In fact, one of the newspaper's writers confessed that "at first, we believed it was some grand speculation that would result in bringing to Mexico all the vagrants, losers, and criminals who, fleeing from the justice of our courts, had taken refuge beyond the Rio Grande, amidst our traditional enemies, those who aided Austin."[30] What class of colonists might potentially return to Mexico continued to be a source of concern, but historical memory was also lengthy, as the reference to Stephen F. Austin, a one-time empresario-colonizer, attests. So, clearly, those who had "helped Austin" (Yankees) would not be allowed into Mexico as colonists. Aside from the rejection of vagrants, losers, and criminals, "another limitation has also been placed on registrations; not admitting either Chinese, blacks, or Yankees." These Yankees were different from Europeans who had remained citizens of their countries of origin, and exceptions were obviously made for certain ethnic groups, as Siliceo's contract specified.[31] Thus, for those "Europeans settled in Texas have often requested registration; then, besides proceeding with great caution, efforts have been made to find out if the applicants were naturalized Americans, or at the very least, had applied for naturalization, as in none of these cases were they admitted."[32] Anti-American sentiment being what it was, even the intention to become a naturalized US citizen was enough to disqualify an individual from Siliceo's repatriation project.[33]

In sum, *El Tiempo* described the nature of the colonists that Siliceo intended to relocate in Mexico as a rugged frontier type. Engaging in wishful thinking, the editor claimed that there were so many of these individuals that Siliceo's resettlement project could potentially involve up to twenty thousand people (even though Siliceo himself consistently promised only one thousand individuals). Later in the article, the number associated with Siliceo's project was quadrupled to perhaps eighty thousand, with the editorial writer concluding that if the "residents of Arizona, New Mexico, [and] California" were also repatriated, "we would have more than half a million . . . compatriots by blood and by heart, who would come to contribute to the progress of Mexico." The writer also assured readers that Siliceo had taken great care to "register each settler" and to "ascertain their background, relationships, [and] position" and "exclude those who either could not give good references of their persons or were notoriously known as lost people."[34]

Given the glowing article, Siliceo must have been quite convincing when he met with the staff at *El Tiempo*. The author of the piece emphasized that Siliceo's colonists would be a great benefit to any community in Mexico that was lucky enough to receive them, because "these hardworking, moralized families [were] educated in the hard school of ostracism." Like recent religious converts, these zealous pilgrims "yearn for the distant homeland as if it were the Promised Land." Siliceo's resettlers were not marginalized victims scarred by the experiences of difference or "people who [had] absolutely nothing to live on"; they were hardworking families who had been toughened by their experiences.[35]

Luis Siliceo's resettlement project from San Antonio, Texas, to various Mexican states did not unfold in isolation from public or political scrutiny, and the release of his contract triggered a fresh round of public discourse in 1895. As the nineteenth century came to a close, economic and environmental conditions had spurred increased migration from Mexico to the United States. In Texas, the non-native Mexican population experienced remarkable growth, expanding eleven-fold from 4,182 to 51,796 between 1850 and 1900.[36] The history of previous debates concerning the potential return of the diaspora resurfaced within the public discourse of Greater Mexico as well as in Mexico City. The quality of potential colonists and the economic prospects of returning to Mexico were once again subject to debate, and the diaspora faced renewed criticism. Questions regarding expatriates' loyalty to Mexico and the motivations behind their northern migration elicited a range of responses, from the contentious to the mundane.

Such diasporic debates were revisited in the autumn of 1895 when Siliceo met with the staff and editor of *El Tiempo*, persuading them that the prospective settlers were "hardworking, moralized families educated in the hard school of ostracism." The reception of Siliceo's colonization contract with the Porfirian government in the Greater Mexico press unveiled a form of folk sociology concerning the type and caliber of individuals returning to Mexico. Debates within the diaspora regarding repatriation and resettlement transcended the boundaries between the two nation-states and captured the attention of a public that projected its own social anxieties onto the phenomena under scrutiny. Such exchanges persisted well into the twentieth century and continue into the twenty-first. Today, there is still no shortage of folk sociology on social media and, particularly, in the mainstream media of both governments.

An exploration into the historical origins of these ideas serves as a reminder that contemporary mass migrations, whether within or outside the realm of the body politic, inevitably leave behind an archive, particularly when the politics of resettlement are at play. Siliceo's experience was no exception, but what set it apart was his unique tool to counter skepticism regarding the type and quality of colonists who would return under his guidance. Part 4 offers a brief analysis of his newspaper, *El Colono*, and its propaganda efforts, including editorial pieces encouraging resettlement and instructions for organizing local *juntas patrióticas*.

PART IV

PRINT CAPITALISM AND *EL COLONO*

CHAPTER 9

EL COLONO AND SETTLER COLONIZATION PROPAGANDA

On 25 November 1895 Luis Siliceo published the first issue of *El Colono*, a newspaper seeking to "provide the Mexican resident on American soil with a special organ to foster the already great desire to return to the homeland, in order to achieve the establishment of a model agricultural colony."[1] The newspaper—more akin to a trade journal—included articles on the latest technological advancements in agriculture, botany, horticulture, homesteading, and livestock raising.[2] One could liken *El Colono* to a Tex-Mex how-to-manual for potential settler-colonists. The newspaper, which ran for approximately five years, was published twice a month, usually on the tenth and twenty-fifth.

The Newspaper: Content, Goals, and Aspirations

Unlike many of the Mexico-Texano newspapers of that era, *El Colono* was notable for its near absence of political content and its zealous propagandizing concerning the benefits for Mexico of resettling Mexico-Texano colonists.[3] If the paper had a political philosophy of any sort, it was clearly pro-repatriation. Additionally, *El Colono* looked to project a positive image of Mexico to appeal to the broader world of "immigrating races" who were settling across the globe. Echoing the logic of the Departamento de Fomento, the newspaper argued that if Mexico-Texanos would resettle in Mexico proper, this in turn would stimulate the global immigration of industrious, assimilable, and morally upright European colonists.

Thanks to advances in maritime technology that reduced transportation costs and expanded cargo spaces, transatlantic vessels were overflowing with European immigrants when Siliceo began to publish *El Colono* in 1895. In the words of historian José Moya, "the trade of the industrial revolution, rather than trade in general, promoted improvements in transportation," greatly reducing both the time and the price required for travel.[4] By the 1890s "the introduction of iron hulls, compound steam engines, and screw propulsion significantly reduced crossing times" to about six days, increasing the number of liner services and the frequency of trips across the Atlantic (and across the world) as the market potential was being realized.[5] Newspapers throughout Mexico and the United States wrote periodically about these mass movements of peoples, especially in the aftermath of the wars for independence.[6] Immigration from abroad continued throughout the nineteenth century, until almost sixty million Europeans had settled in the Western Hemisphere between 1830 and 1930.[7] Contemporary estimates have suggested that between 1846 and 1940, the globe witnessed the migration of 160 million human beings—an event unprecedented in world history.[8] Since the 1970s, the global population residing in a country other than that of their birth has tripled.

Global immigration was at its zenith during the period *El Colono* was in publication, and Siliceo looked to capitalize on the Atlantic flow of immigrants by channeling them toward Mexico. These were not in-depth investigations about the statistical significance of the demography of migration, but rather focused observations in real time. In highlighting the low price of land in Mexico and positive economic opportunities (agricultural and otherwise), the newspaper strove to attract settler-colonists to contribute to the greatness of the nation. Always making sure to highlight their contract with the administration, Siliceo and the staff at *El Colono* wrote,

> It is true that such a newspaper would not have been able to stand on its own a short time ago, but nowadays, when there is already great enthusiasm among the emigrant races to undertake their march to other regions which, like ours, provide them with greater advantages, there is no doubt that such a publication will be received with pleasure, not only by those interested in acquiring detailed reports on the products of our homeland, but also by the federal and local governments in the Republic, since it is not a question of favoring this or that enterprise exclusively, but of contributing our grain of sand to the aggrandizement of our country by means of propaganda and colonization.[9]

Siliceo articulated these objectives when he established *El Colono* in the autumn of 1895, a mere two months after negotiating one of the more favorable colonization contracts during the Porfiriato, especially advantageous for the colonists.[10] As it became evident that a significant portion of the interest in relocation stemmed from Mexico-Texanos and other ethnic Mexicans, the newspaper ceased advocating for European immigration altogether.

El Colono was published consistently twice a month until the end of the century and covered all topics related to settler colonization.[11] While the subject matter of *El Colono* for the most part addressed the concrete knowledge necessary for successful colonization, at least three dozen articles set forth Siliceo's vision and philosophy of repatriation.[12] The 1895 volume of the paper presented recent scientific studies on animal husbandry; current research on the production of coffee, tobacco, ramie, silk, melons, beans, and cotton; and a guide to Mexican laws concerning the export of fruits. Articles on market conditions for various agricultural commodities, butter-making machinery, fruit-sorting equipment, and the promising economics of raising ostriches also featured in its pages.[13] Although the paper did republish articles and opinion pieces critical of the hacendado classes of Mexico, the content reads more like a primer for bilingual settler-colonists. In fact, most of the information is practical and pragmatic, even by today's standards.

A methodical reading of *El Colono* evidences a fetish for the modern accoutrements of science and technology, coupled with a similar zeal for cultural nationalism. The struggle to assimilate all the undeniable advances of science recalls the broader global debates of the era around national belonging and "overcoming modernity," as in the case of the Kyoto School of Japan.[14] According to thinkers of the Kyoto School, the second industrial revolution had given rise to a particular vision of the world that imagined endless advancement, but the innovations of that revolution were accompanied by the Trojan horse of western cultural influences and the potential to dilute Japanese culture.[15] Initially, the staff of *El Colono* walked a similar philosophical path, republishing the latest articles on agro-industry and mechanization but omitting US cultural concepts. As more Mexico-Texanos signed on to Siliceo's repatriation program, the opinion pieces of the newspaper became more nationalistic—even chauvinistic.

Print Capitalism: Diasporic Sacrifice, Suffering, and Imperceptible Insects

Benedict Anderson has convincingly argued that the spread of nationalism during the nineteenth century was partially accomplished via newspapers, or what he calls "print capitalism." Although a number of factors contributed to the diffusion of nationalism, Anderson maintains that "combined, these ideas rooted human

EL COLONO.

BIBLIOTECA NACIONAL DE MÉXICO

TOMO II. MÉXICO, 10 DE MARZO DE 1897. NÚMERO 9

EL COLONO.

LUIS SILICEO, EDITOR PROPIETARIO.

Apartado postal, 51. Bis.
Oficinas, Santa Isabel núms. 11 y 15.

LA REPATRIACION.

Pronto regresará de Michoacán nuestro Director después de dejar establecido en los terrenos de Zacapu el grupo de familias mexicanas repatriadas que á dicho lugar condujo con tal objeto. Este primer grupo aunque poco numeroso vendrá á formar el núcleo de una colonia importante, pues á no dudar al conocer por sí mismas las personas que lo componen, las ventajas excepcionales de que gozarán para dedicarse á sus labores, tanto por la naturaleza misma del suelo y la bondad del clima, como por la protección decidida que les imparte el Supremo Gobierno de la Nación y el Sr. Gobernador del Estado, sin duda, repetimos excitarán á nuestros compatriotas radicados allende el Bravo á reunírseles en el menor tiempo posible, disipando así las dudas que la prensa de mala fé de Texas ha tratado incidiosamente de introducir en sus ánimos con fines nada nobles.

En nuestro próximo número daremos á conocer á nuestros lectores la favorable impresión que han recibido nuestros compatriotas al visitar esa parte del Estado en que van á fundar sus hogares.

Ultimas noticias de México,

MINERIA, FERROCARRILES Y COMERCIO.

Nos complace por todo extremo hacer notar que en países tan importantes como en Inglaterra, y en periódicos tan sérios como el *Financial News* se tratan ya los asuntos de México con la atención que merecen, á diferencia de lo que acontecía antes en países más cercanos: se hablaba de México en los términos más denigrantes, y colocándonos en el centro de la América del Sur.

Reproducimos á continuación una columna del periódico inglés citado, que se refiere en todo á nuestro país:

(Del *Financial News* de Londres.)

Se espera que haya importante desarrollo en asuntos de minería, á lo largo de la línea del Ferrocarril "México, Cuernavaca y Pacífico," que toca uno de los distritos mineros más ricos de la República. La construcción de esa vía se está llevando á cabo rápidamente.

La "Lower California Development Company" se desarrolla de modo notable. Un agente de la expresada Compañía acaba de regresar de un viaje por toda la costa, hasta el Sur de Chiapas, y se asegura que sus informes son muy halagadores. Para calcular la probable cantidad de carga que puede recogerse, la Compañía ha comisionado como agente al Capitán Milton Twing, del vapor "Pacheco" para que recorra todo la costa. Si hay esperanzas de buenos negocios, la misma Compañía pondrá un buque de buenas dimensiones para que haga viajes de San Diego, California á Chiapas.

Esto se anticipará al establecimiento de una rama de la propuesta línea transpacífica en aguas mexicanas.

Mr. Potter, iniciador de esta empresa, dijo que uno de sus primeros resultados sería el establecimiento de una línea de vapores en el litoral mexicano del Pacífico.

La goleta "Josefina" perteneciente á la "Development Company," que ha sido hasta ahora su único medio de transporte, se ha mejorado con la adición de dos máquinas de gasolina, con fuerza de 20 caballos cada una, que la convierten en un vaporcito rápido.

—

El Gobierno Mexicano ha celebrado un contrato con J. Mariowitz, de Galveston, Texas para establecer un servicio de vapores en las costas del Golfo, al Norte y al Sur del puerto de Veracruz. Ofrece hacer un viaje redondo cada semana entre Tampico y Veracruz, y más tar-

The front page of an 1897 issue of *El Colono,* showcasing correspondence from potential settlers and news of ongoing resettlement efforts.
Courtesy of the Hemeroteca Nacional de México, Universidad Nacional Autónoma de México.

lives firmly in the very nature of things, giving certain meaning to the everyday fatalities of existence (above all death, loss, and servitude) and offering, in various ways, redemption from them."[16] Central to cognizing Anderson's critique of nationalism is that "willingness to sacrifice on the part of comfortable classes is food for thought."[17] Anderson's ideas have been challenged since the appearance of his essay, most notably by E. J. Hobsbawm, who suggests that nationalist ideas were not monopolized by those holding power or entrepreneurs with printing presses. Hobsbawm observes that "while governments were plainly engaged in conscious and deliberate ideological engineering, it would be a mistake to see these exercises as pure manipulation from above. They were, indeed, most successful when they could build on already present unofficial nationalist sentiments, whether of demotic xenophobia or chauvinism—the root word itself, like 'jingoism' appears first in the demagogic music-hall or vaudeville—or, more likely, in nationalism among the middle and lower middle classes."[18] Setting the criticisms aside, when examined through the prism of print capitalism, colonists grappling with the challenges of life in a remote frontier of a nascent republic could envision themselves as integral members of a larger nation characterized by a common language, culture, and ideology. This phenomenon was facilitated by profitable newspapers that adhered to a capital-driven logic, skillfully forging "imagined communities" in locations where such bonds had previously been absent.

The content of *El Colono* should be pondered in light of these observations, enhanced by the "commonality between private and official realms" when these petitioners articulated their "appeals for state protection."[19] Thus, displays and projections of nationalism emerged from all directions and classes of peoples, most notably in the form of a basic cultural chauvinism that fostered group solidarity.[20] Though cultural chauvinism is discernible in all human societies across time and space, Hobsbawm and Anderson would agree that modern-day nation-states have been especially proficient at co-opting and exploiting these "imagined communities" for their own ideological engineering.

Both *El Colono* and the Departamento de Fomento y Colonización promoted the advantages of resettlement. However, the editorial section of *El Colono* took the propaganda a step further by appealing to readers on medical and psychological grounds, invoking notions of nationalist sacrifice, nostalgia, family, tradition, and remembrance. The idea of sacrifice, framed as a return to the territorial "womb" through resettlement, was a recurring theme throughout the pages of *El Colono*. This concept aligned closely with a secularized, modern nationalist ideology.[21] For instance, in the article "From Here and There, Love for the Homeland," the staff of *El Colono* argues that "love of country is not entirely the same as patriotism. The former is of all people, times, and circumstances, it is an instinctive and irresistible feeling; in some cases it becomes a physical affliction—nostalgia—which can produce death if the specific remedy is not applied."[22] "Nostalgia" as "a feeling of pleasure and also slight sadness when you think about things that happened in the past" is recast as an emotional/medical condition that "can produce death" if the sentiment is not assuaged.[23] Psychosomatically speaking, advanced stages of this nostalgia for the homeland ran counter to human nature, at least according to this line of thinking. The writers continued, "Patriotism is the love for the homeland taken to its highest point, heroism, and exercised in difficult and solemn situations, distant from the general and routine way of acting of men, and sometimes even against the inspirations of nature itself."[24] In a sense, being outside of their larger spiritual family was a risk to the health and well-being of Mexico-Texanos, and one remedy to alleviate this irresistible, instinctual sentiment was to return to "the country of the future."[25]

In *El Colono*'s understanding of happiness, contentment is to be found not in an empty search for the "American dream," but in being surrounded by your family at the time of your death, then entombed in the country of your birth. Whereas for some Stoic philosophers it is the experience and the struggle of migration, in and of itself, that constitutes "happiness," this particularity is a mere illusion—a *Geist* that leads migrants and their families into an "unhappy consciousness."[26] The physical afflictions that come along with this collective suffering are due primarily to an empty search for happiness that makes one a foreigner in both the place of one's birth and the place of settlement.[27] This was anti-American rhetoric wrapped in the garb of medical discourse and the tropes of illness.

In detailing the struggle of migrant life, *El Colono* philosophizes that "after some years of vicissitudes and upheavals, after having followed the phantom that is called happiness, after having enjoyed all the amusements that life offers, after having travelled through various provinces and nations, and after having provided a comfortable subsistence and secured his future, one feeling remains incessant in the depths of his soul: that of returning to the place where he first breathed."[28] This phantom of unattainable happiness could be exorcised only with a prescription that combined efficacious doses of patriotism with reunification into a greater familial necropolis. This is why "happy is the man who at the end of his days is surrounded by his family in the village where he was born, who remembers with pride in his past glories consecrated to his homeland; who sees the hour approaching when he will go down to the grave, amidst the charms of well-being, having a friendly hand to close his eyes, and loved ones to receive his last breath and shed a tear on the slab of his tomb."[29]

El Colono seemingly affirms Ernest Renan's analysis of the nation-state as a "a spiritual principle resulting from the profound complexities of history—it is a spiritual family, not a group determined by the lay of the land."[30] Resettlement is preferable to the alternative: "abandoned by the whole world, or seeing nothing around them but strange and indifferent physiognomies, they end their existence without hearing an affectionate word, without needing any memory, passing unnoticed and ignored like an imperceptible insect that slithers through the grass we walk on." Thus, Mexico-Texanos risk dying alone in a foreign country. In the absence of a physical family, resettlement offers a "spiritual family" who at your death will not ignore you "like an imperceptible insect that slithers through the grass we walk on."[31]

"Soldiers of Progress": An Agro-Nationalist History of Siliceo's Repatriation Company

Since hundreds of historical interpretations can be gleaned from any dataset, I have opted for one that has a record of development.[32] My historical interpretation is gleaned from two "small histories" in *El Colono* titled "Al vuelo" (On the Fly) from 1898, three years after the publication of the first issue.[33] The two "small histories" were ten pages in length and appeared in two installments during the paper's five-year run. They constitute the few articles that historicize the development of Siliceo's project.

The first piece commences by acknowledging that "not all can be said"—indeed, an accurate statement—and thus the emphasis will be on recounting recent events, and, as the title suggests, the interpretation will likely be "on the fly." The narratological examination arose in response to critiques from the initial group of frustrated colonists tasked with clearing underbrush and trees before cultivating the land. The historical narrative commences with a contingent of 325 settler-colonists departing from San Antonio, Texas, with the objective of founding Colonia Patria in the Guemes (Güémez) district of Tamaulipas on 2 January 1898.[34] Instead of historicizing Siliceo's back-to-Mexico movement from a nationalist point of view, the staff at *El Colono* turned the proverbial table on its critics by sardonically suggesting that the first colonists lacked the necessary ingredient for settlement; namely, sacrifice. Sacrifice in this context included not just love of country, but also willingness to sacrifice labor, time, and skills until regular harvests were established.

The article points out sarcastically that the settler-colonists' main objection is that they have to clear the land in Colonia Patria. The authors proceed to explain away harsh realities by arguing that some colonists lack nationalistic resolve and sacrifice.[35] The article concedes that an exact description of the lands should have been made available to potential colonists, because the lands are essentially unbroken or, as sometimes termed, "uncultivated." Confronted with tropical flora lush with palm trees and undergrowth, the colonists were starting from scratch, which was not the case with the traditional sharecropping arrangements many had known in Texas. In the days before diesel-powered tractors and bulldozers, the uncleared lands in Colonia Patria required backbreaking toil to clear, plow, and prepare for seeding. But instead of focusing on the days, even weeks, it might take to remove one tree stump, the writers of *El Colono* wrote optimistically of these struggles and successes, since "this is the stuff history is made of." In that sense, the colonist will "have at least something to recount; he will have some memories of the founding of the colony . . . in short, there will be material for history."[36] *El Colono*'s historical narrative was retold not as a material struggle between the colonizer and the colonized, but as a spiritual catharsis that combined hard work and nationalist sweat with colonists' own inner spirit and commitment. Having thus set forth the importance of struggle and sacrifice in settler colonization, the authors continue to comment on this first group of colonists.

It is evident from the language used in the article that there were disagreements among various parties, and undoubtedly, there were challenges to overcome during the initial days of settling Colonia Patria. The writers of *El Colono* acknowledged these concerns but sought to place them within a broader context that romanticized the new lands with a somewhat promotional tone. From their historical perspective, and "setting aside what could or could not be, let us focus on what is . . . when the first group of Mexican settlers arrived at the land, one of the first things that undoubtedly impressed them was the overall appearance of the place . . . the never-ending waterwheel, which is picturesque . . . where, naturally, there is some noise, and when you least expect it, you see flocks of parakeets, parrotlets, and parrots flying away in pairs."[37] The writers' strategic rhetorical effort to market the location as a kind of tropical paradise is evident when they describe exotic birds feasting on the colonists' corn and cotton. However, they suggested a different approach when it came to wild turkeys, encouraging colonists to allow the birds to consume enough grain to fatten them up for eventual slaughter.

Gaslighting their audience and readers who might be following the progress of Colonia Patria, the authors convert obstacles to agriculture—such as palm trees—into potential sources of income. Wood from this species could be converted into "gold" or traded for other goods if packaged and sold in the capital of Tamaulipas—only twenty-five kilometers south of the colony.[38] Effectively, the pattern of the article was to show that what some colonists saw as dark and damp land replete with invasive trees and undergrowth to be cleared, others saw as an opportunity to make money. In this interpretation of events, motivation and responsibility are the only ingredients necessary to become a successful settler-colonist. The *Colono* writers describe the various sizes of the families already established in the colony, now under the jurisdiction of Guemes.[39] They assert that a cottage industry has emerged around the harvesting of palm products, with "las señoritas" actively collecting the leaves of these *arecales*. In analyzing the history of the first colonists in Colonia Patria, the article attributes notable agency to the settlers themselves, especially those who regularly attend "meetings and reunions" to discuss the advancement of the colony, but it also employs a sophisticated marketing strategy.

Many colonists were inexperienced in the uprooting of large trees, and they had difficulty securing reliable *peones*, many of whom chose to avoid the grueling labor of clearing land. Based on personal experience, I can hardly blame them. The young men, not surprisingly, were described as working in agriculture and selling their services to fellow colonists. There was no *maquina sembradora* (seeding machine) in Colonia Patria, only draft animals that pulled plows through unbroken earth under human direction. From the perspective of *El Colono*'s writers, "This is how farmers are made, this is how soldiers are made, and this is how the most remarkable men have been made in all branches of industry and the arts, living from birth among the very elements that will later come to be the sustenance and the future of a whole family." Like all good soldiers, the colonists should expect to suffer and should embrace the struggle, because it is through this transformative process that they will contribute to the greatness of Mexico. But the sardonic critique was mixed with a peculiar brand of agro-nationalism. The staff of *El Colono* turned the first years of hardship into a history of stoic resolve by casting the colonists of Colonia Patria as "¡Soldados del Progreso!" Like some Tejano drill instructor snapping them to attention, the article implored these mercenaries of modernity to "stand firm, hand to the plows, turn and till the lands, lead the horses, and march!"[40]

While describing the travails of the first group of colonists in Tamaulipas, the article's authors exhorted potential settlers that "there is no need to take a step back; the Mexican who is determined to return to the country may have some difficulties during the first year," but eventually will get on his feet and become independent. Besides, the living situation is much better in Mexico than in the United States, because "those who stay in North American territory will see themselves sinking deeper and deeper and there will be no one to lend them a helping hand."[41] Unlike the common trope today where the United States serves as the "safety valve" for the globe's surplus population, in this text, Mexico becomes the *elsewhere* to go to escape from late-nineteenth-century American-style modernity—segregated railroad passenger cars and all.[42]

In closing this agro-nationalist rendition of "the history of the repatriation company" (the longest serialized article that appeared in *El Colono*), the writers appeal to the "nationality or race" of colonists' country of residence. Life in Texas is nothing but "disenchantment," because "the Saxon will always be more protected by the Saxon, and this will ultimately result in the Mexican being isolated sooner or later, perhaps even now, and without the help they used to receive from the American landowner." Mexico, thus, offers safety and security unavailable in Texas. Why wait until Mexicans witness the inevitable taking place? the writers ask. "Why wait to be the last when you can and should be the first?"[43] The early trials and tribulations experienced by the first group of settlers in Tamaulipas are thus manipulated into what could aptly be called "positive propaganda."[44] *El Colono* transformed years of suffering into stoic determination via an agro-nationalist history that christened the colonists of Colonia Patria as "Soldiers of Progress!"

CHAPTER 10

LA REPATRIACIÓN AND THE TAXONOMIES OF MEXICO-TEXANO SUPERIORITY

The considerable documentation generated in support of Siliceo's Mexico-Texano colonization project opens an incredibly fruitful space of communication and debate centered on questions of national belonging. Some of the themes woven through the biweekly periodical *El Colono* included citizenship, ethnicity, "race," history, authenticity, instability in Mexico proper, "barbarous Indians," and the promises and pitfalls of frontier life. It was the last-named forces that Siliceo confronted as he looked to embody the historical narrative of "order and progress" into his resettlement project. Theoretically speaking, these points of difference and debate shed light into an arena of Mexican life that provincializes Euro-American sensibilities while illuminating the life worlds of Greater Mexico—a region with a history that predates the formation of the United States.[1] So in addition to confronting critical voices emanating from the Greater Mexico public sphere, Siliceo would also face difficulties with the Porfirian administration, bureaucrats within the Departamento de Fomento, Colonización, e Industria; state and municipal governments; border officials at the *aduana fronteriza* (customs); and tragically, even the microscopic force of mosquito-borne viruses.

La Repatriación: The Series and the Newspaper

One of Siliceo's first articles in *El Colono*, "La repatriación," started what became a regular column in the newspaper and may well have consisted of republished articles from *La Repatriación* newspaper, which Siliceo likely also owned.[2] The "La repatriación" article series typically appeared once a month and had the goal of constructing a derivative historical analysis of late-nineteenth-century resettlement.[3] So in addition to supplying updates on the progress of the colonies, these articles detailed what I call Siliceo's "philosophy of repatriation" and the goals of settler colonization. A few reports foretold some of the challenges, rumors, and obstacles that eventually hindered Siliceo's resettlement project.[4] Due in part to technological advances in printing presses, bilingual newspaper outlets had exploded onto the scene, and a few of them were wary of any scheme that entailed Mexicans in the United States once again organizing to return to Mexico.[5] These new forms of mass communication, in turn, transmitted the intra-ethnic concerns, conflicts, and cooperation among various Mexican American communities throughout the southwestern United States.[6] Siliceo acknowledged criticisms of his project, notably those in a couple of publications that objected to resettlement.

Opposition to repatriation and resettlement can be historicized to several newspapers in the decade after the end of the Mexican-American War in 1848. Media coverage of the 1853 autocolonization junta of Jesús Islas immediately comes to mind, as do examples from *El Clamor Público* in California discussing Andrés Pico's Sociedad de Colonización de Nativos de California para el Estado de Sonora (Native California Settlement Society for the State of Sonora, 1858).[7] The common debates playing out in the press related to the dangers of resettling in mostly desert areas inhabited and defended by indios bárbaros, the social chaos and constant revolts in Mexico, the low prevailing wages in Mexico compared to the United States, and the corruption of Mexican government officials. The primary and secondary sources on colonization conveniently align on these observations as well, and so does the larger corpus of immigrant literature. Nicolás Kanellos observes that "the ethos of Hispanic immigrant literature is based on the premise of return after what authors and community expect to be a temporary sojourn in the land where work is supposedly ubiquitous and dollars are plentiful and the economic and political instability of the homeland is unknown."[8] A growing number of newspapers also started publishing articles in English or bilingually in English and Spanish, illustrating the growing rift between those with nostalgic ties to Mexico versus those with a more assimilationist bent—one that excluded the possibility of ever returning to the homeland.[9] These tropes emerged in the print media every time a substantial resettlement project made news. In the 1890s these intra-ethnic differences of opinion were not insulated from the world around them, including anti-immigrant xenophobia directed at eastern and southern European immigrants arriving in the United States.[10]

In addition to creating an "imagined community," print media in the late nineteenth century could also spread fake news, propaganda, hatred, warmongering, and bigotry.[11] Influenced perhaps by anti-immigrant legislation in the United

States, officials in the Departamento de Fomento turned their focus toward the *calidad* (quality) of colonists who were ostensibly interested in colonizing Mexican lands.[12] The staffs of Mexican consulates in the United States witnessed the multiplicity of European immigrants arriving on the shores of that country, not to mention the anti-immigrant propaganda that usually accompany any instance of resettlement in any country.[13] Although a few sources debated the possibility of settling eastern Europeans in the country, correspondence between Luis Siliceo and the Díaz administration clearly spelled out the only type of immigrants both were interested in: diasporic Mexicans.

Not surprisingly, a few newspapers criticized the colonists as unworthy of resettling in Mexico, which needed experienced farmers, not more "peons." This type of commentary compelled Siliceo to counter with his own folk sociology, noting that "those who were enrolled . . . and who initiated my project of repatriation . . . are industrious . . . moral people, and for the most part quite enlightened."[14] Given that anti-immigrant sentiment was prevalent in the press, it was predictable that Siliceo's project would become a target of criticism, and thus he shrewdly deployed a newspaper outlet that could counter the mixture of realistic analysis and nationalist irrationality that marked this late-nineteenth-century discourse of "order and progress."

The same nationalist (and commercial) spirit of the era outwardly served as Siliceo's life force, and his role as prophetic intermediary is narrated accordingly throughout the pages of the newspaper. After describing his project in glowing terms in an early issue of *El Colono*, he reminds his audience of the systematic nature of his colonization process—adding some humble bragging for good measure:

> As I never intended to boast about my actions during my stay in the United States, this is undoubtedly why the system I have successfully employed for the selection of a thousand or more families who will undoubtedly arrive in our Republic has gone unnoticed. But now that the Government is willing to support the repatriation of its loyal citizens, I will be the first to make an effort to satisfy not only the legitimate objectives of that federal entity but also the needs of a nation that, like ours, is forging ahead towards improvement and progress.[15]

The use of the term "system" here is deliberate, as it signifies a set of principles and methods of organization that generates a structured sequence of procedures. The nineteenth century gave rise to a plethora of "systems" in all academic disciplines and schools of thought, and the use of that term signified that something was practiced, proven, and therefore pragmatic.[16] Accordingly, Siliceo claimed everything he had undertaken had a system, a methodical approach, down to the names of his newspapers and the strategic publication of scientific articles on animal husbandry, agriculture, botany, viniculture, and modern agronomic techniques for the education of settler-colonists. Thereby, he made his case not only to the Greater Mexico press, but also to the Mexican government, considering the contracts it had recently arranged with non-Mexican agents.

The public discourse of self-sacrifice in service of the nation circulated via *El Colono*, however, stands in stark contrast to Siliceo's private correspondence with the Departamento de Fomento. The constant stream of correspondence between the two parties reads like a typical business transaction in which both sides are trying to negotiate the best possible deal. Order and progress was the mantra of the era, and who could better contribute to the country's growth and prosperity than a well-equipped, moral, and industrious group of loyal colonists longing to return to Mexico's booming economy?[17] As Nicolás Kanellos observes in his extensive analysis of this genre, "most Hispanic immigrant literature likewise promotes a return to the homeland and, in so doing, is antihegemonic and rejecting of the American Dream and of the melting pot."[18] Like the resettler-colonists of La Mesilla, New Mexico, who opted to head south in 1872 rather than accept local election results, Siliceo's settler-colonists chose to exchange a late-nineteenth-century version of American modernity for Mexican-style Porfirian "order and progress" governmentality, only this time with American accoutrements and technology.[19]

Siliceo's Views of Race, the Nation, and Sacrifice in *La Repatriación*

Like most individuals in 1895 (just as in 2024), Siliceo projected his own ethnic chauvinism onto the prevailing racialized discourse of that era.[20] The "superior" colonists for Mexico were obviously the ones who had signed on to his project, namely Mexico-Texanos from San Antonio, Texas.[21] Because these were the people of his community and extended family, Siliceo's ideas about them reflected his own imagined "racial worldview."[22] In the 1890s, the population of San Antonio was roughly 50,000 while that of Mexico City was almost 327,000.[23] So comparing these two locales, we in the present can appreciate part of the reason why *El Colono* and other newspapers portrayed Mexico as a country of great opportunity and a country of the future.[24]

Because Siliceo believed that Mexicans in Texas were "superior" to all other "immigrating races," he expected their example would encourage others to join the current of immigration, which was "indispensable for the improvement and enlightenment of the indigenous race in Mexico."[25] Mexico-Texano settler-colonists occupied the top tier of Siliceo's imaginary taxonomy, his newspaper audience, and his contract with the Porfirians. Indigenous peoples ranked second, followed by Spaniards. In at least one manner of thinking, then, Siliceo can be seen as approximating a nationalist in the Científico framework, one informed by a typical nineteenth-century Porfirian indigenismo.[26] The preferred European immigrants whom Siliceo placed in the fourth tier of his imagined racial taxonomy were those most familiar to him in the greater San Antonio area; namely, German immigrants.[27] As Siliceo wrote, "There are very specialized races to enlarge a country, one of them being, and the main one, the Teutonic, for the thousand qualities it enjoys, the principal ones being the energy, the constancy, and the abnegation with which they resist all kinds of vicissitudes; just as the African was never a good colonist, the opposite can be said of the German . . . be it in Africa, in Russia, or in Japan."[28] Siliceo's classification reflected his sociocultural milieu as well as the conditions specified by the Departamento de Fomento: "Germans et al." were among the favored "races" of Europeans mentioned in the contract, even if they were fourth in Siliceo's imagined taxonomy.[29]

Some in the broader Mexican American community viewed the special privileges afforded to Mexico-Texanos in the published contract and in the 1883 Land and Colonization Law as "fictitious," since the lands being offered were located "in the uninhabited places along the frontiers," which inevitably meant conflicts with indios bárbaros.[30] In accordance with Mexican law, colonization contracts of this nature were always published in both government-sponsored and privately owned newspapers and, accordingly, Siliceo published his contract several times over the course of a few years.[31] Publishing his contract in the pages of *El Colono* met the transparency requirement, but it was also a clever marketing strategy that conferred some gravitas to Siliceo's "cultural capital."[32] Members of the public could thereby become familiar with the finer points of the contract and make their analysis known, just like the bureaucrats of Fomento.

El Colono dully fulfilled the publication requirements with the second installment of the "La repatriación" article, which centered on an interpretation of Article 16 of the Mexican Land and Colonization Law of 1883. Article 16 reads, "Mexicans residing abroad who wish to settle in the deserted places on the frontiers of the Republic shall have the right to free cession of land, with the conditions of section III of Art. 3°, up to two hundred hectares in extension, and to the enjoyment, for fifteen years, of the exemptions granted by the present law."[33] Given Siliceo's experience negotiating with the nation's most capable bureaucrats, he understood the generalities of the law well enough to know that this concession did not exclude the possibility of colonizing any other areas in the republic.[34]

Toward the close of the nineteenth century, the menace posed by indios bárbaros had diminished in most regions, with the exception of Sonora and certain areas in Chihuahua. This transformation was particularly pronounced following Geronimo's surrender in 1885. As Mexican historian Friedrich Katz highlights, Geronimo's capitulation marked a significant turning point, leading to a virtual cessation of raids into Mexico. Moreover, Chihuahua experienced a transformative development as it became intricately connected through railroads to both central Mexico and the United States during the same period.[35] So although Mexican settler-colonists who opted for desert lands in the border states qualified for special concessions not available to any other ethnic group, they could also settle in any other part of the republic under the terms spelled out in the 1883 Land and Colonization Law.[36]

From the few US census and Mexican baptism records for Siliceo, his background appears to have included Mexican, French, and Spanish ancestors.[37] It is fair to assume that his cultural particularities would correspond favorably to those nationalities and cultural regions of his genealogical habitus.[38] For instance, he expresses this favoritism as both a lament and a compliment regarding the possibility of Spanish colonization. In an era when anti-Spanish nativism pervaded Mexican political life, Siliceo and *El Colono* ran counter to many in the Científico classes by putting forth a pro-Iberian point of view, at least on colonization.[39] Siliceo ranked Spaniards third in his taxonomy of preferred colonists, comparing Iberians favorably with successful Jewish merchants in New York City and arguing that Mexico should seek remedies to keep them in the country, and by extension, provide lands on which they could settle. His way of thinking is worth examining to better contextualize its historicity:

> The Spanish element in Mexico has shown in all times to be very suitable for colonization, being even more so now than before, since it generally happens that after making a fortune in our country, they spend the last days of their lives on native soil, taking with them not only the money

> but a contingent of our population, since a great part of them have married in Mexico, forming families, which then disappear, transferring their residence, many of them to some other nations, which fortunately does not happen anymore. This element has been for our republic what the Israelite has been in the United States; he is enterprising in everything that is productive, and rarely, in contrast to the Saxon race, do they venture into little-known enterprises; however, he is more than anyone, at least in Mexico, a knowledgeable merchant of a branch that is generally monopolized by that nationality, the grocery stores.[40]

Here, Siliceo makes use of what José Moya has described in the South American context as the "positive side of stereotypes"; that is, labels that "function at one level as signifiers of alterity and mechanisms of exclusion" while simultaneously promoting acceptance.[41] In Siliceo's casting of Spanish settlers, the Iberians are portrayed not as the offspring of conquistadors but as useful entrepreneurs and merchants who will fulfill the needs of their community and start Mexican families. But as the following set of articles will make clear, of all the "migratory races" from which Mexico could select, the "superior" colonists were those whom Siliceo represented: "Mexico-Texanos." While Siliceo and *El Colono* placed Mexicans in Texas atop their imagined racialized hierarchy, this privileged positionality did not forestall contrary opinions from the very community that he was trying to recruit for his colonization project.

Mexico-Texanos and "Race Superiority"

The bulk of the content that *El Colono* published had to do with the practical aspects of settler colonization from the fields science, agriculture, technology, trade, commerce, and the law. Nonetheless, the paper also printed articles from like-minded outlets that disagreed about the viability of resettlement. In responding to their journalistic peers, Siliceo and his staff take an increasingly chauvinistic approach to these critiques, starting with the first installment of the "La repatriación" series. In making the case for Mexico-Texano settlers, *El Colono* argued that "no element is therefore more necessary and suitable to achieve this end as our compatriots across the Bravo; since they have remained some years out of the country, they have acquired new customs, and greater practice and knowledge in modern agricultural matters."[42] This aptitude is central to the writers' solution for how to overcome modernity and adopt new technology while avoiding assimilation into a foreign culture.[43] This know-how will benefit both the settlers and their countrymen, making it especially valuable, because "although the language for the man of the field is not indispensable, they will contribute greatly to quickly spreading this knowledge among the peasants of our republic, most of whom live in ignorance, even of the very culture that they practice."[44] How people residing in their home country could be ignorant of their own culture is not elaborated; Siliceo's purpose here is to cement the position of Mexico-Texanos at the top of the pyramid in terms of preferential treatment.

Almost every public debate about autocolonization throughout the nineteenth century included indigenous peoples, and Siliceo's rhetoric reflected Científico sensibilities of that era.[45] Where Siliceo parted ways with the Científicos was his contention that his colonists had been swimming in a sea of modernity that could benefit any nation that resettled them. Thus, not only were these colonists more modern than any of the other "migrating races," but they shared a larger Mexican culture of which even the very natives of the nation were unaware![46] So aside from the usual chauvinism, he also relied on one of the many logics of settler colonialism that Wolfe alluded to: in addition to displacing indigenous populations under the pretext of improvement, settler-colonists could go further by appropriating indigenous identities as their own in order to legitimize their claims to the land.[47]

Though the 1883 Land and Colonization Law granted preferential treatment to ethnic Mexicans in the United States, people of other ethnic groups believed the terms of colonization were favorable enough that they signed colonization contracts with the Díaz administration. In the same year that *El Colono* began publication (1895), African American colonists arrived in Mexico with a colonization contract in hand.[48] The Porfirian administration clearly did not align itself with Siliceo's taxonomical ideas. This group of around 850 African Americans from Alabama signed a contract to join Colonia Tlahualilo in the state of Durango, but an epidemic decimated the colonists almost immediately, and only 107 managed to return to Eagle Pass, Texas. The tragic events have been well documented, and a number of scholars have written critically about the yellow fever epidemic that doomed the botched colonization project from the beginning.[49] The fallout from the Tlahualilo colonization recalled the experiences of Italian colonists a decade earlier but had wider repercussions that influenced Siliceo's approach. According to *El Colono*, the failure of the Tlahualilo colony brought "displeasures to our Government and material for sensational articles in the American press."[50]

In rebutting their colleagues in the Greater Mexico press, the staff at *El Colono* employed this tragedy to highlight the practicality of their project due to the favored classification of their colonists. The collapse of five of the six Italian colonies founded in the mid-1880s was due primarily to the outbreak of bacterial or viral epidemics of one sort or another (the sixth disintegrated later).[51] In light of these previous incidents, the article affirmed that the "Mexican of whom the Government and our director are concerned is perhaps superior to any other race to colonize our soil, because he is strong and resists the weather and changes of climate more than the Africans themselves, to whom the change of climate, and only that, caused so much harm to them as well as the expenses for the Colonization Company of Tlahualilo."[52] Setting aside the internal charge of sensationalizing the news—a charge that even today would garner a substantial amount of agreement—the worldview of the staff *El Colono*, as evidenced by their thinking regarding human health, climate, and the environment, was derived from the prevailing "scientific views" of the era among their social class.[53]

In the pages of *El Colono* a more pragmatic approach to nineteenth-century colonization is laid out, one in which the individual not only acts upon the environment but has already done so by example. The environment, in turn, also influences the constitution of "the Organism," a process that we might describe as dialectical.[54] In describing the shift from Spencerianism to Pragmatism, Richard Hofstadter argues, "Spencer had been content to assume the environment has a fixed norm—a suitable enough position for one who had no basic grievance against the existing order. Pragmatism, entertaining a more positive view of the activities of the Organism, looked upon the environment as something that could be manipulated."[55] With the recent African American colonization debacle in mind, the staff echo these late nineteenth-century beliefs:

> See how, both on the coasts of the United States and in the swampy areas of the State of Texas, there are thousands of Mexican peasants or laborers, most of whom come from high, cold, or dry regions, such as Zacatecas, Chihuahua, and many other locations in the central plateau of the Republic. It has never been known that diseases such as smallpox or others afflict them more, being, in fact, less healthy in those places than in Tlahualilo.[56]

To drive the point home, the authors note that "almost a majority of the individuals employed in the pine woodcutting operations, not very far from Galveston and Houston, are Mexicans, and despite the fact that the work assigned to them is heavy, they endure it." The writers then ask rhetorically: "to what should it be attributed, when many of them have never engaged in such tasks, if not that their constitution is naturally more resilient?"[57]

According to Siliceo and his staff at *El Colono*, the Chihuahuan deserts, the cold and dry climate of Zacatecas, and the high altitude of the Mesa Central of Mexico whence these Mexicans first migrated developed a "superior human"—a Mexican *Übermensch* dialectically molded from the harsh clays and soils of their environment—prepared to colonize and settle in areas that other "races" were not equipped to handle.[58] Such was the "scientific" thinking during this era, and Siliceo and his staff reflected these fictitious imaginations about "race" and disease in an era that was still struggling to comprehend bacteriology.[59]

These attributes were just the most obvious advantages to resettling Mexican Americans in Mexico proper. The writers of *El Colono* sardonically remarked,

> Some other advantages could be pointed out among those already mentioned. . . . The current generation of those Mexicans residing in the American border states is not a group of individuals who would in no way contribute to the social economy. On the contrary, for the most part, they are communicative, and above all, they have had the opportunity to appreciate the favorable results of the Union and of education, and they know how to collaborate in the realization of some enterprise with the same energy and perseverance as the Anglo-Saxon, as they have already demonstrated and continue to demonstrate.[60]

Siliceo was clearly impressed with the Texas Mexican community in San Antonio, so much so that he eventually made his home and livelihood in the city until his death in 1928.[61] The views Siliceo articulated about his preferred settler-colonists bring to mind a notion that Arnoldo De León once described as "pervasive Tejanismo." For De León, this notion was exemplified by the

LA REPATRIACION

Escriba a Luis G. Siliceo, Director. 317½ W. Commerce St. San Antonio, Texas.

One of many ads in *La Prensa* of San Antonio advertising the repatriation services of Luis Siliceo in the 1920s.

Courtesy of The Portal to Texas History, University of North Texas Libraries. Lozano, Ignacio E., La Prensa (San Antonio, TX), vol. 7, no. 2,098, ed. 1, Tuesday, January 4, 1921.

potentiality of Tejano business enterprise in all spheres of public life, to which autonomy is central.[62] Siliceo, like most individuals of his social class, articulated the enterprising spirit of Tejanos in the ostensibly scientific ideas and discourse of the 1890s.

Within the first three years of Siliceo's enterprise, the relatively moderate discourse of European inclusivity gradually gave way to a more vigorous chauvinism that not only lauded the supposed superiority of Mexico-Texanos but placed them above their North American and European counterparts, arguing that they should be "the first":

> [The Mexico-Texano] better than anyone . . . can rise in their own country even more than the Americans who come to the republic with everything, and these are determined and enterprising men, for a thousand reasons. The first and foremost reason is that they speak the language of the country; second, because the cultivation to which they have dedicated their efforts is carried out under modern systems similar to those that Americans or Europeans residing in the United States could carry out, and many other reasons that we could mention in favor of the repatriated Mexican settler, who is known to all our compatriots.[63]

In short, the resettler was familiar, even at times a "prodigal son" who was part of the larger Mexican "spiritual family."[64] The formation of smaller family units in the form of *juntas patrióticas* would ease and hasten this resettlement; and Siliceo was standing by to channel these organizations into his own contractual *system*.

CHAPTER 11

JUNTAS PATRIÓTICAS AND "HOW TO COLONIZE"

By the late nineteenth century, the resettlement of Mexico-Texanos in Mexico's northern frontier states was not a new phenomenon, and neither was the political economy of state-subsidized Científico propaganda.[1] Between 1893 and 1907, Mexico's economy grew by more than 5 percent annually while the United States experienced the Panic of 1893 and a subsequent recession.[2] In his account of the Panic of 1893, the economist David Whitten states that "the [US] economic contraction began in January 1893 and continued until June 1894." The economy rebounded the following year but slumped once more when it was "hit by a second recession that lasted until June 1897," and one can surmise that the economy was slow for the remainder of that year.[3] The confluence of economic fluctuations in the United States, amid Mexico's burgeoning GDP, with perceptions of the Mexican economy as more robust than its American counterpart at the time undoubtedly heightened the interest among Mexican Americans in repatriation.[4] Donald Keesing argues that the period from 1895 to 1950 saw the Mexican economy "[continue] to grow and progress in countless ways, interrupted only briefly by the turmoil and civil war that centered in the years 1915 to 1917."[5]

The Panic of 1893 also reduced the number of European immigrants arriving in the United States, illustrating how human flows correspond with capital currents.[6] As David Whitten observed, the United States registered "only 270,000 [immigrants] from 1894 to 1898" whereas the country "had averaged over 500,000 people per year in the 1880s and . . . would surpass one million people per year in the first decade of the 1900s."[7] From the vantage point of Siliceo and hundreds of potential settlers, the economic and political situation in Mexico seemed more inviting. Hence, many people crossed the border from the United States into Mexico, which also experienced substantial interstate migration during the same period.

In his study of the state, capitalism, and society in Nuevo León, Juan Mora-Torres describes this period as the "making of the border labor market." Making brilliant use of census data in *Estadísticas Sociales del Porfiriato, 1877–1910*, Mora-Torres documents the increase in out-of-state migrants to the border states of Coahuila, Chihuahua, Nuevo León, Sonora, and Tamaulipas between 1895 and 1910, on the eve of the Mexican Revolution. Measured by rate of growth and contrasting the numbers with the state populations, the proportion of out-of-state migrants in Coahuila ranged from 25.75 to 31.30 percent; this migration was driven by growth in industry, manufacturing, and construction in the state.[8] Similar optimism is reflected in *El Colono*: Siliceo wrote that "Mexico will someday, and not remotely, be the richest and most powerful nation in the New World, being at present the one that enjoys the best government."[9] Viewed in terms of the economic and migration history of the era, therefore, an argument could be made that the financial panic in the United States prompted *El Colono* to publish a questionnaire that perfectly mirrored the variables and queries of the colonists' *declaraciones*, which I discuss in the final chapter.[10]

The Formation of Repatriation Societies in Texas

Siliceo and his staff at *El Colono*, along with their colleagues at *La Repatriación*, reported on large movements of people and the formation of many repatriation organizations throughout Greater Mexico. For several years the growing Mexican economy made that country more attractive for settlement than the United States, and the growing number of repatriation juntas is a useful index for measuring human flows. According to *El Colono*, "in connection with the reorganization of the juntas already established in Texas, Arizona, New Mexico, Colorado, and California, which number more than 40, new associations have been set up all over the country, which will undoubtedly help in the propaganda of the company." A few letters from repatriation juntas were published in the same issue, including ones from Junta Auxiliar de Prairie Lea, Junta Auxiliar de Taylor, Junta Auxiliar de Manor, and Junta Auxiliar de Repatriación de Corpus Christi.[11] Mentions of the formation of additional repatriation juntas in San Antonio, Manor, Luling, and Hutto would continue to pepper many issues of *El Colono* through October 1898.

In addition to describing the hierarchical structure of these organizations, the newspaper often published the minutes of their board meetings.[12] Both the articles and the minutes were written in a very formal and official style that conveyed a soldierly determination, from which one could expect that the junta would support a comparable level of organization once it had established itself in a colonia. The repatriation societies appear to have formed organically when Siliceo looked to harness their energy to expand his colonization project. This particular example of cooperation, at least to some degree, explains Siliceo's earlier claim that his settlers "have had the opportunity to appreciate the favorable results of the Union and of education, and they know how to collaborate in the realization of some enterprise with the same energy and perseverance as the Anglo-Saxon, as they have already demonstrated and continue to demonstrate."[13]

One of the notable articles featured in *El Colono* during its five-year publication span was the highly impactful piece titled "200,000," which appeared in January 1897. This article marked the newspaper's initial reference to the burgeoning number of repatriation societies spontaneously emerging at that time. The authors confidently asserted that "more than 20,000 Mexican families will be able to return to their homeland." At this juncture, Siliceo initiates direct communication with these societies, making a formal request to "direct your correspondence to me, indicating whether you are willing to initiate your departure as soon as I inform you that I can provide you with some advance assistance during the first year of your establishment." He adds, "If you will organize yourselves into groups or Clubs of repatriation, communicate this to me by giving the greatest possible publicity for the present letter among our compatriots." (In other words, help spread the word and feel free to circulate my letter.) In his concluding paragraph, Siliceo underscores that working together is critical: "Remember that unity brings strength, and the realization of your desires depends solely on you. Please let me know as soon as possible if you will be ready to depart when I communicate definitive news that ensures your well-being for one year in the colonies."[14]

Mindful of developments in the political (the 1883 Land and Colonization Law) and economic (the 1893 Panic in the United States) spheres, Siliceo saw an opportunity to capitalize on expatriates' desire to improve their situation. The meager harvest of 1896, exacerbated by a prolonged drought referred to as the "great die-up" (1892–96), provided Siliceo with an additional rationale to advocate for the expeditious return of potential colonists.[15] He later called for the formation of new *juntas auxiliares de repatriación* in order that aid could be more easily distributed. A few months later, the paper reported on the resettlement of Zacapú, Michoacán. It also further formalized the repatriation societies by publishing a "very interesting announcement" for those "Mexicans who want to register to return to their homeland."[16] By June 1897, likely as the US economy was beginning to recover, *El Colono* wrote positively of merchants requesting permission to sell provisions to the repatriates flowing southward into Mexico.[17]

MUY IMPORTANTE.
A LAS
JUNTAS AUXILIARES DE REPATRIACION EN LAS FRONTERAS.
NORTEAMERICANAS.

Siendo ya enteramente indispensable enviar á la Secretaria de Fomento los documentos necesarios relativos á las familias mexicanas que vuelven al país, á fin de que oportunamente quede terminada su tramitación, comunico á los Presidentes de dichas Agencias auxiliares y á los mexicanos que deseen ingresar á las colonias, que deben de proceder desde luego á hacer la remisión de los informes mencionados y listas de lo que cada individuo se propone traer al país, para atender con tiempo su despacho.

México, Agosto 23 de 1897.

LUIS SILICEO, Agente y Concesionario.
Apartado Postal. 54 Bis, MEXICO D. F.

One of several advertisements directed at "auxiliary boards of repatriation" along the borders, asking them to submit "necessary documents" (including itemized lists of household items) required for resettlement in Mexico so that processing can be completed in a timely manner.
Courtesy of the Hemeroteca Nacional de México, Universidad Nacional Autónoma de México.

Like every article on resettlement, this one was tinged with the narrative elements of dynamism, constant flow, and eternal movement.

Instructions for How to Colonize: A Three-Step Process

On 23 August 1897, *El Colono* candidly advised potential settlers on the proper methods of resettlement in a dispatch entitled "Necessary Conditions to Ensure Success in Colonization Enterprises." There is a tone of playful swagger in this piece that seeks to instill a sense of self-assurance in its audience. For the *Colono* writers, trial and error guaranteed success in colonization but, as they liked to remind readers, the prerequisite was a system of colonization, and experience was what mattered most. Brimming with confidence, the authors declared that "once well understood," colonization "is not as difficult as it seems, as it boils down to a perfect understanding of the character of the colonizing races and following the methods employed by expert and experienced agents to the letter" (presumably referring to Siliceo and his company).[18] The "Necessary Conditions to Ensure Success in Colonization Enterprises" served both as a vehicle for boasting of recent achievements and as an instruction manual that distilled what proponents of autocolonization had been debating for decades. Historiographically speaking, it was quite common for members of the Mexican intelligentsia to author and distribute essays that offered guidance on how best to colonize the vast expanses of the republic.[19] Considering this essay in light of the larger narrative tradition, it consciously targeted both prospective colonists and the Científicos at the Departamento de Fomento, Colonización, e Industria. As usual, Siliceo never missed an opportunity to insert strategic marketing for his colonization enterprise.

Debates about how best to colonize sparsely settled areas of the country would continue for the rest of the nineteenth century and through the first half of the twentieth century.[20] In the first decades following independence in the 1820s, the concern was not only whether there should be immigration to Mexico, but also where settlement should take place and what kinds of individuals should be allowed to relocate.[21] In a general sense, colonization for much of the nineteenth century was more concerned with national security than the long-term economic configuration of the colonies and their integration into the national market.

These historical issues were discussed extensively among the many bureaucrats in the Departamento de Fomento, but in their article, the staff at *El Colono* put forth the most pragmatic of all suggestions: resettlement should take place close to towns and cities. Times had changed and the region was now secured from "Indian raiding."[22] So instead of placing a colonia in an isolated area for the purpose of creating a barrier against indios bárbaros, Siliceo suggested that access to the *national market* should be the raison d'être when considering where to found the new settlements. These locales should also have quick access to a broader transportation infrastructure and, by extension, to buyers for the colonists' products, thereby diversifying their streams of income. The experience of resettling Mexico-Texanos had given Siliceo some gravitas and firsthand knowledge of colonization, which he condensed into three "necessary conditions" to assure the success of the endeavor. Naturally, he publicized these to support readers committed to resettlement and to attract those considering it.

The first condition of colonization was that colonies should be established "in the places most immediately adjacent to towns or cities of some importance," so that colonists had easy access to an urban area.[23] The suggestion was as practical as it was radical, because it acknowledged the reality that not all colonists were going to blossom into farmers. Although every nation in the Western Hemisphere desired immigrants who would work the land and make it productive, this was not always the outcome. In an era before background checks and credit scores, there was little colonization companies could do except request some official document testifying to a colonist's good character and claim to be an experienced farmer. Not surprisingly, a number of settler-colonists were either inexperienced in farming or simply unfit for the hard labor it required.[24] The idea of owning ten to fifty hectares of land sounds wonderful until one realizes, as the primary record alludes to, that the land in question needs to be cleared and a dwelling built. The abandonment of a colony—and by extension the property—may seem inconceivable on its face, but if urbanized prospective colonists arrive in a carriage and are unaccustomed to sleeping outdoors, it is easy to understand why they might abandon their hard-earned plots of land, as the Italians had a decade earlier.[25]

Secondly, by being close to an urban center, a family with meager resources could find work to survive until they had the fruits of their first harvest in hand. *El Colono* pointed out that the settlers practiced a kind of mutual aid in which "they help themselves, if necessary, in a thousand ways, by selling firewood, charcoal, bread, sweets, and in general any other industry so as not to abandon in good time the cultivation of their crops." Furthermore, colonists "work throughout the agricultural season in whatever other small businesses can help them with even modest amounts."[26] As students of colonization, Siliceo and the staff at *El Colono* had likely learned some lessons from the government reports that identified disease, abandonment, lack of agricultural knowledge, and unfamiliarity with local crops as the primary reasons why the six Italian colonies had collapsed and were eventually resettled with Mexicans.[27] At the time, the government placed blame for the eventual collapse of these early settlements on the disenchantment of the "lazy Italians."[28] In fact, as was the case for the African American colony of Tlahualilo, the main culprit was yellow fever.[29]

The necessity of access to a market for goods and services led naturally to the third condition, which was easy access to transportation routes to facilitate distribution and sale of products and experimentation with "agricultural industries such as the manufacture of cheese, the raising of chickens and pigs, cold cuts, sale of milk and eggs . . . subsidies that in opportune time, often free the settlers from isolation and misery."[30] The logic was sound because this added layer of food security would solidify the foundation of a colony. The suggestions were not written in a vacuum, and their obvious goal was to streamline the process of resettlement. The "Necessary Conditions to Ensure Success in Colonization Enterprises" are intriguing to peruse and scrutinize, not only for their practicality, but also for the insights they offer into past adverse encounters with colonization.

Two years into his project, Siliceo had observed many scenarios, which shaped the development of his "system of colonization." Meanwhile, the Departamento de Fomento had clearly changed its approach to the colonization process based on its study of earlier colonias. Siliceo had become, as we might say today, a "subject matter expert" in the business of colonization. The staff of *El Colono* did not hesitate to remind readers about the company's ongoing efforts to resettle Mexico-Texanos. But they also assured foreigners interested in colonization that they would be well cared for due to Siliceo's accrued experience with resettlement. The "Necessary Conditions" article concludes by mentioning that another group organized by Siliceo "will arrive this year" and that its procedures will provide many opportunities for "our compatriots to see in practice how true the theoretical principles of good colonization are. Fortunately, for the benefit of the Mexicans returning to the country, our director is well-versed in this matter."[31]

Reglamento de la Unión Fraternal de Repatriación

In contrast to the situation in California during the 1850s, identifying the precise emergence of localized repatriation societies in Texas during the late nineteenth century is challenging.[32] Requests for repatriation, land grants, and related appeals certainly appear in the archival record early on, but there is nothing comparable to what Siliceo later coordinated through repatriation societies. According to *El Colono*, as of 1897 there were already more than forty uniones fraternales de repatriación (fraternal repatriation unions) in the states of Texas, New Mexico, California, Arizona, and Colorado.[33] That we can glean some historicity about these organizations is due in large part to articles in *El Colono* combined with community patterns present in San Antonio at the close of the century. Emilio Zamora observes that the Texas Mexican community was not homogenous, and that "mutual aid, pacifist, Masonic, and union organizations, for instance, at times reflected broadly civic outlooks, highly specialized interests, or narrow instrumental views."[34] Based on the records available and the "highly specialized interest" of Siliceo's project, an examination of the Reglamento de la Unión Fraternal de Repatriación is useful here before I proceed to the basic instructions on how to properly resettle and an overview of correspondence published in *El Colono*.[35]

Uniones fraternales de repatriación make several appearances in the pages of *El Colono*. These repatriation juntas were not part of Siliceo's original plan; however, experience and regional demand compelled him to seek some organizational apparatus to coordinate his resettlement efforts. Seemingly echoing the intentionality of Siliceo and *El Colono*, "mutual aid societies also reinforced a collectivist spirit with resolute statements of purpose in support of nationalist principles and moral values, an active civic role, and strict rules that disciplined their members into conscious Mexicanist proponents of the ethic of mutuality."[36] As with his other endeavors, Siliceo sought to create a system by which settlers enrolled in these uniones fraternales could be channeled toward his project.

José Amaro Hernández, a scholar of Mexican American history, has studied one of the earliest examples of these mutual-aid societies, which he characterized as secular outgrowths of earlier religious brotherhoods, such as the eighteenth-century Penitentes of New Mexico and Confraternity of Brothers of Our Father Jesus of Nazareth. By the late nineteenth and early twentieth centuries, mutual-aid societies had proliferated. At about the time that Siliceo was assembling his colonization project, groups of "distinguished Mexican American families" in Arizona were founding fraternal groups like the Alianza Hispano-Americana (1894).[37] In sum, then, the juntas auxiliaries de repatriación were part of the Greater Mexico landscape of fraternal organizations, in this case, uniting members with a desire for resettlement and colonization.

That a series of laws, instructions, and regulations were required to form a fraternal union of repatriation highlights not only the obstacles to resettlement, but also the "manner of founding and conducting any group established or to be organized." *El Colono* published Siliceo's "Reglamento de la Union Fraternal de Repatriación" two years after the first issue was released, and it can be inferred that these associations developed organically. The lengthy piece begins by detailing the organization's parliamentary procedures; the need for a quorum; the election of officers; and, finally, term limits. Section 1 of Article 2 summarizes the mission of the organization: "To promote among the Mexicans residing in North American territory the patriotic feelings and brotherhood among the members, who of their free and spontaneous will, accept to be subject to the articles of the present regulations, with the purpose of carrying out their repatriation in the best manner." The numerous moral duties of members were also inscribed into a system; for example, how to care for fellow repatriates who become sick or incapacitated; how to assist fellow settlers; and how "to attend to the education of children who unfortunately lose their parents once they are already repatriated."[38] These responsibilities are revealing and highlight Siliceo's impulse toward "systems" and his past experience. For the colonies to take hold, these repatriation unions needed to foster human solidarity prior to, during, and after the process of resettlement.

Altogether, the Reglamento de la Union Fraternal de Repatriación contains eleven articles, which take up almost five pages in this issue of *El Colono*. Most of the articles are procedural in nature, but Article 3 is particularly important because it addresses all "bases, conditions, solicitations, applications, admissions, income, reimbursements, dues, fees, rights, and forfeitures."[39] The rest of the reglamento is a compendium of instructions on parliamentary procedure for organizing the areas of responsibility of each officer and the agenda items for each meeting. The rights and obligations of each settler-colonist were well demarcated in the 1883 Land and Colonization Law, so the reglamento was an added layer of governmentality that enabled Siliceo to micromanage the fraternal organizations. It is much easier to control a group of skilled settlers when an acknowledged leader has been elected by the constituents. This might explain why the reglamento named Siliceo "President for Life and General Agent & Director of the Company."

The conditions for joining a union fraternal de repatriación were not unlike the general requirements for settler colonization in Mexico but were more liberal and charitable. In that sense, "the fraternal union will admit into its fold, as members of the society, only individuals worthy in every respect, of both genders and of any age, even if they are notably poor. They can be protective members of the Union, including Mexicans who, due to their business, may never be able to come to the country in order to establish themselves."[40] There was an initiation fee of fifty cents, which could be paid in installments. Monthly dues of twenty-five cents entitled each member to issues of *El Colono* and *La Repatriación* each month (that is, four issues).

The emergence of mutual-aid groups conveniently intersected with Siliceo's business interests, aspirations, and goal of resettling as many "enlightened" and "superior" colonists in Mexico as possible. Another contributing factor was the relationship between the economic panics of the 1890s in the United States and the organic emergence of repatriation societies in Texas. The 1883 Land and Colonization Law had been in effect for a decade, and repatriation societies appear in the years prior to Siliceo's 1895 contract with the Mexican government. It seems that the stock market crashes of the 1890s contributed to economic disenchantment across the socioeconomic classes of Greater Mexico, opening a space for imagining resettlement in the homeland at a time when the Mexican economy was growing at an annual rate of 5 percent.[41]

PART V

MEETING SILICEO'S SETTLER-COLONISTS

CHAPTER 12

AN ETHNOGRAPHIC GAZE ON SETTLER COLONIZATION THROUGH DECLARACIONES

Nicholas Dirks has presented a compelling case regarding the enduring elements of British corporate colonialism in India. He posits a transition from history to anthropology as the primary mode of epistemological domination, particularly noticeable after the mid-nineteenth century. He describes the new practice as the "ethnographic state."[1] In an effort to make sense of the many "Hindu tribes and castes," British authorities attempted to catalogue the multiplicity of different ethnic groups via the social classification and organization of empirical data, especially after the 1857 rebellion.[2] The logic of some colonial authorities was that if more ethnographic information could be gathered, then future rebellions could be prevented and populations controlled—in other words, statistics could be employed in the service of state repression.[3] But in the process of gathering this data, particular caste categories were reinscribed upon a population who had not been as strict about social differentiations prior to colonial rule.[4] As a result, British-style corporate colonialism reinforced "ancient" caste distinctions in an effort to divide and conquer a territory and its people through an administrative ethnographic reclassification system.

The Ethnographic State in Mexico

The term "ethnographic state" captures well the kind of census gathering that had been taking place in Mexico for centuries. Indeed, Mario Luis Fuentes Alcalá and Saúl Arellano Almanza's main thesis in *Nuevo ensayo político-social de la República Mexicana* is that "behind the design and content of the questionnaires through which the information is collected, there is a vision of power and society; that is, the governing groups have decided what is important to know, based on the ideas or notions they have of development and the information required to make decisions that enable and stimulate it."[5] The same will to power was at play when

Siliceo submitted numerous declarations containing census data on his colonists directly to Manuel Fernández Leal, head of the Departamento de Fomento in Mexico.[6] Quantifying the entirety of Siliceo's file enables detailed evaluation of the demography of these particular settler-colonists in order to identify some general characteristics of the colonists that resettled under Siliceo's watchful eye.

All settler-colonists were required to sign contracts making them the primary contractual agents initiating resettlement in Mexico proper as eventual property owners. Every modern nation-state has some type of official form for anyone crossing its borders, and formal declaration of one's belongings is usually required before entry. The declarations Siliceo's colonists completed are analogous to the US Customs and Border Protection (CBP) Declaration Form 6059B, which Americans traveling abroad must fill out to reenter the United States. According to the CBP, this form provides "basic information about who you are and what you are bringing into the United States, such as agricultural and wildlife products, and whether or not you have visited a farm prior to traveling to the United States."[7] A returning citizen is also asked about the prices and quantity of items purchased abroad.

Like all government surveys, the declaration forms are surveillance mechanisms that reduce money laundering and trafficking, but they also hold many histories. In the case of Siliceo's expatriate settlers, they had favored status under the 1883 Land and Colonization Law, which granted them lower taxes, larger tracts of land, relief from military service, and exemptions on property taxes for the first several years of settlement. Moreover, the law also exempted the following items "destined for the colony": "internal duties on foodstuffs, farming implements, tools, machinery, household goods, construction materials for living quarters, furniture for use, and livestock for breeding and husbandry."[8] It is my contention that historians can glean much from these declaration forms, which, as I will show, can aid in triangulating other primary and secondary sources. This documentation detailing the movements of people, goods, and livestock offers fascinating historical insight into the migratory patterns observed within the scope of Siliceo's project between 1985 and 1900.

Several other observations can be made from the data about settler-colonists who ultimately ended up resettling in three locations: La Sauteña and Colonia Patria in Tamaulipas; and Zacapú in Michoacán (although the declarations do not specify each colonist's eventual destination).[9] The 239 petitioners brought with them 638 family members, for a total of 877 settler-colonists, a large figure in comparison to the settlers in other colonies. The list is certainly not

INFORME No. 145 Grupo 3°

NOMBRE DEL COLONO: Guadalupe Jurado — RESIDENCIA ACTUAL: Manor. Texas

NACIONALIDAD: Mexicano

EDAD 40 AÑOS. — ESTADO Casado

NOMBRES	EDAD	SEXO	SEXO	SABE LEER	SABE ESCRIBIR	SABE INGLES	PARENTESCO	NACIO EN
Guadalupe Jurado	40.	m.		si	si	si	Esposo	Chihuahua
Andrea G. "	37.		f.	"	"	"	Esposa	Nuevo. Mex.
Adolfo "	22.	m		"	"	"	hijo	" "
Alejandro "	18.	m		"	"	"	"	" "
Carolina "	16.		f.	"	"	"	hija	" "
Dolores "	12.		f.	no	no	"	"	Manor Texas
Manuel "	10.	m.		"	"	"	hijo	" "
Josefa "	8.		f.	"	"	"	hija	" "
Alfredo "	7.	m		"	"	"	hijo	" "
Juana "	4.		f.	"	"	no	hija	" "
Andrea "	2.		f.	"	"	"	"	" "
María B. ?	60		f.	"	"	"	Tía.	Chihuahua
TOTALES	12	5	7	5 si 7 no	5 si 7 no	9 si 3 no		

OBSERVACIONES: Solamente agricultor

Instrumentos, Animales de Cría y de Trabajo; Vehículos y muebles que posee el interesado.

VEHICULOS Y ANIMALES		INSTRUMENTOS Y UTILES		MUEBLES DE USO Y BULTOS	
Guayines		Cultivadoras		Estufas	1.
Carros expresos		Arados en general	2.	Sillas y sillones	4.
Carretones		Sembradoras		Camas	1.
Caballos		Hachas	2.	Colchones	5.
Yeguas		Talaches	2.	Cajas con enceres de cocina	2.
Mulas		Palas	2.	" " ropa y otros	4.
Bueyes		Azadones	6.	" " misceláneа	3.
Vacas		Barras		Semillas en general, kilos	100.
Burros		Serrones	1.	Sillas de montar	
Cerdos de raza		Otras piezas de labranza		Guarniciones	2.
Gallinas finas	11.	Cajas con útiles de herrería		Carabinas	1.
Ganzos		" " " " carrocería		Pistolas	
Ganado menor		" " " " carpintería		Máquinas de coser	1.

Lo inscrito en lista es propiedad del interesado y se compromete á no carecer de los útiles é instrumentos para la agricultura, ó la industria, los animales de cría y trabajo con sus aperos, obligándose á reponer lo que faltare ó adquirir lo más necesario llegado el caso.

(Firma)

NOTAS: Trae además 4 piezas de muebles y una guitarra

Copy of a typical declaration form filled out by all settler-colonists returning to Mexico under Siliceo's Mexican Colonization Enterprise.

Courtesy of the Hemeroteca Nacional de México, Universidad Nacional Autónoma de México.

comprehensive—historical archives never are—but still the forms reveal another layer of state sociology.[10] In these particular declaration forms, demographic data is followed by queries about the declarant's current city and state of residence; place of birth; and level of literacy in both Spanish and English; as well as the ages of all accompanying family members, their civil status, and their relationship to the head of household. Given the limitations of space, I will focus on a few general themes, including place of birth and identity, some common characteristics of the entire sample, and sizes of the family units.

National and Regional Identities of Siliceo's Settlers

The question of Mexican American identity in Texas history continues to be a subject of considerable research. This case study of settler-colonists who returned to Mexico in the late 1890s confirms many of the conclusions that have been reached by quantitative analyses of the region in this period. A number of the statistical inferences from this dataset noticeably overlap with Kenneth Stewart and Arnoldo De León's rigorous sociohistorical investigations, from which they deduced that the Mexican American experience was "fundamentally diverse and complex." This is why my overview of the declaration forms likewise takes a "quantitative approach to show the heterogeneity of the nineteenth-century Tejano community."[11]

Given that the group of settlers included individuals from various states in Mexico whose children were mostly born in the United States, these family units could aptly be labeled as "Mexico-Texano." In fact, five declarants self-identified as "Mexico-Texano" or "Mexico-Tejana," which explains why I have chosen to use this term here.[12] Of the 239 persons whose declaraciones are archived in the AHTN, which supposedly contains "everything related to said contract" with Siliceo, all but two were of Mexican origin and most were born in Mexico.

Although most of the heads of household were born in Mexico proper, the declarations also reveal that when family groups are quantified, more than 42 percent of colonists listed the United States as their place of birth while 57 percent hailed from a dozen states in northern and central Mexico. The vast majority gave their nationality as either "Mexicana" or "Mexicano," excepting one colonist who self-identified as English and another as German; these two were both married to Mexicans.[13] Evaluating this data against Siliceo's contractual obligations, he clearly fulfilled Article 1, which called for him to resettle members of his own "raza."[14] Beyond that, however, the settler-colonists who returned to

Mexico under Siliceo's supervision were not a homogenous group in terms of state or region of origin, age, gender, or rate of literacy in English and Spanish.

According to Stewart and De León's pioneering sociohistorical investigations of the US federal census from 1850 to 1900, estimates of the Tejano population were between 13,900 and 23,200 in 1850 and increased to 165,000 by 1900. This population explosion of 1,086 percent over the course of five decades "was largely the result of immigration from Mexico rather than natural reproduction of the Native Mexican population." By 1900 non-native Tejanos made up 41 percent of this total while 59 percent were identified as "native."[15] Comparing these figures with Siliceo's final tally suggests that, among his colonists, the percentages were largely reversed, in that close to 57 percent of the settlers were born in Mexico while a little more than 40 percent could be considered "native Tejanos." There is an interesting generational and intra-familial dimension that correlates more closely in that wives and children constituted the majority of individuals born in Texas. This data point also correlates with the high percentage of English speakers among the wives and children.[16] As a traditional region of out-migration, it is unsurprising that the mid-central Mexican state of San Luis Potosí comes in second as place of origin, with 10 percent (90) of all colonists naming this mid-central state as their birthplace. Sharing a 230-mile border with Texas, Tamaulipas was the third most common state of birth, named by 10 percent of the settlers.

Given how profoundly environment and climate can affect human migration flows, a regional comparison of the north, central, and southern ecological zones can offer insight into patterns of migration and settlement. In that regard, 28 percent (243) of the settlers in Siliceo's enterprise were born in the border states of Coahuila, Sonora, Chihuahua, Nuevo León, and Baja California. Phrased in a different way, 28 percent of the individuals in this group were *norteños* who most likely migrated to Texas under labor contracts or were recruited there through newspaper advertisements.

Children and Spouses of the Returning Settlers

The family, like all human institutions, has an extensive historiography.[17] Likewise, the historiography of the Mexican American family is extensive, rich, and consonant with some of the extrapolations to be made from the settlers' declaration forms. Although there are many excellent studies of the Greater Mexico family, the research of Arnoldo De León and Kenneth Stewart is the most statistically rigorous and tightly focused on the state of Texas in the latter half of the nineteenth century. That makes their findings the most relevant for comparison with the numerical data in the declaraciones.

A general overview of the declaration forms reveals that 67 percent (159/239) of declarants were adults (average age of 39), married with children, and traveling as a family unit.[18] The remaining 32 percent were single men (60) and older widowers (18). Three of the 239 petitioners were widows; together, widows and widowers represented 11 percent of the declarants.

These findings align closely with De León and Stewart's observations on single-family homes in the 1900 US census. In their analysis of five different Tejano living arrangements in Texas between 1850 and 1900, single-family households accounted for 67 percent of the total. Among non-natives (that is, Mexican migrants) 66 percent lived in single-family households, compared to 67 percent of US-born Tejanos. In their analysis, and as my own research shows, "single-family dwellings were the norm among Tejanos in the nineteenth century when single-family arrangements outnumbered multifamily situations in the Mexican community of Texas by a margin of two to one."[19] The percentage of multifamily units—which could include grandparents, uncles, aunts, or other relatives—was not comparable with the declaración data. The prerequisites for migration and movement might help explain why a disproportionate number of single males (60) signed up with Siliceo's project in the late 1890s. Even today, young, single men are the most desirable for national economies.

Single men made up 25 percent of my sample, and more than a few of them declared only "the shirt on their back," one saddle, one horse, and one harness.[20] By contrast, De León and Stewart conclude that in 1900 the number of single-person households among native Tejanos in Texas was 6 percent, while the figure for non-natives was 8 percent.[21] If the 21 widows and widowers are counted among the single-person households, the percentage of single heads of household increases to 33 percent of all declarants. Seen in this light, settler colonization was clearly a family affair: two-thirds of the declarants belonged to traditional nuclear families.

The composition of the family units in the declaraciones sheds light on a few other generational details when coupled with age and civil status. For example, while the average age of a declarant was 39 years of age, petitioners ranged from as young as 20 to upwards of 67 years of age.[22] The average age of a settler-colonist's wife was 32 years, with a range from as young as 14 up to 56 years old. A fourteen-year-old bride was not all that unusual in this time period. As De León and Stewart note "among wedded Tejanos aged 14–24 years, the average

age at marriage was 17.9 at the turn of the century"; the corresponding figure for Anglos was 19 percent.[23] What is striking about Siliceo's sample, in my own estimation, is not necessarily the ages per se, but the disparity of percentages when contrasting single travelers vis-à-vis family units.

Residential Patterns of Settler-Colonists: The Blackland Prairie

A close-up view of Texas counties and cities yields insight into the type of environment the settler-colonists left to resettle in Mexico. Of the settler-colonists in Siliceo's enterprise, 61 percent were residing in six towns within four counties. Keeping in mind that most of the settler-colonists in the sample were born in Mexico, 41 percent of all family units (98) lived in three locales: San Antonio (Bexar County), Manor (Travis County), and Georgetown (Williamson County).[24] San Antonio was the largest city in Texas in the 1890s, with 53,000 residents, all in Bexar County. Back then, its size was but a shadow of the sprawling San Antonio metropolitan area today. Among the declarants, 32 family units comprising 101 individuals (12 percent) came from Bexar County. However, if the individuals living in what is now the greater San Antonio metropolitan area are included (Bexar, Atascosa, Comal, and Gonzalez Counties), then the figure increases to 155 settler-colonists, or 18 percent.

Focusing on the counties these settlers came from, Caldwell County, which was an important agricultural area in the 1890s, is interesting to isolate. Not all petitioners correctly identified their county of residence, many substituting the name of their town instead. When all the residents from small towns within Caldwell County are added together, it becomes the location where most of Siliceo's colonists were residing when they signed on to his resettlement project. The breakdown is as follows: 18 families (76 individuals) from Luling, 21 families (72 individuals) from Prairie Lea, and 18 families (55 individuals) from Lockhart, for a total of 57 families (203 individuals), or 23 percent of all colonists.

In the 1890 US census for Caldwell County, the recorded 477 native Mexicans represented a mere 3 percent of the population. By 1910 ethnic Mexicans composed 17 percent of the county population, a demographic increase of 4,113 people—or a bit more than 760 percent. Local research on Caldwell County suggests that the area became a magnet for Mexican migration right as the local economy shifted from a cattle industry to one more heavily dependent on cotton. Historian Vivian Elizabeth Smyrl notes that "in 1890 the 38,710 acres planted in cotton represented nearly 30 percent of the county's improved acreage, and the yield of 21,326 bales was nearly three times higher than the

1880 harvest." By "1900 farmers planted more than 90,000 acres in cotton, or nearly 70 percent of the improved land."[25] Similar patterns were repeated elsewhere in the region.

Like modern-day San Antonio, Austin is also becoming a megacity and now covers an area that includes Travis, Williamson, and Hays Counties in central Texas. Grouping Siliceo's settler-colonists in accordance with modern-day Austin's larger metropolitan area yields an interesting perspective on Mexican American settlements in that region. For example, in the 1890s, the city of Austin had a population of 14,575, while the town of Manor had "population estimates reaching 500 by 1892."[26] According to the declaración records, 37 families (150 individuals) from the town of Manor signed up for resettlement. These individuals accounted for 17 percent of the settlers but perhaps 30 percent of the residents of Manor, meaning the town would have experienced a considerable population decline. Twenty-nine family units (around 85 settlers) came from Williamson County, which today is part of the larger Austin metropolitan area. If the neighboring counties of Williamson and Manor are considered in their current configurations, then the number of settler family units from the larger Austin area increases dramatically to 66 (235 individuals). Hence, it is reasonable to suggest that the greatest proportion of individuals (27 percent) in Siliceo's resettlement project came from what is now the greater Austin metropolitan area.

Occupational Status of the Settler-Colonists

Based on the material possessions reported by the settler-colonists, more than 90 percent of the 239 heads of households can be classified as "agricultores," or agriculturalists.[27] During this era, deliberate use of the term "agricultores" carries substantial cultural and sociological implications of elevated socioeconomic standing. Consequently, this usage played a pivotal role in shaping the ongoing debates surrounding the diaspora in the Greater Mexico press.[28] Based on the meticulous details encapsulated within the questionnaires, it can be asserted with assurance that nearly all declarants who did not list an occupation were, in fact, agriculturalists. This conclusion is substantiated by the fact that every colonist brought along the essential tools of their agricultural trade, notably plows and the domestic animals required for their operation.[29] Additionally, the places of residence of most of the petitioners are located in an area known as the Blackland Prairie. Based on his research on cotton farmers in the Blackland Prairie of

Texas, Neil Foley notes that these particular tenant farmers "occupied a higher class position on the agricultural ladder than did sharecroppers, mainly because they owned their own plows, work animals, and tools."[30]

Moreover, there is another source to consider in evaluating the occupational status of these settler-colonists: the words, promises, and contractual obligations of Luis Siliceo himself. In both his contract and in his newspaper, Siliceo consistently called for agricultural workers to return to Mexico and work the soil. In one of his first "La repatriación" editorials, Siliceo describes the occupation of the settler-colonist he aims to recruit for his *patria*. Note his use of the term "nuestros campos" and of flowery nationalist prose about service to the state.

> Those who were registered during my stay in San Antonio, and those who initiated my repatriation project, are undoubtedly the kind of individuals needed in our fields. In addition to being hardworking, they are morally upright and, to a great extent, quite educated. They are by no means like the large majority of migrants to the United States were some years ago. Most of these Mexicans possess all the modern tools and equipment required for agriculture; many of them own some heads of cattle and horses; and, finally, these laborers are not mere field workers but rather *medieros* [tenant farmers] who live with some comfort, yet for a thousand reasons, they yearn to return to the place of their birth.[31]

It remains ambiguous which category of immigrants Siliceo was drawing parallels with regarding his settler-colonists, or if he was alluding to recent migrations from Asia and eastern and southern Europe.[32] Either way, Siliceo used the contrast with these other immigrants to underscore his settlers' industriousness, morality, intelligence, and occupational status as medieros, not mere braceros. Medieros occupied a social class between laborers and landowners, splitting their harvests and profits with the owner of the land they farmed by *medio*, or in half.

The material history of the declarations along with Siliceo's assertion that these colonists were "quite enlightened" offer some corroborating evidence for the characterization of the colonists as medieros. Siliceo consistently maintained that the individuals who resettled under his project were the most modern settler-colonists because of their position on the well-known "agricultural ladder" theory of his era. Following this ladder, an individual could rise to proprietorship by working as wage laborer, then sharecropper, then tenant farmer, and finally landowner. In Siliceo's opinion, his Mexico-Texano colonists were well on their way toward the decisive step in the agricultural ladder; namely, landownership in Mexico. As Siliceo observed,

> It is not possible for the settler to be an educated man; but it is natural that, being so, he remains in this condition for only a few years and then moves into the category of property owner. Therefore, we must speak about things as they generally are, without taking exceptions and rarities into account. We shall say, then, that settlers occupy a middle ground, both in terms of knowledge and possessions, between laborers and property owners. Their interest also falls in between the two, as they work with more enthusiasm than the former, who only look to get through the day, and with less than the latter because they are concerned only with the duration of their lease. We can say that the settler aspires to make progress in his work, while the property owner aims for its longevity.[33]

According to Siliceo's sociological and class analysis, these potential settler-colonists from the Blackland Prairie had accrued farming and agricultural knowledge through their experience as tenant farmers with *arrendamientos* (leases). They had animals and modern tools and knowledge. What they lacked were titles to their own surveyed plots of land. In his "Arrendamiento" article, Siliceo cleverly underscored the mutual benefits of colonization and how both the colonizer and the colonized could contribute to the nation. Specifically, the "interest of agriculture in general is also the interest of the nation, *and both* are primarily concerned with properties being cultivated by their rightful owners, with the property owner possessing as much land and agricultural improvements as they can effectively manage, without compromising sound administration." In short, substantive improvement of the land could only come with the long-term thinking associated with ownership. Siliceo left "no doubt that *el hombre* takes better care of his own property than that of others" by highlighting that those who had signed on to his project had the most suitable status for resettlement. In this case, "rural properties" were always "better administered by their owners than by colonists, and better administered by the latter than by foremen or managers."[34] Landownership would develop economic and cultural roots that could only come with guarantees of land concessions.

As the preceding analysis of the settlers' residential patterns showed, 64 percent of all settler colonists in Siliceo's project were residing in counties clustered within the Blackland Prairie triangle that Foley mapped in his insightful analysis of Texas cotton farms. As Foley underscores, the ecological and geographical amalgamation of cotton with cattle, as outlined by Donald Meinig, marks a crucial intersection where the "plantation and the hacienda" truly converge. Moreover, the Mexican population of the Blackland Prairie predominantly resided in San Antonio and the adjacent counties of Hays and Travis.[35] That almost two-thirds of all settler families hailed from this region further substantiates the other pieces of evidence suggesting that these individuals were primarily agricultores.

Taking into account certain historiographical intersections with the research of other scholars alongside the insights gleaned from archival and material records, it becomes pertinent to scrutinize the self-descriptions of the settler-colonists. A minority of declarants reported two or three professions in addition to agricultor. These other professions included *albañil*, *hojalatero*, *horticultor*, *industrial*, *peluquero*, *carpintero*, *sastre*, *herrero*, *carrocero*, *comerciante*, *zapatero*, and *profesor de primeras letras*. Vicente González of Corpus Christi, Texas, for instance, was a specialist in three trades: carpintero, carrocero, and agricultor (carpenter, carriage repairer, and agriculturalist). Hilario Luna, age thirty, from Manor, Texas, reported that he was both an agricultor and a horticultor (agriculturalist and horticulturalist).[36] Each of these men recorded the appropriate tools and materials for those professions in their declaraciones, thus authenticating their occupational status.

A statistical overview of the characteristics of the settler-colonists who returned to Mexico under the direction of Siliceo's Mexican Colonization Enterprise between 1895 and 1900 reveals that the majority were tenant farmers who "occupied a higher class position on the agricultural ladder than did sharecroppers."[37] Due either to Siliceo's micromanagement or sheer chance, a sizable quantity of primary and legal documentation related to Siliceo's contract is archived, including signed sworn statements by the colonists and 239 declaration forms recording varying levels of detail on 877 individuals. When organized statistically, the data revealed that the majority of settlers were families, largely from the San Antonio and Blackland Prairie areas, and with an average age of forty. Alongside some surprising impressions, the occupational data of the sample was the most revealing because several other pieces of evidence corroborate the settlers' declaration forms. In chapter 13, I continue analyzing some of the typical characteristics of these colonists by comparing literacy rates, ages, and birthplaces of the heads of household with those of their spouses and children.

CHAPTER 13

CHARACTERISTICS OF A TYPICAL SETTLER-COLONIST

The term "head of household" may be confusing because of its current meaning in the US tax code, but I employ the term here because of the way the declaration's questionnaire is structured. In the declaración, "name of the Colono" is the same person as the "declarant" and hence constitutes a "head of household."[1] Just as the components of speech are interrelated and get their meaning from the broader structure of the surrounding language, I apply the same approach to the analysis of the census data, which all points to the settler-colonists' agricultural vocation.

Characteristics of Heads of Household

Based on the declarations archived in Siliceo's contract file, 95 percent (228 of 239) of the heads of household were born in Mexico, and all but three were males. As described in the previous chapter, 25 percent (60 of 239) of the declarants were single bachelors (*solteros*); that proportion jumps to 33 percent if the 18 widowers and 3 widows in the sample are included. All told, then, one of out of every three heads of household was widowed or unmarried. The average age of the declarants was almost 40, and there was a large range of 47 years between the youngest declarant (age 20) and the oldest (age 67), which is accounted for by the solteros.[2]

Of the declarants born in Mexico, 20 percent (49) were from the central state of San Luis Potosí. This large proportion reflects both railroad networks and historic patterns of migration from the region.[3] As Miguel Ángel González-Quiroga writes, "the railroad expanded the scope of migration; after 1880 more people began the trek north from states such as Jalisco, Zacatecas, and Guanajuato."[4] Although most northward migration likely took place in carriages and animal-powered vehicles, railroad networks were growing by the day at the close of the nineteenth century. It is no surprise, therefore, that the largest share (44 percent) of colonists hailed from the northern border states of Nuevo León (33, or 13 percent),

Tamaulipas (29, or 12 percent), Coahuila (28, or 12 percent), and Chihuahua (16, or 7 percent). Another 42 percent of heads of household were from the central states of San Luis Potosí, Zacatecas, Guanajuato, Jalisco, and Aguascalientes. Overall, 86 percent of the heads of household hailed from the northern and central regions of Mexico, while eight declarants (3.35 percent) were from Texas. This stands in stark contrast to their predominantly US-born children.

While 95 percent of the declarants listed Mexico as their place of birth, their family units cannot be characterized as expatriate Mexicans. The spouses', extended family members', and especially children's countries of birth were more diverse. The contemporary stereotypes of migrants and sharecroppers in the twenty-first century do not always align seamlessly with the nineteenth-century realities. Many of these individuals were not only mobile but also entrepreneurial, possessing sufficient capital to enable their migration. For example, 67 percent of the declarants (161 of 239) were married. Examining the birthplaces of dependent family members more closely reveals that several of the spouses (32) and most of

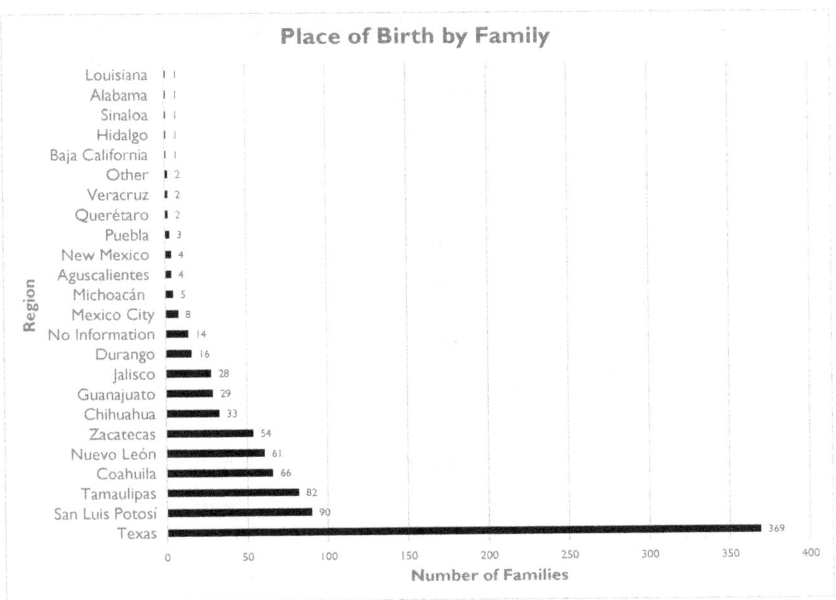

Map highlighting the places of birth of all members of the families that returned to Mexico under Siliceo's Mexican Colonization Enterprise. When quantifying all 877 settlers by states, including children, the largest share (42 percent) were born in Texas. *Graph by author.*

the children (314) were born in the United States, constituting what today might be called a "mixed-status" family.[5]

Another way of breaking down the data in a more granular fashion is to focus on the ages and language levels of the heads of household. According to the completed questionnaires, 66 percent of all male declarants (married, single, and widowed) could read Spanish while 43 percent "knew" English. The proportion of declarants who could also write in Spanish was slightly lower (60 percent). One of the settlers was trilingual, being able to speak Comanche in addition to English and Spanish. Citing official statistics from 1895, historians of literacy in Mexico set the general country-wide literacy rate at around 18 percent, reaching perhaps as high as 50 percent in Mexico City.[6] By comparison, the United States had an 87 percent literacy rate.[7] So, contradicting the newspaper criticism about the poor quality of settlers in Siliceo's enterprise, these colonists had a significantly higher literacy rate than the general population of Mexico and approaching that of the general population of the United States.

Throwing the elevated literacy level of Siliceo's colonists into sharp relief, they also enjoyed a significantly higher literacy rate than Texans with comparable occupations at the close of the nineteenth century. In their granular analysis of demographic statistics for the state of Texas from 1850 to 1900, Arnoldo De León and Kenneth Stewart found that 36 percent of "Anglo workers" in the agricultural sector were literate. Moreover, restricting the sample to US-born Tejanos at midcentury, the literacy rate was 50 percent; in 1880 the rate was 37 percent, and in 1890 it was 22 percent.[8] Thus, compared to their Tejano and "Anglo" counterparts in terms of occupation, the colonists in Siliceo's "Mexican Colonization Enterprise" were marked by a significantly higher literacy rate.

Characteristics of Spouses

Having taken a closer view of the overall family units and heads of household, I would be remiss if I did not conduct an equally measured examination of the spouses who accompanied the declarants to Mexico. Women accounted for 44 percent of the colonists (384 of 877) in the sample. Of these, 155 were registered as spouses (18 percent) with an average age of 32.3 years. Their occupational status is not recorded, but it would be safe to assume that they were agriculturalists to some degree. Like settler colonization, agricultural work in the nineteenth century was a family affair.

In terms of birth country, the population of spouses in the sample was more diverse than the male heads of household. Whereas 95 percent of male declarants were born in Mexico, only 81 percent of their wives were born in that country.[9] Thirty of the 155 wives (19 percent) were born in the state of Texas, compared to only eight of their husbands. This "mixed-status" among family units was not unusual during the period, as Siliceo himself later married Sunny Mendoza, a "Mexico-Tejana." The fact that 43 percent of the male declarants were bilingual may also help to explain the high rate of intermarriage diversity.[10] As for why such a high percentage of wives were born in Texas, we can infer that many of their husbands migrated to Texas as young men and later married into Mexico-Tejano families. Since Spanish was the lingua franca among Tejanos and Mexican migrants, it stands to reason that such mixed-status families were common.

From a regional Mexican perspective, the distribution of spouses exhibits a notable balance. Mexico emerges as the predominant place of birth for the majority of spouses. Nevertheless, it is worth noting that 44 percent of this cohort were born in the customary migration zones located in the northern frontier states, while 30 percent traced their origins to the central states of Mexico. In this context, a remarkable congruence emerges between wives and husbands regarding their birthplaces, with both groups predominantly originating from the central or northern regions of Mexico. Like their male counterparts of similar ages, spouses from the northern states of Coahuila (24), Nuevo León (16), Tamaulipas (14), and Chihuahua (4) constituted 37 percent of the total.[11] Finally, 30 percent of spouses registered birthplaces in central Mexico.[12]

One question that arises in this statistical exercise concerns potential correlations between place of birth and literacy in Spanish, English, or both. If elements of modernity in 1895 were defined by occupational status and knowledge of modern forms of agriculture and machinery, do literacy and bilingual aptitude factor into what it meant to be "more modern" at this time?[13] Intentionally or not, modern notions of literacy are automatically tied to questions not only of a nation's development, but also of a population's "intelligence quotient." Unfortunately, the data in this sample is insufficient for a robust analysis. Bearing in mind that adult men outnumbered adult women, which could skew the results, the literacy rate (reading and writing Spanish) for married women was a little more than half that of married men: 36 percent of married women could read Spanish and 31 percent could also write in that language, whereas 66 and 60 percent of all male declarants could do so. However, the literacy rate of females is still double the average national literacy rate in Mexico (18% at that time). Recalling De León and Stewart's data, the literacy rate of these Mexican American women was practically identical to that of "Anglos" working in agriculture in

Texas in 1880 (36 versus 37 percent). Spouses in the sample presented by Siliceo thus had a higher literacy rate than their male Anglo and Tejano counterparts in the same period. Moreover, 30 percent of wives were bilingual speakers in two languages, which at least by modern-day standards, is an index for intelligence.

Characteristics of Children

Collectively, children represented 51 percent (448 of 877) of the settler-colonists who returned to Mexico as part of Siliceo's colonization project. Of the children, 55 percent (243) were male and 45 percent (205) were female. Almost three-quarters of the children (326 of 448, 73 percent) were US citizens born in Texas. The children ranged in age from as young as a few months to 33 years old, with the average age being 10.3 years. In sum, then, 73 percent of the children, 19 percent of the spouses (Texas almost exclusively), and only 3 percent of male declarants (Texas) were US-born.

The remaining 27 percent of the children who were not Tejanitos (little Tejanos) were born in the following states: Tamaulipas (37), Zacatecas (16), San Luis Potosí (14), Chihuahua (12), Coahuila (12), and Nuevo León (7). Here it is important to note that the northern Mexican states bordering the United States are disproportionately represented once more. That is, 15 percent (68) of the children were from northern frontier states while 9 percent (41) hailed from central Mexican states. The contrast with the regions of birth of the parents is also quite telling. Whereas a low proportion of children were born in central states of Mexico (9 percent), 42 percent of heads of household and 30 percent of their wives reported having been born in that region.

The levels of education across mothers, fathers, and children in settler families, evaluated in terms of literacy rates, serve as another window into late-nineteenth-century social life. Literacy rates are an interesting proxy for the effectiveness of a state's bureaucratic reach via educational institutions, especially the primary schools that flourished under President Porfirio Díaz.[14] When the 1900 US census was conducted in Texas, the *illiteracy* rate for native Tejanos was 49.4 percent; for native Texans it was 38.7 percent; and for non-native Texans (usually someone from another state or an immigrant from another country) it was 53 percent.[15] Siliceo's heads of household appear to enjoy a literacy rate significantly higher than that of native Texans, but something different appears to have happened with their children when analyzing their literacy rates compared to their ages.

It would seem reasonable from our standpoint that literacy rates would increase significantly after five or six years of age, which is when most children started attending primary schools in both Mexico and the United States.[16] The ability to read and write Spanish run quite parallel after the age of six, but the rate of literacy stalls at around 20 percent after the age of 18. Recall that 66 percent of the heads of household and 36 percent of the wives could read Spanish, and 60 percent of the former and 31 percent of the latter could also write in that language. By contrast, 20 percent of the children could read Spanish and 19 percent could write it as well. Only 32 percent of the children spoke English, which is a bit higher than the rate for their mothers, at 29 percent, but lower than the rate for male heads of household at 43.5 percent. It would seem from this sample that the heads of household were the most literate of all the family members and 95 percent more likely to have been born in Mexico. Considering both structure and agency, the higher literacy rate among the parents of these children could perhaps be explained by the growth of primary education in Mexico between 1878 and 1900. A total of 5,194 primary schools existed in Mexico in 1878; that number more than doubled to 12,016 by 1900, and one could speculate that several of the declarants were the beneficiaries of these early Porfirian institutions of primary education before they emigrated to the United States.[17] But without more data, one can only speculate at this point.

Reasons for the low literacy rate among the children could be the small sample size or the average age of the children, which as I noted, was 10.3 years. However, the literacy rate is most likely related to the intermittent school attendance of the children of agricultural workers, who often worked before and after school—especially during harvest season.[18] Some of the families may also have been migratory, constantly following the harvest seasons, which would further disrupt the children's schooling. In fact, there appears to be a significant correlation between literacy and school attendance rates. The rate of Tejano school attendance, lower in the 1870s, did increase to 29 percent by 1900.[19] These upswings in attendance could correlate with rising literacy rates or explain the 32 percent of resettler children who knew English. "More relevant," argue De León and Stewart, "was the impact of inequality in the development of Texas schools, a point documented by statistics on literacy in the various sections of the Mexican settlement region."[20] Tejano literacy in the 1850s was at 25 percent and had increased to 42.4 percent by 1900 for the central Texas region.

Analyzing the characteristics of declarants, spouses, and children reveals a few factors that demonstrate the diversity of these Mexico-Texano families. Most notable is their high literacy rates vis-à-vis their compatriots in Mexico as well as US-born Tejanos. Data from each group of family members also uncovered insights into historical migration patterns between numerous states in Mexico and various counties in Texas.[21] One out of every five spouses was born in Texas but triangulation with secondary and other relevant primary sources highlights the diversity of and historic connections between Mexico and Texas. Thus, while most of the children were born in the United States, their fathers were primarily from Mexico.

In regard to migratory labor and larger economic forces, it is difficult to overestimate the centrality of agriculture during this period and the rise of agro-industry in the decades to come. The vast majority of settler-colonists in Siliceo's contingent were composed of family units and were employed primarily in some occupation in the agricultural sector. In chapter 14, I further complexify these declaration forms by examining the declarants' material possessions, showing that the tools and implements they brought with them further supports their occupational status as experts in modern agriculture.

CHAPTER 14

SETTLER-COLONISTS' COMPANION SPECIES, TOOLS, AND MATERIAL HISTORY

The last chapter discusses the material histories of these settler-colonists and sheds light not only on agricultural commodities, but more importantly, on the objects, tools, and animals registered in their declaration forms. This added material history authenticates the information in *El Colono* regarding the residential patterns, occupational status, and expertise of these agricultores.

Settler-Colonists and Their Tools of Colonization

The material culture of the settler-colonists is congruent with some of the statistical observations made about the heads of household and their wives and children presented in the previous chapter. The data detailing tools and machinery also speaks to the "quality" of these colonists, an issue that very much concerned Siliceo and the Greater Mexico press. Quantifying all their possessions, including some of the more mundane belongings, draws a more colorful picture of these "soldiers of progress." An examination of this granular statistical data—seeds, tools, machines, replacement parts, and companion species—further reinforces the occupational status of these settler-colonists. Thus, even when declarants did not list their occupation, the evidence of several horses, plows, farming implements, seeds, and replacement parts embedded in their declaration forms speaks to their agricultural expertise.

The idea that everyday objects have a social life was put forth by Arjun Appadurai in a collection of essays titled, appropriately, *The Social Life of Things* (1986). Appadurai theorized a radical claim in proposing "the idea that persons and things are not radically distinct categories, and that the transactions that surround things are invested with the properties of social relations."[1] In our twenty-first-century world of global flows of ideas, peoples, and commodities, his contention seems commonsensical; archaeologists have long observed that the ancient wares, tools, ceramics, and objects associated with once-forgotten locales can identify the possessor's social class, occupational status, diet, and cultural milieu.[2] In his analysis of "historical materialism," the mid-nineteenth-century philosopher-turned-historian Karl Marx understood well this assemblage of humans, modes of production, and manufactured objects.[3] These ideas were clarified in a 1938 essay in which Joseph Stalin, general secretary of the Communist Party of the Soviet Union, underscored that "historical materialism" is essentially "an application of the principles of dialectical materialism to the phenomena of the life of society, to the study of society and of its history."[4] So what can the personal possessions, tools, devices, machines, objects, animals, household items, and other material tell us about the lives, history, and society of the settler-colonists who participated in Siliceo's back-to-Mexico movement?

Although efforts to count and quantify populations date back to the Han Dynasty in China, these particular declaraciones appear to be part and parcel of a larger statistical impulse in the late nineteenth century.[5] For example, Herman Hollerith invented an electromechanical tabulating machine to process data for the 1890 US census.[6] The British historian Lawrence Goldman suggests that this "era of statistical enthusiasm" during the nineteenth century was a direct result of state growth and power. He argues that "nations grew in political sophistication as their populations increased, as their economies became more diverse and their trade more complex, so more numbers were available, more were collected, and more were needed for better regulation of these new societies." In short, "large scale statistics [were] a byproduct of the rapidly expanded census activities undertaken by various government agencies."[7] The influence of statistics on the American historical imaginary can easily be traced to the so-called frontier thesis (1893), which took a publication by a superintendent of the US Census Bureau as its primary basis for ruminating on the "American character."[8] It is no surprise that the settlers' declaraciones resemble the census surveys typically employed in both the United States and Mexico.[9]

In general, most of the material items declared fell into the categories of vehicles and animals, instruments and tools, and furniture and large baggage (*bulto*). These categories collectively encompass the material history of the settler-colonists in quantifying their vehicles, companion species, agricultural implements, and household wares and provisions. As more settlers signed up for Siliceo's project, the lists of itemized goods and the descriptions in the notes grew longer. Based on the preponderance of evidence, this material record supports the characterization of the colonists as tenant farmers, defined by Neil Foley as individuals who "occupied a higher-class position on the agricultural ladder than did sharecroppers, mainly because they owned their own plows, work animals, and tools."[10]

In 1895, transportation was undergoing rapid evolution, yet the predominant mode of land travel remained vehicles propelled by companion species such as horses, donkeys, mules, or oxen. These vehicles ranged from two-wheeled carts to buggies, covered wagons, and more modern, four-wheeled carriages. Animal-drawn carriages were starting to be replaced by mechanical and electrical vehicles, which eventually came to displace animal power—although not uniformly. Karl Benz of Germany was the first to develop an internal combustion engine in 1885 for his Motorwagen, but it appears that the first motorized vehicles did not appear in the United States until the mid-1890s. According to the Texas Transportation Museum website, the "first recorded horseless carriage in San Antonio, an electric vehicle, was delivered to the Staacke Brothers livery service on Commerce Street in 1899." More to the point, "this is the same year that most historians agree the first gasoline powered car arrived in Texas."[11] Thus, it seems that those settlers traveling farther south into states like Michoacán made use of animal power to the international border, then rail transportation to their final destination. The large numbers of vehicles and livestock speak not only to the colonists' entrepreneurialism as tenant farmers but also to the particularities of the agricultural sector in which they were most experienced. In conjunction with the examination of vehicles and companion species, an appraisal of the seeds imported into Mexico may provide valuable insights into the agricultural practices and crops cultivated in Texas.

One of the items that appears in all the declarations is an assortment of seeds, though the plant varieties are not always specified. Seeds may seem unassuming and only come to mind in spring for gardeners, or as an annoying question on declaration forms when reentering the United States from abroad. But when seeds are analyzed structurally in the context of other material possessions and tools of the profession, they can reveal some historicity of a particular class of individual.[12] Although the amount varied by settler, on average each settler returned to Mexico with 390 pounds of assorted grains and seeds. When quantifying all the declaration forms, I calculated about 93,110 pounds (42,233.95 kilograms or 46.5 tons) of assorted seeds, including maize, melon, *caña*, fruit, peanut, and livestock grasses.[13] Cotton seeds alone totaled 5,750 pounds (2,608.15 kilograms), which would average out to 24 pounds per each of the 239 declarants—around

8 percent of the seeds documented on the declaration forms. The first group of settler-colonists listed a larger quantity of cotton seed compared to later groups, increasing the likelihood that not all the colonists were cotton growers.

Aggregating the seed with the farming tools, machines, agricultural implements, and companion species yields a broader assemblage of a type of settler-colonist conditioned by labor migration and experience working plots from farmsteads to larger acreages. It is also important to note that many of the settler-colonists, primarily the single men, returned with very few tools, animals, or material possessions. In short, this large group was diverse in occupational status, level of literacy, level of wealth, and even agricultural specialty. Different seeds require specialized knowledge of the seasons and methods of pruning, and propagating—topics that were covered regularly in *El Colono.*

Companion Species

It is opportune to touch briefly upon the growing importance of animal studies alongside the material histories already considered.[14] Animals and companion species are key factors in our collective human history, especially prior to the widespread adoption of engines and other machines.[15] There is unfortunately not enough space to discuss the fascinating debates concerning animal and horticultural domestication in human history, but I will discuss three important categories that illuminate the social lives, occupational statuses, and interspecies cooperation that characterized these settler-colonist households.[16] The first category is carts, carriages, or wagons. The second is the livestock—horses, mules, donkeys, or oxen—required to power those vehicles. The third grouping consists of firearms, saddles, and of course, animal harnesses.

The number of carriages powered by companion species totaled 184. The declaraciones listed three kinds of vehicles, *guallines* (coaches), *carros* (carts), and *carretones* (carts); however, these were not the only kinds of vehicles recorded in the declarations. Horse-drawn buggies, for instance, appear occasionally, but coaches made up 50 percent of all the vehicles declared. *Guallin* is a Mexicanization of the English word "wagon," *gualla*, coupled with the Spanish diminutive *-in*, as in "small wagon"; an 1894 Spanish-English dictionary suggests the translation "stagecoach."[17] In the absence of visual evidence, this information supplies at least a semblance of a description of the vehicle in question. If guallines were similar to stagecoaches, then carretones would be akin to American four-wheeled covered wagons. Carretones accounted for approximately 14 percent of all vehicles, while the proportion of carros was more than twice that at 36 percent.[18] Without more description of these items, or an indication of their size or value, it is difficult to determine whether the possession of these vehicles reveals anything about the social class of each family.

Carros and *carretas* (with only a few of the latter listed) typically consisted of open carts featuring two substantial wheels. These carts were designed to accommodate bales of hay and bushels of cotton, serving as a cushion for a rider who guided the animals harnessed to a yoke at the front. That a few of the declarants identified their occupations as "hojalatero," "herrero," or "carrocero" is interesting in that these trades are directly tied to the manufacturing, repair, or operation of these vehicles. To a small degree, these trades exist today primarily for body work on older-model automobiles. Expertise in these trades required specific skills in metalworking and mechanical repair, as well as knowledge of hardware such as nuts, bolts, and cylinder sleeves for animal-powered vehicles. This would help explain why settlers also carried with them 447 pounds of nuts and bolts, 118 pounds of horseshoes, and 1,250 pounds of nails and assorted metal bars. The metal bars were used for smelting, making nails for house construction, and manufacturing and repairing parts for vehicles and assorted machinery.

A total of 1,339 animals went with the settler-colonists on their return to Mexico; in addition there were a few dogs, goats, turkeys, sheep, and pigeons not itemized in the original declarations.[19] It could be argued that more farm animals than people journeyed to Mexico as part of Siliceo's resettlement initiative. But these numbers are a bit deceiving because they suggest each declarant (and thus family unit) had an average of 5.6 animals. Of the 1,339 animals, around 57 percent were fowl such as chickens (754), and geese (24). It is not clear why most of the fowl were chickens; perhaps they were particularly popular US chicken breeds that might not be available in Mexico, simply intended for consumption on the long journey, or both. The 754 chickens would average out to 3.15 birds per household.

Among the four-legged animals, the declarations recorded 561 mammals with cows (35) and pigs (63) accounting for the smallest numbers. Cows made up only 2.6 percent and pigs 6.2 percent of all four-legged farm animals. Francisco Gregory, aged 46, of Corpus Christi, owned 22 of the 35 cattle that were declared.[20]

Equines were preferred to cattle as draft animals. Horses—identified as *yeguas* (mares), *caballos* (stallions), *potrancos* (colts)—totaled an estimated 378 animals. The number increases to 463 when mules and burros are added in. This works out to an average of 1.93 equines per settler family; however, cows and oxen could also be used to pull a wagon or a plow. If we add the cattle to the number of animals used for work and transport, then each family would average around

2.08 equines and bovines. Even today, the maintenance of companion species is not inexpensive, and it is agreed that the size of a family's herd says something about the family's social standing in a community.

It is also relevant to describe the material condition of the single men (solteros) who were making their way back to Mexico.[21] Solteros returned with 108 horses, 27 mules/burros, and 4 cows—139 equines and bovines in total—or 1.78 per individual. In addition, single men and widowers declared 21 saddles and 41 vehicles of all the types described earlier. A few solteros owned nothing more than their horse and their clothing on their backs, but collectively, they owned 53 firearms. This means that 68 percent of them were armed. Is there some correlation between the high literacy rates of this group and the high percentage of gun ownership, which was an index of material wealth? Among the 239 family units in the sample, 212 firearms were recorded, indicating that 88 percent of the families were armed with a carbine, rifle, musket, or pistol. The data suggests that married men with families were more likely to be armed than single or widowed men. Regardless of how one chooses to analyze this data, it is clear that this group of individuals was heavily armed by any standard.[22] Weaponry during this era was essential for frontier survival, but more relevant for our purposes, it was also an index of technology transfer.

Tools, Machines, and Agricultural Implements

Tools and tool making predate the human species and have been a central feature of hominin evolution.[23] According to John Hands, "the earliest species is thought to be *Homo habilis*, fossils of which are claimed from 1.9 to 1.5 million years ago in Kenya and Tanzania, with some fossils accompanied by extremely primitive stone tools called Oldowan; similar tools have been claimed to date from 2.6 million years ago."[24] Here, I follow a general definition of a tool as "the external employment of an unattached environmental object to alter more efficiently the form, position, or condition of another object, another organism, or the user itself."[25] These tools, in turn, helped humans create modern technologies and more sophisticated "equipment."[26] New tools bring about new ways of doing things and, subsequently, distinctive technologies—and vice versa. Tools are part of our human evolution and, today, are also stratified in accordance with social class, trade, profession, and technological expertise.[27] In short, tools say a thing or two about an individual's persona, occupation, interests, hobbies, and so on.

Fast-forward to nineteenth-century Mexico, where "productive technologies" before the 1870s "differed little from those used in the late eighteenth century," according to Edward Beatty. Prior to the late nineteenth century, "Mexico was in many ways a nation of isolated and localized markets where most business activity was based on personal relations, a result of 50 years of post-independence political instability and economic stagnation." Just prior to the election of General Díaz in 1876, "productive technologies" began to be updated. The return of Díaz in 1884 accelerated this trend, as "a flood of foreign technologies swept Mexico between 1870 and 1910—a not uncommon experience for societies outside the North Atlantic in the latter half of the century." Beatty's work challenges a number of prevailing historiographical interpretations around technology transfer and its relationship to economic dependence; he points out that newer "approaches to technological change have largely evolved through studies of change within societies and have not been systematically applied to the transfer of technologies between societies."[28] It is in this context that I situate this section on tools, machines, and other equipment by describing a migratory modality of technology transfer via the resettlement of what *El Colono* called "enlightened" modern Mexicans from Texas. The available sample here is limited, but given the amount of data that overlaps with the history of technology in Mexico during the nineteenth century, I think studies of technology transfer via repatriation will be a fruitful avenue of research in the future.[29]

The first salient point is that there are more farm tools than heads of household, just as there are more animals (1,339) than people. Restricting the count to farming tools, the declarations list 62 plows, 423 agricultural hoes, 135 shovels, 340 *talachos* (mattocks), 425 axes, and 30 steel digging bars. These are all basic tools that humans have used for millennia, tools still employed in the clearing, cutting, tilling, and sowing of land—not to mention a staple of giant home improvement stores in Mexico and the United States. The important feature is that the tools recorded by the Mexican customs were made of steel and most likely mass manufactured in the United States.

It is not difficult to identify the technology transfer of mechanized items that the settler-colonists declared, because the descriptions are literally "machines." In addition to hundreds of handheld tools and agricultural implements, settlers in Siliceo's project brought with them an estimated 38 *maquinas de cultivar* (cultivation), 42 *maquinas de sembrar* (seeding), and 48 *maquinas de coser* (sewing), along with firearms (212) and accordions (2).[30] The variety of agricultural machines provides us with a more complex view of the settlers' expertise. Maquinas de sembrar, presumably machines for seeding or planting, constituted one of the most modern innovations in US farming technology at the time, although there is no way to determine whether the colonists owned cutting-edge equipment. Several of these agricultural machines are advertised in numerous editions of *El Colono.*[31] Although still powered by animals, from a technological perspective, these new technologies were evolving and competitively patented.[32] At the time, factories were still producing animal-drawn machines but quickly transitioning to models powered by combustion engines running on fossil fuels.

In pondering the quantity and category of tools the settler-colonists declared, plows and farming implements merit further discussion. *Piezas de labranza* can be translated as "farming implements," while plows as we traditionally understand them are typically labeled *arados.* A total of 462 plows and 655 farming implements were recorded on the declaration forms. Today, farming implements, at least those that can be attached to a tractor or some sort of animal harness, can encompass machines for seeding, harvesting, cutting, or any number of agricultural tasks. Unfortunately, the declaration forms do not itemize these machines by purpose but instead lump them into a single category. The total of 655 agricultural implements averages out to 2.74 pieces of equipment per family unit, which seems reasonable.

Plows have a 10,000-year history in agriculture throughout the world.[33] A total of 462 agricultural plows, powered by companion species, were recorded in Siliceo's forms, or 1.93 plows for every family. In other words, every head of household owned an average of almost two agricultural plows. Without visual evidence, it is impossible to know how modern they were. What is clear is that the colonists were farmers who owned their own animals, tools, and farming machinery, so they ranked somewhere above sharecroppers but below landowners.[34]

This closing chapter analyzed the material possessions, companion species, tools, and machines that the setter-colonists whom Siliceo recruited imported into Mexico. When examined collectively, the statistics, objects, material possessions, tools, technology, and general household items unmistakably identified the majority of the settler colonists as agriculturists. When combined with all the other evidence, the material history of these settlers confirms Siliceo's claims that he would resettle modern, enlightened colonists in Mexico. Given that anxieties over the quality of colonists permeated the Greater Mexico press, it is important to recognize that his characterization appears accurate. The preceding section also concludes my transition from a planetary to a granular analysis, as initially outlined in my analogy of Matryoshka nesting dolls.

Material history has enjoyed an immensely fruitful philosophic and ideological conversation for centuries; my approach was to demonstrate that the disproportionate numbers of farming tools, seed, and agricultural machinery compared to people crossing the border provides supporting evidence for the more than 90 percent of declarants who stated their occupation as "agricultor." I undertook a similar discussion of companion species because animal power was essential for operating nineteenth-century farming implements. While companion species are part of earth's history, they are inextricably linked to the life and evolution of humans. Animals have domesticated *Homo sapiens* as much as *Homo sapiens* have domesticated animals.[35] That these settler-colonists returned to Mexico with so many different companion species not only humanizes them but also reveals that most of them had expertise as tenant farmers. While animals typically accompanied settler-colonists in their quest for new lands prior to the twentieth century, they were particularly important in this transitional phase to the rise of modern agriculture and the invention of diesel-powered tractors.[36]

EPILOGUE

Luis Siliceo's resettlement project from San Antonio, Texas, to Mexico between 1895 and 1900 got off to a rough start in the face of some opposition from the Greater Mexico press. Siliceo was quite cautious, perhaps too cautious, and can easily be described as a micromanager in modern parlance. In a letter to the Secretaría de Fomento y Colonización, Siliceo complained that he had been the victim of the "unjustified and constant opposition of the Mexico-Texano press," which he had been able to counter through the "profound influence of my newspaper 'El Colono.'"[1] Despite the perennial debates within the public sphere about the possibilities and pitfalls of expatriates' return to Mexico, Siliceo secured a contract with the Mexican government, started at least two (maybe three) newspapers dedicated to his enterprise, and eventually resettled several groups of families (877 individuals) in Tamaulipas and Michoacán.[2] Aside from Siliceo's contract, however, these efforts were never included in the government's tallies when the Secretaría de Fomento published subsequent annual *memorias*.[3]

In fact, a substantial portion of the documentary record consists of requests from Siliceo for the duty-free importation of settlers' material goods, animals, carts, and assorted equipment. In all the cases, officials in the Secretaría de Fomento and the Secretaría de Hacienda agreed to waive import duties and allow Mexico-Texano settlers and their animals to enter the country duty-free. This decision is notable, not only for what it says about the political position of the Porfirian administration with respect to diasporic populations, but also because this policy was later adopted by other political parties, most notably the Partido Liberal Mexicano (PLM): Article 35 of the PLM's program states, "For the Mexicans residing abroad who so solicit, the government will provide repatriation, paying for the transportation costs and allotting them lands that they can cultivate."[4] With Siliceo's project, the government granted all requests for duty-free importations, free travel by rail, and exemptions from certain documentary requirements. In fact, for those families traveling to Michoacán, the government also subsidized their train travel and transport for their animals, vehicles, and agricultural equipment. In the case of one disgruntled colonist, the government even paid for his return to Tamaulipas from Michoacán.[5]

In their initial accounts of colonization, the team at *El Colono* focused on the early colonists in Tamaulipas and aimed to emphasize the nationalist narrative of settlers' sacrifices. These writers were aware of the challenges faced by the early colonists but lacked sympathy for their struggles. While tenant farming was undeniably demanding, the fields these colonists had previously leased in Texas had already undergone extensive cultivation or rotation, sparing the farmers from the laborious task of clearing the land. However, the lands granted to the settlers in Mexico had never been cultivated before, necessitating the grueling tasks of chopping down timber and palm trees and removing the stumps. Without the aid of machinery, this process could take months. On hearing some rumblings from the colonists, the staff at *El Colono* responded that "this is how farmers are made, this is how soldiers are made, and this is how the most remarkable men have been made in all branches of industry and the arts, living from birth among the very elements that will later come to be the sustenance and the future of a whole family." In the pages of *El Colono*, the first efforts at resettlement were recast as the expression of a stoic resolve via a history that sought to embolden the colonists of Colonia Patria with a militant form of agro-nationalism: "Soldiers of Progress, stand firm, hand to the plows, turn and till the lands, lead the horses, and march . . . !"[6]

Siliceo acknowledged that "the results of my efforts have not been satisfactory to me," but stated that unforeseen circumstances and expenses had arisen in the repatriation project, expenditures he occasionally paid out of his own pocket. For example, he gave assistance to settlers waiting at the border for entry, subsidized his agents' trips to several states in Mexico, published numerous supplements, and remitted "some money to 'Colonia Patria' during the time of the fatal epidemic that invaded the state of Tamaulipas." According to Siliceo, thirty of the colonists whom he had resettled in this colony had perished during the epidemic.[7] The epidemic did not end his resettlement efforts, but there was no way to put a positive spin on the scourge of yellow fever, which had devastated the African American colony of Durango only a few years earlier.[8] Always the propagandist, Siliceo noted that although his enterprise had encountered some difficulties, he had seen some very favorable results, including numerous families already preparing to resettle lands in the district of Balleza in Chihuahua and perhaps fifty more families predicted to resettle there by the end of the year.[9]

Sticking to the Script: Longue Durée of Autocolonization

The final pieces of correspondence between Siliceo and the Secretaría de Fomento in May 1900 effectively terminated the colonization contract in accordance with the terms agreed to by both parties.[10] However, there are obviously more than two sides to any story, and Siliceo's longest letter gives his perspective of the past—one naturally predisposed to support his effort to renegotiate particular aspects of his expiring contract. Siliceo started his letter to engineer Manuel Fernández Leal by stating that he was aware that he was "near the expiration of the [contract] term" and expressing "my regret that I have not been able to achieve as much as I earnestly and wholeheartedly aimed for during the period when I received the requested increase of 150 pesos over the original amount allocated for the support of the aforementioned newspaper."[11] Apparently, Siliceo had managed to secure a raise in his monthly stipend, elevating it from 350 to 500 pesos. Nevertheless, this agreement was now drawing to a close, just like his colonization contract.

The response from the Secretaría de Fomento on behalf of the Díaz administration arrived almost six weeks later and, as was typical, was laden with contractual legalese. Repeating verbatim the essence of Siliceo's own words—including his own auto-critique—the final letter effectively reiterated the terms of the contract and declared it "expired."[12]

Siliceo's project is one microhistory within a larger history of many resettlement projects that took place throughout the nineteenth century. Although the number of contracts the Mexican government cancelled is difficult to calculate, we can derive some historicity from Fomento's annual reports, which indicate that the agency either rescinded or declined to extend or renew more than half of all colonization contracts. Of all the colonization contracts published by Fomento in its many outlets when Siliceo secured his concession, 55 percent were voided or rescinded between 1892 and 1896.[13] The report for these years recorded twenty-nine new contracts awarded to various colonization companies, of which five had been modified or perhaps renegotiated at that point, six had been rescinded, and ten had been cancelled. Thus, out of twenty-nine contracts, sixteen were no longer in effect and the remaining thirteen were in the initial stages of the approval process. In sum, more than half of the colonization contracts between the Díaz administration and private companies in 1892–96 were voided and therefore went unfulfilled. By any standard—historical, cultural, or economic—this is an astonishing number of cancelled contracts.[14] Although several historians of the Mexican Revolution have accused land and colonization companies of accumulating millions of hectares of land, none of this complexity over colonization contracts has ever been considered.[15] It is one thing to read a signed contract involving thousands of acres, but it is quite another matter to analyze what actually happened to the land at the end of the agreement.

As for Luis Siliceo, he probably stayed in Mexico City after his colonization contract ended in 1900, because the following year he began giving free English classes at the National Conservatory of Music in Mexico City.[16] Siliceo evidently also enjoyed modern Mexican bourgeois life. Once the social and political situation in Mexico City was no longer favorable after the resignation of Díaz in 1911, he joined the growing migrant streams headed north and relocated to San Antonio, Texas, where he smelled new opportunities. Siliceo continued to advertise himself as a "repatriation agent" and to maintain an office in downtown San Antonio well into the 1920s, suggesting that he maintained amicable relationships with the administrations of General Venustiano Carranza and later General Alvaro Obregón. The continuing operation of his agency also provides evidence that the Mexican government was still involved in the business of colonization and in resettling Mexico-Texanos.[17]

Administrative changes were taking place within the bureaucracy at the Secretaría de Fomento, including the publication in 1906 of the agency's most important assessment of colonization by the jefe of the Primera Sección, engineer José Covarrubias. Titled *Algunas observaciones acera la inmigración y de la colonización en las naciones independientes de América* (Some Observations on Immigration and Colonization in the Independent Nations of America), the study appeared in many outlets, including the *Revista Positiva* in 1907, which was the main journal of the Científicos.[18] Covarrubias narrated what would be the agency's most comprehensive global history of colonization throughout Latin America, including the United States, before outlining a series of policy recommendations. The major thesis, in my estimation, is Covarrubias's recommendations about the quality and kind of colonists who should be privileged in the settlement of *terrenos baldíos.* Covarrubias effectively confirmed the standing policy of autocolonización, which all political sectors of Mexican society supported, including the anarchist wing of the PLM. Prior to writing his 1906 study, Covarrubias had signed off on many of Siliceo's requests and had gained intimate knowledge of earlier back-to-Mexico movements. Autocolonization was the consensus prior to the start of the revolutionary era in 1910.

Covarrubias termed settler-colonists hijos del país (children of the country). After surveying an admirable archive detailing decades of experience with colonization, Covarrubias concluded, "It must always be borne in mind that the nationals will be the main element in the colonization of the new lands." In other words, "the colonization of new lands is almost entirely done by sons of the country, who emigrate with their families to unpopulated places, but with good prospects for agriculture, in search of a future." Reinforcing the contemporary Porfirian indigenism of his political class, he wrote that "perhaps the Indian's love of the land will make them a colonist, and later a citizen." Echoing verbatim the writings of *El Colono* Covarrubias also noted that "foreigners will only present themselves as colonists in appreciable numbers when, due to the rise in wages, a stream of immigrants is formed, and until it is possible for a part of them to save a small amount of capital."[19]

Two years later, the prominent Mexican sociologist Andrés Molina Enríquez amplified Covarrubias's "masterful work" by citing the monograph on at least four separate occasions and agreeing on all points. However, applying his own systematic taxonomy to the question of colonization, Molina Enríquez put forth a slightly different interpretation about the viability of European colonists. Seemingly flipping Herbert Spencer's survival of the fittest philosophy on its proverbial head, Molina Enriquez reasoned that Europeans had become soft and unfit for colonizing the difficult terrain of the northern Mexican deserts. The future "intellectual author of the Mexican Revolution" regurgitated Siliceo's chauvinism when he maintained that "in quality of immigrants properly stated, Europeans will also not come—in a general manner of course—because it will be impossible to sustain the struggle for life against the lower national unities considerably stronger than themselves." As this and other statements about the "superiority" of the more "modern Mexican migrants"—who were often compared to Europeans, Asians, Africans, and North Americans—show, racialized thinking was tied to a vulgar Spencerian view about the natural environment. And as we have already seen, Siliceo and his staff had made similar arguments on several occasions more than a decade earlier. Like Siliceo, Molina Enríquez believed northern Mexicans (and by extension Mexican Americans) had adapted to the difficult living conditions on the frontier. Inviting Europeans was all well and good, but the question was whether they could survive in the rugged desert environs where mestizos and other "national unities" had learned how to survive economically and defend themselves against the indios bárbaros. Molina Enríquez argued that mestizos, being "superior to Europeans," could thrive where the latter could not, and that promotion of European colonization was unscientific.[20] And, naturally, contemporaries of Molina Enríquez and Covarrubias had ample empirical evidence at hand, exemplified by the debacle of five out of the six Italian colonies a decade prior.

In the years when Covarrubias and Molina Enríquez were opining on the pitfalls of European colonization, the discourse of racial superiority came to be applied more generally to Mexican laborers migrating to the United States. The ongoing mass migration of Mexican laborers to the United States—and later repatriations to come—alarmed local and federal officials alike. Ignacio Mariscal, Mexican consul general in Tucson, Arizona, published an article in the October 1906 issue of *El Boletín de la Secretaría de Fomento* in which he criticized the low wages hacendados paid their workers. Mariscal argued that these structural conditions explained the continued mass migration of laborers to the United States. Mexicans' work ethic, as Siliceo had consistently claimed, was very attractive to companies right across the international boundary. For this reason Mariscal, too, believed that "all the border companies have the firm experience that the Mexican laborer is a powerful nerve of unquestionable energy that propels them in work that requires selflessness and firmness of character, and that they can face the toughest jobs, which they alone can overcome."[21]

Rómulo Escobar Zerman of Chihuahua repeated something similar when he attempted to sound the alarm to Mexican officials about the growing wave of northward migrations. He argued that radical structural and cultural changes were necessary in Mexico in order to maintain the viable labor force that competitors across the border were now recognizing. As *El Colono* had suggested a decade before, companies in the United States had come to realize that the Mexican worker was industrious because in "his endurance he surpasses many kinds of foreign workers that abound in the United States, if not because his physical constitution gives him that *superiority* then because his diverse rusticity of character by necessity makes him *superior*. This is to be admired; but it can be explained because the Mexican laborer, brought to the United States, obliged by necessity and the orders of foreign foremen, works better than he does for us."[22] Higher wages were the only material factor that could build a dike high enough to contain this latest wave of hard-working "superior" Mexican braceros.

But setting aside all the ideological banter over racial taxonomies, it seems clear that larger structural factors like economic recessions combined with land concessions and marketing are more revealing of the motivations for back-to-Mexico movements. The labor economist Victor Clark observed something similar with regard to northward migration when he concluded that "a large part of this immigration is not stimulated, except by general economic conditions."[23] We saw evidence for his argument in the 1893–97 economic recession in the United States, which explains some of Siliceo's success with his Mexican Colonization Enterprise. A similar case is the deportation of hundreds of Mexican workers to the border town of Ciudad Juárez in 1907 due primarily to an economic depression in the United States that year.[24] Clark suggests that "on the Mexican Central Railway, which moves more immigrants than any other single road in Mexico, the official estimate of third-class passengers (laborers) crossing the frontier northward during the twelve months ended with August 1907 was 50,000, and the return traffic during the same period was estimated to be 37,000."[25] The noted Mexican historian Friedrich Katz points out that during the financial crisis of 1908–10, "The United States proclaimed a ban on Mexican immigration, and more than 2,000 Mexicans were given railway tickets by the companies to El Paso, where they crossed into Chihuahua, swelling the ranks of the unemployed."[26] But these northward and southward movements of laborers were only the beginning of a trickle when compared to the millions of Mexican migrants who would eventually crisscross between the United States and Mexico after the so-called revolution of 1911.

While all successful nations have been shaped by colonization and empire building, Mexico's state formation in the Western Hemisphere followed a trajectory different from those of other settler colonial states. Whereas millions of European immigrants arrived to displace the indigenes and transform the landscape in other countries, the mass of migrants overlooked Mexico. The frontier regions of Mexico were inhabited by dozens of independent indigenous groups who had been resisting US, indigenous, and Mexican encroachment upon their traditional lands for centuries. As a consequence, the Mexican nation was forced to look inward to its own expatriate citizens to solve the dilemma of populating its frontiers and fortifying its national boundaries. In stark contrast to Wolfe's "elimination of the native," Mexican American theologian Virgilio Elizondo offers a distinct perspective from his hometown of San Antonio. In his 2000 essay, *The Future Is Mestizo*, Elizondo contends that strolling through the city's streets unveils a profound truth: "You easily recognize the native faces of the present-day descendants of the Apache, Comanche, Chichimeca, and other pre-Columbian inhabitants of this land." Elizondo emphasizes that these indigenous descendants are not consigned to extinction or reservation life; rather, they seamlessly integrate into the "complex organic mosaic that makes up this city on the great frontier between the United States and Latin America." Mexican settler colonization employed hijos del país as frontier colonists in a centuries-long struggle to settle the frontiers of the republic.

NOTES

Introduction

1. The term "Mexico-Texano" means Texas-Mexicans and denotes any ethnic Mexican residing in Texas who does not specify recent migration to that state. This is a term that several colonists employed when describing their "nationality," and I employ it here to appreciate its historicity. For example, José María Rodríguez self-identified as "Mexico-Texano" with a birthplace of "Texas," and Teodora Castillo Garza of Laredo, Texas, is one of the few widows who self-identified as "Mexico-Tejana" also born in "Texas." See, respectively, informe no. 38, folio 123, and informe no. 45, folio 143, in "Luis Siliceo. Contrato sobre compra-venta y colonización de terrenos en varios Estados de la República, y todo relativo a dicho contrato," 8 July 1895, exp. 452, 1.29 (32), Archivo Histórico de Terrenos Nacionales, Secretaría de la Reforma Agraria (hereafter AHTN). This archive is managed by the Secretaría de Desarrollo Agrario, Territorial, y Urbano (SEDATU). It holds many of the records from the Secretaría de Fomento, Colonización, e Industria (the agency in charge of colonizing the frontier areas of Mexico). Also see César Arturo Velásquez Becerril, "Intelectuales y poder en el Porfiriato. Una aproximación al grupo de los Científicos, 1892–1911," *Revista Fuentes Humanísticas* 22, no. 41 (2010), 7–23.
2. "Más sobre colonización en la República," *El Colono* 2, no. 7, 10 April 1897, 7. Copies of *El Colono* dating from November 1895 to October 1898 are located in the Biblioteca Nacional, UNAM, Fondo Reservado.
3. "Probabilidades favorables," *El Colono* 2, no. 7 (10 April 1897), 7, UNAM, Fondo Reservado. All translations from the original Spanish are mine.
4. "Probabilidades favorables," *El Colono*, 10 April 1897, 7, UNAM, Fondo Reservado.
5. José Angel Hernández, *Mexican American Colonization during the Nineteenth Century: A History of the US-Mexico Borderlands* (Cambridge: Cambridge University Press, 2012), 225–31; Alejandro González Milea, *El silencio de las aldeas. Urbanismo militar y civil del noreste mexicano, siglo XIX* (Monterrey: Consejo Nacional para la Cultura y las Artes, 2014); William Douglas Taylor, "La repatriación de mexicanos de 1848 a 1980 y su papel en la colonización de la región fronteriza septentrional de México," *Relaciones* 18, no. 69 (1997): 198–212; Martín González de la Vara, "El traslado de familias de Nuevo México al norte de Chihuahua y la conformación de una región fronteriza, 1848–1854," *Frontera Norte* 6, no. 11 (January–June 1994): 9–21; Moisés González Navarro, "La política colonizadora del Porfiriato," *Estudios*

Históricos Americanos (1953): 183–239; *La colonización en México, 1877–1910* (México: Talleres de Impresión de Estampillas y Valores, 1960); and *Los extranjeros en México y los mexicanos en el extranjero* (México: El Colegio de México 1993): 2:356, 367–70; Enrique Cortés, "Mexican Colonies during the Porfiriato," *Aztlán* 10 (Fall 1979): 1–14; Evelyne Sánchez, "Regresar a la madre patria. La repatriación de los mexicanos durante el Porfiriato," in *Fronteras y sensibilidades en las Américas*, ed. Salvador Bernabeú and Frédérique Langue (Madrid: MASCIPO-CNRS: 2011): 259–82; José Angel Hernández, "The Decree of 19 August 1848: First Repatriation Commissions and Postwar Settlements along the US-Mexico Borderlands," *Maryland Journal of International Law* 33, no. 1 (2018): 1–37; Ángela Moyano Pahissa, *Antología: Protección consular a mexicanos en los Estados Unidos, 1849–1900* (México: Archivo Histórico Diplomático Mexicano, 1989); Manuel Ceballos Ramírez, "Consecuencias de la guerra entre México y Estados Unidos. La traslación de mexicanos y la fundación de Nuevo Laredo," in *Nuestra frontera norte*, ed. Patricia Galeana (México: Archivo General de la Nación, 1997): 39–59; Jaime R. Águila, "Protecting 'México de Afuera': Mexican Emigration Policy, 1876–1928" (PhD diss., Arizona State University, 2000); Alejandro González Milea, "Colonias militares y civiles del siglo XIX: una aproximación a las utopías urbanas del norte de Coahuila," *Estudios Fronterizos* 13, no. 25 (2012): 191–219; Patrick Wolfe, "Settler Colonialism and the Elimination of the Native," *Journal of Genocide Research* 8, no. 4 (December 2006), 387–409.

6. "Ley de 15 de Diciembre de 1883, mandando deslindar, medir, fraccionar y valuar los terrenos baldíos o de propiedad nacional, para obtener los necesarios para el establecimiento de colonos," in *Código de colonización y terrenos baldíos de la República Mexicana, formado por Francisco F. de la Maza y publicado según el acuerdo del presidente de la república, por conducta de la secretaría de estado y del despacho de fomento, años de 1451 a 1892*, ed. Francisco F. de la Maza, (México: Oficina Tipográfica de la Secretaria de Fomento, 1893), 936–45.
7. "La repatriación," *El Colono* 1, no. 2, 25 November 1895, 1–2, UNAM, Fondo Reservado.
8. For the Mexican case, see Martin S. Stabb, "Indigenism and Racism in Mexican Thought: 1857–1911," *Journal of Inter-American Studies* 1, no. 4, October 1959: 405–23; and T. G. Powell, "Mexican Intellectuals and the Indian Question, 1876–1911," *Hispanic American Historical Review* 48, no. 1 (February 1968): 19–36. For Argentina, see Juan Bautista Alberdi, *Bases y puntos de partida para la organización política de la República Argentina* (Buenos Aires, 1852); Sam Schulman, "Juan Bautista Alberdi and His Influence on Immigration Policy in the Argentine Constitution of 1853," *The Americas* 5, no. 1 (July 1948): 3–17; and especially José C. Moya, *Cousins and Strangers: Spanish Immigrants in Buenos Aires, 1850–1930* (Berkeley: University of California Press, 1998). For Brazil, see George Reid Andrews, *Blacks and Whites in São Paulo, Brazil, 1888–1988* (Madison: University of Wisconsin Press, 1991); and Samuel L. Baily and Eduardo José Míguez, *Mass Migration to Modern Latin America* (London: Rowman & Littlefield, 2003).
9. Natalia Priego, *Positivism, Science, and "The Scientists" in Porfirian Mexico: A Reappraisal* (Liverpool, UK: Liverpool University Press, 2016), 11.

10. Moisés González Navarro, *La colonización en México, 1877–1910* (México: Talleres de Impresión de Estampillas y Valores, 1960).
11. "La Colonia Patria" and "La colonización de los indios. La colonia de Zacapú," *El Colono* 2, no. 7, 10 April 1897, 4–5, UNAM, Fondo Reservado.
12. Nicolás Kanellos, *Hispanic Immigrant Literature: el sueño del retorno* (Austin: University of Texas Press, 2011), chap. 3.
13. "La colonización de los indios," *El Colono*, 10 April 1897.
14. José Angel Hernández, "From Conquest to Colonization: Indios and Colonization Policies after Mexican Independence," *Mexican Studies/Estudios Mexicanos* 26, no. 2 (Summer 2010): 285–315; Moisés González Navarro, *La política colonizadora del Porfiriato*; also *La colonización en México*; and especially *Los extranjeros en México*; Ignacio González-Polo y Acosta, "Colonización e inmigración extranjera durante las primeras décadas del siglo XIX," *Boletín bibliográfico de la Secretaria de Hacienda y Crédito* 412 (1973): 4–7; Dieter Berninger, "Immigration and Religious Toleration: A Mexican Dilemma, 1821–1860," *The Americas* 32, no. 4 (April 1976): 549–65; José B. Zilli Mánica, "Proyectos liberales de colonización en el siglo XIX," *La Palabra y el Hombre* 52 (October–December 1984): 129–42; Jan de Vos, "Una legislación de graves consecuencias: el acaparamiento de tierras baldías en México con el pretexto de colonización, 1821–1910," *Historia Mexicana* 34, no. 1 (July–September 1984): 76–113; finally, David K. Burden, "Reform before La Reforma: Liberals, Conservatives, and the Debate over Immigration, 1846–1855," *Mexican Studies/Estudios Mexicanos* 23, no. 2 (Summer 2007): 283–316.
15. On the changing role of science in society, see the excellent work of David Wootton, *The Invention of Science: A New History of the Scientific Revolution* (New York: HarperCollins, 2015), chaps. 1, 13–14; For some information on the Mexican context, see Priego, *Positivism, Science, and "The Scientists,"* 16–44.
16. "Condiciones necesarias para asegurar un éxito en las empresas de colonización," *El Colono* 2, no. 20, 23 August 1897), 4–5. It is notable that *Algunas observaciones acerca la inmigración y de la colonización en las naciones independientes de América* (1906), a book by engineer José Covarrubias (head of a later iteration of the Department of Colonization), was serialized in the *Revista Positiva*, the main publication of The Scientists. See Covarrubias, "La inmigración y colonización en las Américas," *Revista Positiva: Científica, Filosófica, Social, y Política* 7, no. 77 (1907): 4–14, 94–121; "La inmigración y colonización en las Américas IV. La inmigración y colonización en la República Argentina," *Revista Positiva: Científica, Filosófica, Social, y Política* 7, no. 81 (23 April 1907): 297–325; and "La inmigración y colonización en las Américas V. La colonización artificial," *Revista Positiva: Científica, Filosófica, Social y Política* 7, no. 81 (23 April 1907): 363–98.
17. Powell, "Mexican Intellectuals and the Indian Question," 19–36.
18. "La colonización de los indios," *El Colono* 10 April 1897.
19. *Encyclopaedia Britannica Online*, s.v. "Mestizo": "any person of mixed blood. In Central and South America, it denotes a person of combined Indian and European extraction. In some countries—e.g., Ecuador—it has acquired social and cultural connotations; a

pure-blooded Indian who has adopted European dress and customs is called a mestizo (or cholo). In Mexico the description has been found so variable in meaning that it has been abandoned in census reports. In the Philippines "mestizo" denotes a person of mixed foreign (e.g., Chinese) and native ancestry." https://www.britannica.com /topic/mestizo.

20. For a fascinating genealogy of these rebellions and revolts, see the essays in Gerald E. Poyo, ed., *Tejano Journey, 1770–1850* (Austin: University of Texas Press, 1996). For changes in colonization policy, see Hernández, "From Conquest to Colonization."
21. Adam McKeown, "Global Migration, 1846–1940," *Journal of World History* 15, no. 2 (June 2004): 155–89; Hernández, "From Conquest to Colonization."
22. Luis Aboites Aguilar, "La Comisión Nacional de Colonización y la Expansión de la Pequeña Propiedad Rural en México, 1947–1963," *Historia Mexicana* 68, no. 3 (January–March 2019): 1165–1204. For an example of resettlement during the 1930s, see Manuel Gamio, *The Influence of Migrations on Mexican Life*" (n.p., 1931) Nettie Lee Benson Latin American Collection, University of Texas at Austin.
23. Severiano Galicia, *La auto-colonización en México. Discurso del señor ingeniero Severiano Galicia, en apoyo de su proyecto de ley sobre la colonización de los terrenos despoblados de la república por los mismos mexicanos, pronunciado en la sesión del Congreso Nacional de Agricultura efectuada la tarde del día ocho de marzo de 1893 en el congreso de la unión* (México: Tipografía de "El Correo Español," 1893), 8–9.
24. Covarrubias, *Algunas observaciones acerca la inmigración y de la colonización*, 51, 153–55. My italics.
25. Covarrubias, *Algunas observaciones acerca la inmigración y de la colonización*, 157.
26. The best definition of the field appears in Lorenzo Veracini, "Settler Colonialism," in *The Palgrave Encyclopedia of Imperialism and Anti-Imperialism*, ed. Immanuel Nes and Zake Cope (New York: Palgrave Macmillan, 2019), 1. Also see *The World Turned Inside Out: Settler Colonialism as a Political Idea* (London: Verso, 2021).
27. Here I am paraphrasing the historian David J. Weber in his introduction to *Bárbaros: Spaniards and Their Savages in the Age of Enlightenment* (New Haven, CT: Yale University Press, 2005).
28. Some notable exceptions that describe this collaboration in exquisite detail are Matthew and Oudijk, *Indian Conquistadors*, especially Schroeder's introduction; Laura E. Matthew, *Memories of Conquest: Becoming Mexicano in Colonial Guatemala* (Chapel Hill: University of North Carolina Press, 2012).
29. On questioning the colonial period, see Jaime E. Rodríguez O., *"We Are Now the True Spaniards": Sovereignty, Revolution, Independence, and the Emergence of the Federal Republic of Mexico, 1808–1824* (Stanford, CA: Stanford University Press, 2012), 7. On questioning the conquest, see Susan Schroeder's introduction to *Indian Conquistadors: Indigenous Allies in the Conquest of Mesoamerica*, ed. Laura E. Matthew and Michel R. Oudijk (Norman: University of Oklahoma Press, 2007), 5–27; also Colin M. MacLauchlan and Jaime E. Rodríguez O., *The Forging of the Cosmic Race: A Reinterpretation of Colonial Mexico* (Berkeley: University of California Press, 1980), 1–4.

30. Matt S. Meier, *Mexican Americans: From Conquistadors to Chicanos* (New York: HarperCollins, 1972).
31. Beth Saler, *The Settlers' Empire: Colonialism and State Formation in America's Old Northwest* (Philadelphia: University of Pennsylvania Press, 2014), 1–2.
32. An excellent overview and model of transnational research is Moya, *Cousins and Strangers*.
33. See González Navarro, *La política colonizadora del Porfiriato*; *La colonización en México*; and *Los extranjeros en México*, 2:356, 367–70; Cortés, "Mexican Colonies during the Porfiriato"; Sánchez, "Regresar a la madre patria."
34. González Navarro, *La política colonizadora del Porfiriato*; *La colonización en México*; and *Los extranjeros en México*, 2:356, 367–70; Cortés, "Mexican Colonies during the Porfiriato."
35. Iberians during the colonial period and Mexicans thereafter distinguished between "indios civilizados" and "indios bárbaros." An excellent discussion can be read in Weber, *Bárbaros*.
36. Dan L. Thrapp, *The Conquest of Apacheria* (Norman: University of Oklahoma Press, 1975); Pekka Hämäläinen, *The Comanche Empire* (New Haven, CT: Yale University Press, 2008); and Hämäläinen, *Lakota America: A New History of Indigenous Power* (New Haven, CT: Yale University Press, 2019).
37. See Mark Reisler, *By the Sweat of Their Brow: Mexican Immigrant Labor in the United States, 1900–1940* (Westport, CT: Greenwood Press, 1976), 269. It is important to note that Mexican emigration to the United States had a long history preceding the establishment of the international boundary in 1848. See M. Colette Standart, "The Sonoran Migration to California, 1848–1856: A Study in Prejudice," *Southern California Quarterly* 58, no. 3 (Fall 1976): 333–57.
38. González Navarro estimated that there were 30,591 foreigners in Mexico in 1842, most likely including the thousands of Anglo-American settlers in Texas, which was still part of the Mexican Republic. His next estimate was 36,196 foreigners in 1857, followed by 45,601 foreigners in Mexico twenty-eight years later in 1885. See *Los extranjeros en México*, 2:271.
39. "Más sobre colonización en la República," *El Colono* 2, no. 7, 10 April 1897, 7.
40. For the 1894 law, see Secretaría de Fomento, *Ley sobre ocupación y enajenación de terrenos baldíos de los Estados Unidos Mexicanos* (México: Oficina Tipográfica de la Secretaría de Fomento, 1894), Art. 6.
41. A good chronology of the evolution of these pieces of legislation can be located in Vos, "Una legislación de graves consecuencias."
42. Wistano Luis Orozco, *Legislación y jurisprudencia sobre terrenos baldíos* (México: Imprenta el Tiempo, 1895), 354. Orozco also appears to have been an "apoderado de una compañía deslindadora." Original: "con más razón podrán denunciar y adquirir dichos terrenos los Mexicanos residentes en el extranjero, sobre todo, si conservan conforme a derecho la nacionalidad Mexicana." See José Alfredo Rangel Silva, *Ave de las tempestades: Wistano Luis Orozco y las contradicciones del porfiriato en la provincia, 1884–1910* (San Luis Potosí: El Colegio de San Luis, 2019).

43. "Luis Siliceo. Contrato sobre compra-venta y colonización de terrenos en varios Estados de la República, y todo relativo a dicho contrato," 8 July 1895, 1.29 (32), exp. 452, Archivo Histórico de Terrenos Nacionales, Secretaría de la Reforma Agraria (hereafter AHTN). For the final version of the contract, see "Contrato celebrado con el Sr. Luis Siliceo para la compra-venta y colonización de terrenos baldíos y nacionales en los estados de Chihuahua, Coahuila, Guerrero, México, Michoacán, Puebla, y Veracruz, 1895," 1.29 (06), exp. 365, AHTN.
44. Borrowed from Edward Gibbon Wakefield, ed., *A View of the Art of Colonization; with Present Reference to the British Empire; in Letters between a Statesman and a Colonist* (London: John W. Parker, 1849).
45. Veracini, "Settler Colonialism," 1.
46. Hernández, *Mexican American Colonization*, 225–31. For an excellent overview of these repatriated and national colonies, see González Milea, *El silencio de las aldeas*; Taylor, "La repatriación de mexicanos de 1848 a 1980"; González de la Vara, "El traslado de familias de Nuevo México al norte de Chihuahua."
47. "Decreto de 27 de Noviembre de 1846 estableciendo la Dirección de Colonización," in de la Maza, *Código de colonización*, 345–47.
48. "Reglamento de 4 de Diciembre de 1846 para la Dirección de Colonización," in de la Maza, *Código de colonización*, 347–48.
49. Veracini, *World Turned Inside Out*; González Milea, *El silencio de las aldeas*; also González Milea, "El 'poblamiento español' en la colonización del norte mexicano: la voz de los ingenieros entre la Independencia y la Posrevolución," *edA Esempi di Architettura*, 7 no. 2 (2020): 105–15.
50. Junta Directiva de Colonización, México, *Proyectos de colonización presentados por la Junta Directiva del Ramo* al Ministerio de Relaciones de la República Mexicana en 5 de Julio de 1848 (México: Imprenta de Vicente García Torres, 1848), 12–13.
51. An absorbing approach to anarchist history is James C. Scott, *The Art of Not Being Governed: An Anarchist History of Upland Southeast Asia* (New Haven, CT: Yale University Press, 2009).
52. "Más sobre colonización en la República," *El Colono* 2, no. 7, 10 April 1897, 7.
53. Wolfe, "Settler Colonialism and the Elimination of the Native."
54. Guillermo Bonfil Batalla, *México Profundo: Reclaiming a Civilization* (Austin: University of Texas Press, 1996), 46.
55. Bonfil Batalla used the term "México profundo" to describe Mesoamerican civilization and culture. For an excellent overview and interpretation of the book, see Claudio Lomnitz-Adler, *Deep Mexico, Silent Mexico: An Anthropology of Nationalism* (Minneapolis: University of Minnesota Press, 2001).
56. Simón Tadeo Ortiz de Ayala, *Resumen de la estadística del imperio mexicano, 1822: estudio preliminar, revisión de texto, notas y anexos de Tarsicio García Díaz* (México: Biblioteca Nacional, UNAM, Reimprimido 1968), 21.
57. Veracini, *Settler Colonialism: A Theoretical Overview* (Palgrave, 2010), 20.
58. An obligatory starting point on these comparative cases of settler colonization would be Veracini, *World Turned Inside Out.*

59. Weber, *Bárbaros*, 257–78. Pekka Hämäläinen makes a similar observation of absorption/incorporation that he attributes to indigenous kinship practices of collaboration and cooperation in North America. See *Indigenous Continent: The Epic Contest for North America* (London: W. W. Norton, 2022).
60. At least in terms of the longer historiography of colonization, I believe that the obligatory starting point for these questions should be the classic corpus of González Navarro: *La política colonizadora del Porfiriato*; *La colonización en México, 1877–1910*; and especially *Los extranjeros en México*. See also González-Polo y Acosta, "Colonización e inmigración extranjera, 4–7; Berninger, "Immigration and Religious Toleration"; Zilli Mánica, "Proyectos liberales de colonización en el siglo XIX"; Vos, "Una legislación de graves consecuencias."
61. The most comprehensive historiographical analysis of the evolution of the internal colonial model is John R. Chávez, "Aliens in Their Native Lands: The Persistence of Internal Colonial Theory," *Journal of World History* 22, no. 4 (December 2011): 785–809. Indeed, after his excellent survey of the literature Chávez concludes on page 809 with, "Understood as a subset of the colonial paradigm, including formal colonialism, neocolonialism, post colonialism, and borderlands theory, post nationalism, internal colonialism remains a viable theory." One is tempted to add settler colonialism to his growing list of available theories.
62. See Mario Barrera, *Race and Class in the Southwest: A Theory of Racial Inequality* (South Bend, IN: Notre Dame University Press, 1979); Rubén Martínez, "Internal Colonialism: A Reconceptualization of Race Relations in the United States, *Humboldt Journal of Social Relations* 10, no. 1 (1982): 163–76, http://www.jstor.org/stable/23261862; Armando Navarro, *Mexicano Political Experience in Occupied Aztlán: Struggles and Changes* (Walnut Creek, CA: Altamira Press, 2005), 1–12.
63. The earliest instance of legally sanctioned Mexican resettlement that I have encountered occurred in 1831 and involved Mexican citizens in New Orleans. In "Número 74: Enero 18 de 1831: Resolución facultando al Ejecutivo para invertir la cantidad necesaria en el regreso de las familias mexicanas pobres existentes en Nueva Orleáns," in de la Maza, *Código de colonización*, 244. Also see José Angel Hernández, "Contemporary Deportation Raids and Historical Memory: Mexican Expulsions in the Nineteenth Century," *Aztlán: A Journal of Chicano Studies* 52, no. 2 (Fall 2010): 115–41.
64. See, especially, Veracini's discussions around the relationship of suburbia to settler colonialism in *World Turned Inside Out*, 171, 206, 265.
65. Here, it is important to point out that Mexican intellectuals of the past have covered similar ground (such as distinguishing between ethnocide versus genocide and homicide), with the best example being Guillermo Bonfil Batalla's classic monograph *México Profundo*.
66. Wolfe, "Settler Colonialism and the Elimination of the Native," 387–409; Lorenzo Veracini, "Obituary: Patrick Wolfe (1949–2016)," *Settler Colonial Studies* 6, no. 3 (2016), 189–90, DOI: 10.1080/2201473X.2016.1176393. For a critique, see Tim Rowse and Len Smith, "The Limits of 'Elimination' in the Politics of Population," *Australian Historical Studies* 41, no. 1 (2010): 90–106, DOI:10.1080/10314610903317598.

67. Wolfe, "Settler Colonialism and the Elimination of the Native." In *Los extranjeros en México*, González Navarro observes that during the Porfiriato most of the colonies were located along the frontiers of the North and South Pacific and the Gulf of Mexico. The eleven colonies located in central Mexico were either cases of autocolonization or were considered loyal (2:134). For an interesting discussion of the geographical distribution of contemporary DNA, see Martin Bodner et al., "The Mitochondrial DNA Landscape of Modern Mexico," *Genes (Basel)* 12, no. 9 (21 September 2021): 1453, DOI: 10.3390/genes12091453.
68. For an excellent overview of these debates in short essays by several twentieth-century authors, see Roger Bartra, *Anatomía del mexicano* (México: Plaza y Janés, 2002).
69. Pablo Sánchez Olmos, "López Obrador: 'La Conquista fue un rotundo fracaso,'" *El Mundo*, 13 August 2021, https://www.elmundo.es/internacional/2021/08/13/6116b83ffdddffb30d8b45f5.html.
70. Wolfe, "Settler Colonialism and the Elimination of the Native," 390. Here, it is important to point out that the noted Mexican sociologist and jurist Pablo González Casanova alluded to colonization as structure half a century ago in a series of essays written during the 1960s. In 2006 González updated some of his theories and argued, "The practical and political value of the category of internal colonialism may be distinguished from other categories in that they provide, above all, a psychological and evaluative analysis, useful for designing policies of communication, propaganda, and education, while the notion of internal colonialism is not only psychological but structural, and moreover structural." Original: "El valor práctico y político de la categoría del colonialismo interno quizá se distingue de otras categorías (de Lerner, Mac Clelland, Hoselitz) en que éstas proporcionan sobre todo un análisis psicológico y valorativo, útil para el diseño de políticas de comunicación, propaganda y educación, en tanto que la noción de colonialismo interno no es sólo psicológica sino estructural, y más bien estructural." Pablo González Casanova, "El colonialismo interno," in *De la sociología del poder a la sociología de la explotación: pensar América Latina en el siglo XXI*, ed. Marcos Roitman Rosenmann. (México: Siglo XXI Editores, 2015), 156.
71. Patrick Wolfe, "Settler Colonialism, Time, and the Question of Genocide," in *Empire, Colony, Genocide: Conquest, Occupation, and Subaltern Resistance in World History*, ed. A. Dirk Moses (New York: Berghahn Books, 2008), 102–32.
72. Peter A. Stern, "Social Marginality and Acculturation on the Northern Frontier of New Spain" (PhD diss., University of California, Berkeley, 1985).
73. I take the regional and temporal approach adopted by Friedrich Katz in "Labor Conditions on Haciendas in Porfirian Mexico: Some Trends and Tendencies," *Hispanic American Historical Review* 54, no. 1 (February 1974): 1–47. On the geographical location of the sixty colonies founded during the Porfiriato, see González Navarro, *Los extranjeros en México*, 2:134.
74. Mauricio Tenorio-Trillo, *Mexico at the World's Fairs: Crafting a Modern Nation* (Berkeley: University of California Press, 1996), 170, 239, 250.
75. Wolfe, "Settler Colonialism and the Elimination of the Native," 393–94.
76. Wakefield, *View of the Art of Colonization.*

77. Veracini, *World Turned Inside Out*, passim.
78. On structures structuring structures, see Pierre Bourdieu, *Outline of a Theory of Practice* (New York: Cambridge University Press, 1977), 72–90.
79. Quoted in Jorge Chávez Chávez, *Los indios en la formación de la identidad nacional Mexicana* (Ciudad Juárez, Chih.: Universidad Autónoma de Ciudad Juárez, 2003), 11.
80. González Casanova, "El Colonialismo Interno," 156.
81. Rodríguez O., *"We Are Now the True Spaniards,"* 7. Also worthy of mention is the earlier work by Rodríguez O. and MacLachlan, *Forging of the Cosmic Race*, 1–4.
82. Max Weber, *Max Weber: Essays in Sociology* (London: Routledge, 1946), 78. The use of monuments and public statues has a long history and an extensive historiography. A good place to start is Christina Bueno, *The Pursuit of Ruins: Archaeology, History, and the Making of Modern Mexico* (Albuquerque: University of New Mexico Press, 2016).
83. Enrique Florescano, *National Narratives in Mexico: A History*, trans. Nancy T. Hancock (Norman: University of Oklahoma Press, 2002), 291.
84. Hernández, "Decree of 19 August 1848."
85. "Greater Mexico" refers to "all the areas inhabited by people of Mexican descent—not only within the present limits of the republic of Mexico but in the United States—as well as in a cultural rather than a political sense." See Américo Paredes, *A Texas-Mexican Cancionero: Folksongs of the Lower Border* (Austin: University of Texas Press, 1995), xiv.
86. Lance R. Blyth, *Chiricahua and Janos: Communities of Violence in the Southwestern Borderlands, 1680–1880* (Lincoln: University of Nebraska Press, 2012); Thrapp, *Conquest of Apacheria*; Hämäläinen, *Comanche Empire* and *Lakota America*.
87. González Navarro, states, "During the long government of Porfirio Díaz, there were established, with very unequal success, 16 official colonies and 44 private, 60 in total." *Los extranjeros en México*, 2:133–34. Though his tally may be incomplete, there is enough data to conclude that ethnic Mexicans composed 69 percent of the official colonies (11/16) and more than 27 percent of the private colonization projects (12/44), during the Porfiriato. González Navarro, *La política colonizadora del Porfiriato*, *La colonización en México*, and *Los extranjeros en México*, 2: 133. Also see Cortés, "Mexican Colonies during the Porfiriato."
88. See Ranajit Guha, "On Some Aspects of the Historiography of Colonial India," in *Selected Subaltern Studies*, ed. Ranajit Guha and Gayatri Chakravorty Spivak (Oxford: Oxford University Press, 1988), 37–43.
89. John S. Wilkins, "Darwin," in Aviezer Tucker, ed., *A Companion to the Philosophy of History and Historiography* (Chichester, UK: John Wiley & Sons, 2008), 404–15. Also Gilles Deleuze and Félix Guattari, *Anti-Oedipus: Capitalism and Schizophrenia* (New York: Viking Press, 1977).
90. "Ley de 15 de Diciembre de 1883," in de la Maza, *Código de colonización*, 936–45.
91. Veracini's *World Turned Inside Out* puts to rest the notion that the process of colonization is restricted to any one nation, European or otherwise.
92. For similar approaches, see Yuval Noah Harari, *Sapiens: A Brief History of Humankind* (New York: Harper, 2015); David Christian, *Maps of Time: An Introduction to*

Big History (Berkeley: University of California Press, 2011); Jared Diamond, *Guns, Germs, and Steel: The Fates of Human Societies* (New York: W. W. Norton, 1997); John Hands, *Cosmosapiens: Human Evolution from the Origin of the Universe* (New York: Abrams, 2017); and, especially, Edward O. Wilson, *The Social Conquest of Earth* (New York: Liveright, 2012).

93. *Encyclopaedia Britannica Online Dictionary*, s.v. "Colonize," https://www.britannica.com/dictionary/colonize.
94. "New Research Confirms 'Out of Africa' Theory of Human Evolution." *ScienceDaily*, 10 May 2007, https://www.sciencedaily.com/releases/2007/05/070509161829.htm.
95. For an overview of at least six "explanatory hypotheses" on human emergence, I highly recommend the wonderful monograph by John Hands, *Cosmosapiens*, 449–55.
96. Christian, *Maps of Time*, 180–84; Hands, *Cosmosapiens*, 431–44.
97. Svante Pääbo, *Neanderthal Man: In Search of Lost Genomes* (New York: Basic Books, 2014); Harari, *Sapiens*, especially chap. 1.
98. Friedrich Wilhem Nietzsche, *On the Advantage and Disadvantage of History for Life* (London: Hackett, [1872] 1980), 20–22.
99. Matthew and Oudijk, *Indian Conquistadors*; Murillo, *Urban Indians in a Silver City*; Eugene B. Sego, "Six Tlaxcalan Colonies on New Spain's Northern Frontier: A Comparison of Success and Failure," (PhD diss., Indiana University, 1990); Adams, *Tlaxcalan Colonies of Spanish Coahuila and Nuevo León*; Sean F. McEnroe, *From Colony to Nationhood in Mexico*.
100. See, for instance, Restall, *Maya Conquistador*; Matthew and Oudijk, *Indian Conquistadors*; Matthew, *Memories of Conquest*.
101. In some form or fashion, the project of colonization continues well into the middle of the twentieth century, at least according to some historians. See Aboites Aguilar, "La Comisión Nacional de Colonización."
102. *Junta Directiva de Colonización, Proyectos de colonización*.
103. See Veracini, *World Turned Inside Out*, 1–26, for examples of "Neo-Europes." The classic work is Alfred W. Crosby's *Ecological Imperialism: The Biological Expansion of Europe, 900–1900*, 2nd ed. (Cambridge: Cambridge University Press, 2004).
104. Siliceo's contract and his story are recorded in the *memorias* of the Secretaría de Fomento, but the three colonies where he resettled Tejanos are not mentioned in any of these records. For the government's tally, see González Navarro, *Los extranjeros en México*, 2:133–34.
105. Audrey Smedley, "History of the Idea of Race . . . and Why It Matters," paper presented at the Race, Human Variation and Disease: Consensus and Frontiers conference, 14–17 March 2007, Warrenton, VA.
106. I am using "morality" in the nineteenth-century sense that Friedrich Nietzsche employed in *Beyond Good and Evil* (1886).
107. "La repatriación," *El Fronterizo*, no. 868, 27 July 1895, 1.
108. It would be a mistake to mention only the United States as a source of ideas. Throughout its many iterations, the Department of Colonization repeatedly offered global comparisons when discussing colonization policy, even though it ultimately adopted

a policy of autocolonization. For a hemispheric analysis, see Covarrubias, *Algunas observaciones acerca la inmigración y de la colonización*. Colonization discussions in the historical record at the Secretaría de Relaciones Exteriores are replete with examples from Argentina. A good starting point is the index of González Navarro, *Los extranjeros en México*, 2:465.

109. For an example of how past conflicts continue to generate trauma in the historical memory of US academics, see Samuel P. Huntington, *Who Are We? The Challenges to America's National Identity* (New York: Simon & Schuster, 2005).
110. For some early migrations northward, see Juan Mora-Torres, *The Making of the Mexican Border: The State, Capitalism, and Society in Nuevo León, 1848–1910* (Austin: University of Texas Press, 2001), 24–41; and Miguel Ángel González Quiroga, *War and Peace on the Rio Grande Frontier, 1830–1880* (Norman: University of Oklahoma Press, 2020), 106–19.
111. González Navarro, *Los extranjeros en México*, esp. 3:193–331. Also see David Fitzgerald's excellent examination of how the Mexican state manages this emigration in the twentieth century and his analysis of a new kind of citizenship in *A Nation of Emigrants: How Mexico Manages Its Migration* (Berkeley: University of California Press, 2009).
112. Veracini, *World Turned Inside Out*, 1–26; González Milea, "El 'poblamiento español.'"
113. Carsten Schäfer, "China's Diaspora Policy under Xi Jingping: Content, Limits, and Challenges," *Stiftung Wissenschaft und Politik Research Papers*, German Institute for International and Security Affairs (October 2022). https://www.swp-berlin.org/10.18449/2022RP10/.

Chapter 1

1. J. J. Hublin et al., "New Fossils from Jebel Irhoud, Morocco, and the Pan-African Origin of *Homo sapiens*," *Nature* 546 (2017): 289–92, DOI: 10.1038/nature22336.
2. Johannes Krause and Thomas Trappe, *A Short History of Humanity: A New History of Old Europe* (New York: Random House, 2021); David Reich, *Who We Are and How We Got Here: Archaeogenetics and the New Science of the Human Past* (New York: Pantheon Books, 2018); Lorena Becerra-Valdivia and Thomas Higham, "The Timing and Effect of the Earliest Human Arrivals in North America," *Nature* 584 (2020): 93–97. For a definition of colonization, see *Merriam-Webster Dictionary*, s.v. "colonization," https://www.merriam-webster.com/dictionary/colonization.
3. Daniel Lieberman, *The Story of the Human Body: Evolution, Health, and Disease* (New York: Knopf Doubleday, 2014).
4. One of the more interesting examples in my opinion comes from the Philippines. Bruce Bower, "An Indigenous People in the Philippines Have the Most Denisovan DNA," *Science News*, 12 August 2021. https://www.sciencenews.org/article/indigenous-people-philippines-denisovan-dna-genetics.
5. It is well established that most human populations whose ancestors came from somewhere outside of Africa have between 1 percent and 3 percent Neanderthal DNA. See Pääbo, *Neanderthal Man*; Reich, *Who We Are and How We Got Here*; Brian

Handwerk, "In Groundbreaking Find, Three Kinds of Early Humans Unearthed Living Together in South Africa," *Smithsonian Magazine Online*, 2 April 2020, https://www.smithsonianmag.com/science-nature/homo-erectus-australopithecus-saranthropus-south-africa-180974571/.

6. "The Origins of Homo Sapiens with Professor Chris Stringer," *YouTube* video, July 1, 2022, 27:01, https://youtu.be/mG4nxegSTCg.
7. Lilly Tozer, "Did Our Human Ancestors Eat Each Other? Carved-up Bone Offers Clues," *Nature News*, 26 June 2023. https://www.nature.com/articles/d41586-023-02082-x. Also, Peter Bellwood, ed., *The Global Prehistory of Human Migration* (John Wiley & Sons, 2014), 18–25.
8. Reich, *Who We Are and How We Got Here*, xi–xxv.
9. Carl Zimmer, "A Blended Family: Her Mother Was Neanderthal, Her Father Something Else Entirely," *New York Times*, 22 August 2018, https://www.nytimes.com/2018/08/22/science/neanderthals-denisovans-hybrid.html.
10. I am aware of the historiographical debates challenging the "collapse" or "decline" of Rome by referencing the Eastern Roman Empire. A good introduction is Timothy A. Gregory, *A History of Byzantium* (Oxford: Blackwell, 2005), 21–33.
11. For an example of Greek and Roman colonization see Guy Bradley and John Paul Wilson, eds., *Greek and Roman Colonization: Origins, Ideologies, and Interactions* (Oakville, CT: Classic Press of Wales, 2006).
12. Carolina López-Ruiz and Michael Dietler, eds., *Colonial Encounters in Ancient Iberia: Phoenician, Greek, and Indigenous Relations* (Chicago: University of Chicago Press, 2009).
13. Iñigo Olalde et al., "The Genomic History of the Iberian Peninsula over the Past 8000 Years," *Science*, 15 March 2019: 1234.
14. Olalde et al., "Genomic History of the Iberian Peninsula," 1230; also Fulvio Cruciani et al., "Tracing Past Human Male Movements in Northern/Eastern Africa and Western Eurasia: New Clues from Y-Chromosomal Haplogroups E-M78 and J-M12," *Molecular Biology and Evolution* 24, no. 6 (June 2007): 1300–11.
15. Cruciani et al., "Tracing Past Human Male Movements," 1300.
16. Reich, *Who We Are and How We Got Here*, xxii.
17. Ardelean, C.F., Becerra-Valdivia, L., Pedersen, M.W. et al. "Evidence of Human Occupation in Mexico around the Last Glacial Maximum," *Nature* 584 (2020): 87–92, DOI: 10.1038/s41586-020-2509-0.
18. Martin Sikora et al., "The Population History of Northeastern Siberia since the Pleistocene," *Nature* 570, 182, DOI: 10.1038/s41586-019-1279-z.
19. Reich, *Who We Are and How We Got Here*, 155–85.
20. Arun Durvasula and Sriram Sankararaman, "Recovering Signals of Ghost Archaic Introgression in African Populations," *Science Advances* 6, no. 7 (2020), DOI: 10.1126/sciadv.aax5097.
21. Reich, *Who We Are and How We Got Here*, 155–56.
22. Philip Carl Salzman, "Tribes," *Oxford Research Encyclopedia of Anthropology*, 28 September 2020, DOI: 10.1093/acrefore/9780190854584.013.185.

23. María del Carmen Rodríguez Martínez et al., "Oldest Writing in the New World," *Science* 313, no. 5793 (15 September 2006): 1610–14, DOI: 10.1126/science.1131492.
24. I would suggest the interpretation provided by Christian Duverger, *El primer mestizaje: La clave para entender el pasado Mesoamericano* (México: Taurus, 2007).
25. Peter G. Tsouras, *Warlords of Ancient Mexico: How the Mayans and Aztecs Ruled for More Than a Thousand Years* (New York: Skyhorse, 2014); Ross Hassig, *Aztec Warfare: Imperial Expansion and Political Control* (Norman: University of Oklahoma Press, 1995).
26. Frances F. Berdán et al, *Aztec Imperial Strategies* (Washington, DC: Dumbarton Oaks Research Library and Collection, 1996), 211.
27. Duverger, *El primer mestizaje*, 560–97.
28. Scott, *Art of Not Being Governed*, 117.
29. Historicizing the term *bárbaros* takes one back to the etymology of the term as employed by the Greeks to denote all foreigners who did not speak their language. *Encyclopaedia Britannica Online*, s.v. "barbarian," https://www.britannica.com/topic/barbarian.
30. On Iberian and Nahuatl shared notions of blood, see Lomnitz-Adler, *Deep Mexico, Silent Mexico*, 35–57.
31. Ida Altman, *The War for Mexico's West: Indians and Spaniards in New Galicia, 1524–1550* (Albuquerque: University of New Mexico Press, 2010).
32. On state legibility see James C. Scott, *Seeing Like a State: How Certain Schemes to Improve the Human Condition Have Failed* (New Haven, CT: Yale University Press, 1998).
33. Lockhart, *Nahuas after the Conquest*, 429; MacLachlan, *Imperialism and the Origins of Mexican Culture*, 5.
34. For challenges to traditional perspectives on Spanish colonization, a good place to start is the collection of essays in Galen Brokaw and Jongsoo Lee, eds., *Fernando de Alva Ixtlilxochitl and His Legacy* (Tucson: University of Arizona Press, 2016). An excellent analysis of how Mexican historians in both Europe and Mexico influenced European interpretations of the so-called New World can be read in Jorge Cañizares-Esguerra, *How to Write the History of the New World: Histories, Epistemologies, and Identities in the Eighteenth-Century Atlantic World* (Stanford, CA: Stanford University Press, 2001).
35. This narrative "from below" was reinscribed with the intellectual influence of subaltern studies in Mexican history. One example of this trend can be read in Eric Van Young, *The Other Rebellion: Popular Violence, Ideology, and the Mexican Struggle for Independence, 1810–1821* (Stanford, CA: Stanford University Press, 2001). Mexicanist Alan Knight found Van Young's arguments "wrong headed," "irritating," "unconvincing, and even contrived. . . . Fundamental interpretations—especially those concerning long-dead Indian peasants—are bound to be partly subjective, based on how we think the world works." Alan Knight, review of *The Other Rebellion: Popular Violence, Ideology, and the Mexican Struggle for Independence, 1810–1821*, *The Americas* 59, no. 4 (April 2003): 606–11.
36. There is no need here to regurgitate the "Histories" of Herodotus for the genealogy of this civilization-versus-barbarism dichotomy. One of the best overviews of these nationalist historiographies is Florescano, *National Narratives in Mexico*.

37. Rodríguez O., *We Are Now the True Spaniards*, 7.
38. This arbitrary periodization can be found in almost any contemporary Mexican history textbook, most of which borrow outlines from older studies. For an excellent overview of these historiographies see Enrique Florescano, *Historia de las historias de la nación mexicana* (México: Taurus, 2002).
39. Meier, *Mexican Americans*; Stacy Finz, "Matt S. Meier—Started Chicano Studies Programs," *SF Gate*, 20 August 2003, https://www.sfgate.com/bayarea/article/Matt-S-Meier-started-Chicano-studies-programs-2594642.php. The interpretive overlap among Guillermo Prieto, Pablo Casanova, and Meier is apparent.
40. Duverger, *El primer mestizaje*.
41. Guadalupe Alonso Coratella, "Cortés no quiso la Conquista sino el mestizaje: Christian Duverger," *Milenio*, 1 August 2021. https://www.milenio.com/cultura/laberinto/hernan-Cortés-no-quiso-la-conquista-sino-al-mestizaje.
42. Duverger, "La idealización del mestizaje," *Nexos*, 1 May 2019; "Hernán Cortés quiso independizar México para crear un reino mestizo: Duverger," *México Desconocido*, https://www.mexicodesconocido.com.mx/hernan-Cortés-quiso-independizar-mexico-para-crear-un-reino-mestizo-duverger.html.
43. Duverger, *El primer mestizaje*; Luis Prados, "Hernán Cortés, the Humanitarian," *El País*, 12 February 2013, https://english.elpais.com/elpais/2013/02/12/inenglish/1360672838_941682.html.
44. Gregory Rodriguez, *Mongrels, Bastards, Orphans, and Vagabonds: Mexican Immigration and the Future of Race in America* (New York: Vintage Books, 2008).
45. Rodriguez, *Mongrels, Bastards, Orphans, and Vagabonds*, 4–5. William H. Sewell, *The Logics of History: Social Theory and Social Transformation* (Chicago: University of Chicago Press, 2005), 6–12. I mention Sewell here because I think his statement about how historians think about the past as "lumpy, uneven, unpredictable, and discontinuous" is applicable in these debates over the periodization of "contact, conquest, and colonization."
46. On "monumental histories," please see Friedrich Wilhem Nietzsche's 1872 essay, *On the Advantage and Disadvantage of History*.
47. Inga Clendinnen, *Ambivalent Conquests: Maya and Spaniard in Yucatan, 1517–1570* (Cambridge: Cambridge University Press, 2003).
48. Rodriguez, *Mongrels, Bastards, Orphans, and Vagabonds*.
49. Prasenjit Duara, *Rescuing History from the Nation: Questioning Narratives of Modern China* (Chicago: University of Chicago Press, 1996).
50. Michael C. Meyer, William L. Sherman, and Susan M. Deeds, *The Course of Mexican History* (New York: Oxford University Press, 2018); William H. Beezley and Michael C. Meyer, eds., *The Oxford History of Mexico* (New York: Oxford University Press, 2010).
51. Rodriguez, *Mongrels, Bastards, Orphans, and Vagabonds*, 4.
52. See Peter A. Stern, "Social Marginality and Acculturation on the Northern Frontier of New Spain" (PhD diss., University of California, Berkeley, 1985).
53. Rodriguez, *Mongrels, Bastards, Orphans, and Vagabonds*, 4.

54. Gabriela Martínez-Cortés et al., "Admixture and Population Structure in Mexican-Mestizos Based on Paternal Lineages," *Journal of Human Genetics* 57 (2012) 568, DOI: 10.1038/jhg.2012.67.
55. Reich, *Who We Are and How We Got Here*, 230.
56. Michel-Rolph Trouillot, *Silencing the Past: Power and the Production of History* (London: Beacon Press, 1995).
57. Failed expeditions could also threaten the colonial social order. A fascinating read is Captain Bernardo de Vargas Machuca, *The Indian Militia and Description of the Indies* (Durham, NC: Duke University Press, 2008). Another wonderfully written book of a failed expedition is Andrés Reséndez, *A Land So Strange: The Epic Journey of Cabeza de Vaca* (New York: Basic Books, 2007).
58. Juan-Camilo Chacón-Duque et al., "Latin Americans Show Wide-Spread Converso Ancestry and Imprint of Local Native Ancestry on Physical Appearance," *Nature Communications* 9, article 5388 (2018), DOI: 10.1038/s41467-018-07748-z.
59. One interpretation ("Indigenista") can be read here: Juan Manuel Pérez Zevallos and Héctor Cuauhtémoc Hernández Silva, *México a través de los siglos: historia general y completa del desenvolvimiento social, político, religioso, militar, artístico, científico y literario de México desde la antigüedad más remota hasta la época actual: obra única en su género,* ed. *D. Vicente Riva Palacio* (México, Ballescá y Compañía; Barcelona Espasa y Compañía, 1882), vol. 1, chap. 3. On similar experiences with conquest and colonization see Susan Schroeder, "Introduction: The Genre of Conquest Studies," in Matthew and Oudijk, *Indian Conquistadors*, 5–27.
60. Sean McEnroe, *From Colony to Nationhood in Mexico: Laying the Foundations, 1560–1840* (Cambridge: Cambridge University Press, 2014); Matthew and Oudijk, *Indian Conquistadors*; Dana Velasco Murillo, *Urban Indians in a Silver City: Zacatecas, Mexico, 1546–1810* (Stanford, CA: Stanford University Press, 2016); Eugene B. Sego, "Six Tlaxcalan Colonies on New Spain's Northern Frontier: A Comparison of Success and Failure" (PhD diss., Indiana University, 1990); David Bergen Adams, "The Tlaxcalan Colonies of Spanish Coahuila and Nuevo León: An Aspect of the Settlement of Northern Mexico" (PhD diss., University of Texas, 1971); Charles Gibson, *Tlaxcala in the Sixteenth Century* (New Haven, CT: Yale University Press, 1952).
61. Lockhart, *Nahuas after Conquest*, 5; also MacLachlan, *Imperialism and the Origins of Mexican Culture*, 5; Bradley Benton, *The Lords of Tetzcoco: The Transformation of Indigenous Rule in Postconquest Central Mexico*; Emma Pérez-Rocha and Rafael Tena, *La nobleza indígena del centro de México después de la conquista* (México: Instituto Nacional de Antropología e Historia, 2000).
62. For a definition of "Mexicanization" see Bartra *Anatomía del mexicano*. The quoted phrases come from Wolfe, "Settler Colonialism and the Elimination of the Native," 393–94.
63. The phrase "new figure" is a play on—and an homage to—Enrique Florescano's brilliant argument that "the conquest" created a "new protagonist of the historical narration:

the conquistador." See *National Narratives in México*, 100–26. Narratively speaking, Florescano is correct; however, my point here is that there were always more Nahuas than Iberians, and thus the majority of "conquistadors" and soldiers who manned the presidios, missions, and various military forts were indigenous and later mestizo. On the concept of world historical figure, consult Georg Wilhelm Friedrich Hegel, *Lectures on the Philosophy of World History*, trans. H. B. Nisbet (Cambridge: Cambridge University Press, 1975), 11–24.

64. McEnroe, *From Colony to Nationhood*; Matthew and Oudijk, *Indian Conquistadors*; Velasco Murillo, *Urban Indians in a Silver City*; Sego, "Six Tlaxcalan Colonies"; Adams, "Tlaxcalan Colonies"; Gibson, *Tlaxcala in the Sixteenth Century*.
65. José E. González, *Algunos apuntes y datos estadísticos que pueden servir de base para formar una estadística del estado de Nuevo León* (Monterrey: Imprenta del Gobierno, 1873), 16; quoted from Juan Mora-Torres, *Making of the Mexican Border*, 15.
66. McEnroe, *From Colony to Nationhood*, 5.
67. Schroeder, "Introduction: The Genre of Conquest Studies," in Matthew Oudijk, *Indian Conquistadors*, 14; Andrea Martínez Baracs, "Colonizaciones tlaxcaltecas," *Historia Mexicana* 43, no. 2 (1993): 195–250, http://www.jstor.org/stable/25138897; Raquel E. Güereca Durán, "Las milicias tlaxcaltecas en Saltillo y Colotlán," *Estudios de Historia Novohispana* 54 (January–June 2016): 50–73.
68. Matthew, *Memories of Conquest*, 90.
69. Rocío Gómez et al., "Y Chromosome Diversity in Aztlán Descendants and Its Implications for the History of Central Mexico," *iScience* 24, no. 5, 102487, DOI: 10.1016/j.isci.2021.102487.
70. Güereca Durán, "Las milicias tlaxcaltecas en Saltillo y Colotlán."
71. Matthew and Oudijk, *Indian Conquistadors*; Martínez Baracs, "Colonizaciones tlaxcaltecas"; Güereca Durán, "Las milicias tlaxcaltecas en Saltillo y Colotlán."
72. Max L. Moorhead, *The Presidio: Bastion of the Spanish Borderlands* (Norman: University of Oklahoma Press, 1991).
73. Martínez Baracs, "Colonizaciones tlaxcaltecas."
74. McEnroe, *From Colony to Nationhood*, 39.
75. Martínez Baracs, "Colonizaciones tlaxcaltecas" 195–196; Güereca Durán, "Las milicias tlaxcaltecas en Saltillo y Colotlán."
76. Another instance of the "diaspora model" perhaps? See Florescano, *National Narratives in Mexico*, 45.
77. Matthew, *Memories of Conquest*, 98.
78. On indigenous militias, see Güereca Durán, "Las milicias tlaxcaltecas en Saltillo y Colotlán." On "immigrant Indians" see Andrés Reséndez, *Changing National Identities at the Frontier: Texas and New Mexico, 1800–1850* (Cambridge: Cambridge University Press, 2005), 15–55; González Quiroga, *War and Peace*, 114–21; James David Nichols, *The Limits of Liberty: Mobility and the Making of the Eastern U.S.-Mexico Border* (Omaha: University of Nebraska Press, 2018), 49–56.
79. Eva Maria Mehl, *Forced Migration in the Spanish Pacific World: From Mexico to the Philippines, 1765–1811* (Cambridge: Cambridge University Press, 2016), 157.

80. Mehl, *Forced Migration in the Spanish Pacific World*, 13, 15. Also see Rafael Bernal, *México en Filipinas: estudio de una transculturación* (México: UNAM, 1965).
81. Gilles Deleuze and Félix Guattari, *Nomadology: The War Machine* (Seattle, WA, 2010), 98–99.

Chapter 2

1. Ortiz de Ayala, *Resumen de la estadística del imperio mexicano.*
2. Teodoro de Croix, *Teodoro de Croix and the Northern Frontier of New Spain, 1776–1783: From the Original Document in the Archives of the Indies, Seville* (Norman: University of Oklahoma Press, 1941).
3. Spain opened its lands to foreign settlement in 1820. For an example of early fears of US expansion, see José Cortés, *Views from the Apache Frontier: Report on the Northern Province of New Spain*, ed. Elizabeth A. H. John, trans. John Wheat (Norman: University of Oklahoma Press, 1989).
4. Aldon S. Lang and Christopher Long, "Land Grants," *Handbook of Texas Online*, accessed April 13, 2022, https://www.tshaonline.org/handbook/entries/land-grants.
5. Weber, *Bárbaros*, 91–137.
6. David Weber, *The Mexican Frontier, 1821–1846: The American Southwest under Mexico* (Albuquerque: University of New Mexico Press, 1982), 179–206.
7. Tomás Almaguer, *Racial Fault-Lines: The Historical Origins of White Supremacy in California* (Berkeley: University of California Press, 1994), 47.
8. Lang and Long, "Land Grants."
9. Reséndez, *Changing National Identities*, 35–37.
10. Weber, *Mexican Frontier*, 181–82.
11. Lang and Long, "Land Grants."
12. Lomnitz-Adler, *Deep Mexico, Silent Mexico*, 29–32.
13. George Dieter Berninger, "Mexican Attitudes towards Immigration, 1821–1857" (PhD diss., University of Wisconsin, Madison, 1972); Hernández, "From Conquest to Colonization."
14. José Angel Hernández, "*Indios Bárbaros* and the Making of Mexican Colonization Policy after Independence: From Conquest to Colonization," in *Transnational Indians in the North American West*, ed. Andrae M. Marak and Clarissa Confer (College Station: Texas A&M University Press, 2015).
15. Enrique Delgado López, "El clima y la raza como parte de la historia de México en la primera mitad del siglo XIX," *Revista de Historia de América* 146 (January–June 2012): 113–33.
16. Berninger, "Mexican Attitudes towards Immigration," 149.
17. Covarrubias, *Algunas observaciones acerca la inmigración y de la colonización*, 155–57.
18. González Navarro, "La política colonizadora del Porfiriato," and *La colonización en México*, 105–22.
19. Hernández, "From Conquest to Colonization." On "El Indio" as the biological and cultural basis of Mexican identity, see Bartra, *Anatomía del mexicano*, 203–14.

20. Chávez Chávez, *Los indios en la formación de la identidad nacional* (Ciudad Juárez, Chih.: Universidad Autónoma de Ciudad Juárez, 2003), 26–27. Original: "para alcanzar estas metas, tuvieron que implementar una serie de acciones políticas, entra las que destacaron: el imponerles un Nuevo tipo de educación donde se les enseñara los nuevos valores culturales y olvidaran los suyos; procurar la colonización extranjera para lograr el mestizaje biológico y cultural; someterlos y más aún, exterminarlos por medio de la represión armada si se resistían en forma drástica (como la rebelión o insurrección) a la nueva colonización. Esto, con el único fin de hacer que indios abandonaran sus diversas identidades culturales, creadas y recreadas durante la Colonia, para incorporarlos a otra, la mexicana."
21. For early arguments on autocolonization, see González-Polo y Acosta, "Colonización e inmigración extranjera"; Covarrubias, *Algunas observaciones acerca la inmigración y de la colonización*, 155–57.
22. Berninger, "Mexican Attitudes towards Immigration," 28. The "contractual obligation" to Mexicanize is even more pronounced during the Porfiriato. Rodriguez mentions a number of earlier laws encouraging Iberians to form marital unions with indigenous women. See *Mongrels, Bastards, Orphans, and Vagabonds*, 19–29.
23. Saler, *Settlers' Empire*, 1–2.
24. "La legación Mexicana comunica que se le ha presentado al Sr. Juan Ross, Jefe de la Tribu de Indios Llamados Cherokees, manifestando sus deseos de saber si el gobierno admitiría gustoso en su territorio a dicha tribu, molestada y perseguida por el Ejecutivo de los EUA., 1835," exp. 2-13-2965, Archivo Histórico Genaro Estrada, Secretaría de Relaciones Exteriores (hereafter AHSRE); Isidro Vizcaya Canales, *Incursiones de indios al noreste en el México independiente, 1821–1855* (México: Gobierno de Nuevo León, Archivo General del Estado, 1995).
25. Hernández, "Mexican Expulsions and Indian Removal during the Early Period of Global Mass Immigrations," *World History Bulletin* 30, no. 2 (Fall 2014): 30–34.
26. This question deserves more research, especially regarding the number of indigenous groups that requested lands to colonize in Mexico. The Cherokees in the 1820s and 1830s are one case, but there are apparently others, including a request from Cherokees in 1901 for lands in Sonora. See "Indios Cherokees desean adquirir terrenos en Sonora, 1901," exp. 3742-18, AHSRE.
27. A few examples can be seen in "Indios Comanches y Mescaleros que pretenden concertar tratados con el Gobierno Mexicano, 1869," exp. 1-5-970, AHSRE; "Indios Lipanes, permiso para establecerse en Santa Rosa, Coahuila, 1877–78," exp. 1-14-1628, AHSRE; and "Indios Creek, compra de terrenos en México, 1908," exp. 15-20-96, AHSRE.
28. Deleuze and Guattari, *Nomadology*, 98–99.
29. Florescano, *National Narratives in Mexico*, 45.
30. Gregory D. Smithers, *The Cherokee Diaspora: An Indigenous History of Migration, Resettlement, and Identity* (New Haven, CT: Yale University Press, 2015), 27–57. Mary Whatley Clarke observes that their given Algonquin name points to Pennsylvania. See *Chief Bowles and the Texas Cherokees* (Norman: University of Oklahoma Press, 1971), 4.

31. Jason C. Nelson, "The Application of the International Law of State Succession to the United States: A Reassessment of the Treaty between the Republic of Texas and the Cherokee Indians," *Duke Journal of Comparative and International Law* 17, no. 1 (Fall 2006): 6, https://scholarship.law.duke.edu/djcil/vol17/iss1/1.
32. Quoted in Smithers, *Cherokee Diaspora*, 30–31.
33. Clarke, *Chief Bowles and the Texas Cherokees*, 79–80; Ernest William Winkler, "The Cherokee Indians in Texas," *Quarterly of the Texas State Historical Association* 7, no. 2 (October 1903): 95–165.
34. Smithers, *Cherokee Diaspora*, 27.
35. Nelson, "Application of the International Law," 1–48.
36. Clarke, *Chief Bowles and the Texas Cherokees*, 3–17.
37. Clarke, *Chief Bowles and the Texas Cherokees*, 79–80; Winkler, "Cherokee Indians in Texas," 14.
38. Clarke, *Chief Bowles and the Texas Cherokees*, 79–80; Winkler, "Cherokee Indians in Texas," 20; Smithers, *Cherokee Diaspora*, 7, 21.
39. Clarke, *Chief Bowles and the Texas Cherokees*, 24; Smithers, *Cherokee Diaspora*, 8.
40. Smithers, *Cherokee Diaspora*, 8.
41. Clarke, *Chief Bowles and the Texas Cherokees*, 60–61; Nelson, "Application of the International Law," 10.
42. Clarke, *Chief Bowles and the Texas Cherokees*, 70.
43. Nelson, "Application of the International Law," 17.
44. Paul D. Lack, "The Córdova Revolt," in *Tejano Journey, 1770–1850*, ed. Gerald E. Poyo (Austin: University of Texas Press, 1996), 89–109; Nelson, "Application of the International Law," 13.
45. Clarke, *Chief Bowles and the Texas Cherokees*, 79–80.
46. Nelson, "Application of the International Law," 13–14.
47. Clarke, *Chief Bowles and the Texas Cherokees*, 114.
48. Dianna Everett, *The Texas Cherokees: A People between Two Fires, 1819–1840* (Norman: University of Oklahoma Press, 1990), 109.
49. González Milea, *El silencio de las aldeas*, 194–204.
50. "La legación Mexicana comunica que se le ha presentado al Sr. Juan Ross," exp. 2-13-2965, AHSRE; "Indios Comanches y Mescaleros que pretenden concertar tratados," exp. 1-5-970, AHSRE; "Indios Lipanes, permiso para establecerse en Santa Rosa," exp. 1-14-1628, AHSRE; "Solicitud de Indios Osaje para pasarse a la Republica, 1885," 15-2-38, AHSRE.
51. Hegel, *Lectures on the Philosophy of World History*, 136.
52. Ranajit Guha, "The Prose of Counter-Insurgency," in *Subaltern Studies II: Writings of South Asian History and Society*, 2–42 (Oxford: Oxford University Press, 1983), section 2.
53. Duara, *Rescuing History from the Nation.*
54. Bryan Burrough et al., *Forget the Alamo: The Rise and Fall of an American Myth* (New York: Penguin Random House, 2021).

55. González Navarro, *La política colonizadora del Porfiriato, La colonización en México,* and *Los extranjeros en México.*
56. See "Circular de 4 de Diciembre de 1846, recomendando la exacta observancia de las medidas que contiene el decreto expedido para el establecimiento de la Dirección de Colonización," in de la Maza, *Código de colonización,* 360. Original: "Se han dado leyes unas después de otras, relativas a este objeto, y se han ajustado contratos de fundaciones de colonias, pero sin efecto ni resultados. La única que se ha establecido y prosperado, es la que se rebeló en Texas, porque el pensamiento de su establecimiento no fue de una empresa económica o mercantil, sino de usurpación de nuestro territorio, aprovechando el candor juvenil con que la Republica abría sin recelo sus brazos a todas las naciones extranjeras en los primeros días de su existencia independiente. Este hecho patentiza que las leyes de colonización eran inadecuadas."
57. Historian David J. Weber does an excellent analysis of how Mexico tried to secure its northern frontier by granting huge land grants to various empresarios in Texas; see *Mexican Frontier,* 179–206. Reséndez enumerates thirty-nine empresario grants in the New Mexico Territory between 1821 and 1853 in *Changing National Identities at the Frontier*, 36–37. On historical narratology, see Jerzy Topolski, "Historical Narrative: Towards a Coherent Structure." *History and Theory* 26, no. 4 (1987): 75–86, DOI: 10.2307/2505046.
58. *Memoria del Ministro de Relaciones Interiores y Esteriores D. Luis G. Cuevas leída en la Cámara de Diputados el 5 y en la de Senadores el 8 de Enero de 1849* (México: Imprenta de Vicente García Torres, Ex-Convento del Espíritu Santo, 1849), 8.
59. *Memoria de la Secretaría de Estado y del Despacho de Fomento, Colonización, Industria y Comercio de la República Mexicana, escrita por el Ministro del Ramo, D. Manuel Siliceo, para dar cuenta con ella al Soberano Congreso Constitucional* (México: Imprenta de Vicente García Torres, 1857).
60. Manero, Vicente E., *Documentos interesantes sobre colonización: los ha reunido, puesto en orden cronológico y los publica, Vicente E. Manero, gefe de la Sección 1ª del Ministerio de Fomento* (México: Imprenta de la V. E Hijos de Murguía, 1878) 43–52; also *Memoria de la Secretaría de Estado . . . escrita por . . . Manuel Siliceo,* 41. Original: "En vista de estos funestos resultados, no faltará quien crea que la introducción de extranjeros para poblar nuestros desiertos terrenos, compromete la seguridad de la nación; y efectivamente así sucederá siempre que se proceda con la misma imprevisión con que se puso en planta la colonización de aquel Departamento, pues no se tuvo presente la inmensa distancia que lo separaba del centro de la República, ni su inmediación a una potencia de primer orden, que desde tiempos anteriores había manifestado los deseos que tenia de que formara parte de su territorio, para lo cual no tenía más que extender la mano, mientras el gobierno de México para impedirlo tenía que atravesar algunos centenares de leguas, desiertas en gran parte, y sin recursos para sostener un ejército."
61. The obvious anthropomorphizing of the nation's political evolution need not concern us here but is too obvious not to acknowledge.

62. One of the best studies problematizing the mythic notion of manifest destiny is Thomas R. Hietala, *Manifest Design: American Exceptionalism and Empire*, rev. ed. (Ithaca, NY: Cornell University Press, 2003).
63. *Memoria de la Secretaría de Estado . . . escrito por . . . Manuel Siliceo*, 41; Manero, *Documentos interesantes sobre colonización*, 43–52. Original: "De esto resultó que al admitirse en Tejas como colonos a ciudadanos de los Estados-Unidos no se hizo otra cosa que extender el territorio de éstos, faltando únicamente que se hiciera una expresa declaración de que les pertenecía de derecho ya que de hecho lo poseían, supuesto que sus naturales lo ocupaban conservando sus costumbres, idioma y relaciones sin modificación alguna, por la falta de población mexicana, que hubiera podido neutralizar las tendencias de hacer un todo de las colonias con el país de donde habían salido y del que solo estaban separadas por un rio."
64. Here I am thinking of Pekka Hämäläinen's *Comanche Empire*, which effectively argues that the presence of a Comanche empire along Mexico's foremost northern regions prevented settlement there, thus facilitating the execution of the Mexican-American War (1846–48). This narrative, in my estimation, undermines the entire thesis of manifest destiny as a linear process guided by ideology instead of the global market.
65. Currently, 29 Amerindian reservations are located along the international boundary between the United States and Mexico. For a listing of these autonomous communities, see https://naepc.com/border-tribes/.
66. For an interesting interpretation of this process, see Conor O'Dwyer's, "Runaway State Building: How Political Parties Shape States in Postcommunist Eastern Europe." *World Politics* 56, no. 4 (2004): 520–53. http://www.jstor.org/stable/25054274.
67. *Memoria de la Secretaría de Estado . . . escrito por . . . Manuel Siliceo*, 45; Manero, *Documentos interesantes sobre colonización*, 43–52.
68. *Memoria de la Secretaría de Estado . . . escrito por . . . Manuel Siliceo*, 45; Manero, *Documentos interesantes sobre colonización*, 43–52.
69. See, for example, *Junta Directiva de Colonización, Proyectos de colonización*.
70. This was made quite clear during the term of General Carlos Pacheco. See *Memoria presentada al Congreso de la Unión por el Secretario de Estado y del Despacho de Fomento, Colonización, Industria y Comercio de la República Mexicana, General Carlos Pacheco, corresponde a los años trascurridos de diciembre de 1877 a diciembre de 1882* (México: Oficina Tipográfica de la Secretaria de Fomento, 1885), 1:3–4.
71. Brian Hamnett, "The Comonfort Presidency, 1855–1857," *Bulletin of Latin American Research* 15, no. 1 (1996): 81–100.
72. Hernández, "Mexican Expulsions and Indian Removal," 30–34.

Chapter 3

1. On reconquista rhetoric (and practice) from as early as 1837 through the 1840s, I recommend consulting Raúl Ramos, *Beyond the Alamo: Forging Mexican Ethnicity in San Antonio, 1821–1861* (Chapel Hill: University of North Carolina Press, 2008), 177–90.

2. See Nancy Shoemaker, "Settler Colonialism: Universal Theory or English Heritage?" *William and Mary Quarterly* 76, no. 3 (July 2019): 369–74.
3. Richard J. Salvucci, *Politics, Markets, and Mexico's "London Debt," 1823–1887* (Cambridge: Cambridge University Press, 2009), 131–41, quotation on 141.
4. "Almonte to Luis G. Cuevas," quoted in Faustino A. Aquino Sánchez, *Intervención francesa, 1838–1839. La diplomacia mexicana y el imperialismo del libre comercio* (México: Instituto Nacional de Antropología e Historia, 1997), 209; quotation from Salvucci, *Politics, Markets, and Mexico's "London Debt,"* 141.
5. Salvucci, *Politics, Markets, and Mexico's "London Debt,"* 141.
6. "Decreto de 27 de Noviembre de 1846 estableciendo la Dirección de Colonización," in de la Maza, *Código de colonización*, 345–47.
7. González Navarro, *Los extranjeros en México*, 1:253.
8. *Memoria de la primera Secretaria de Estado y del Despacho de Relaciones Interiores y Esteriores de los Estados Unidos Mexicanos, leída al soberano Congreso constituyente en los días 14, 15, y 16 de diciembre de 1846* (México: Imprenta de Vicente García Torres, 1847), 81.
9. See Richard Blaine McCornack, "The San Patricio Deserters in the Mexican War," *The Americas* 8, no. 2 (October 1951): 131–42.
10. For a fascinating read on immigrant soldiers, desertion, and employment, see Peter Guardino, *The Dead March: A History of the Mexican-American War* (Cambridge, MA: Harvard University Press, 2017), esp. chap 6.
11. *Memoria de la primera Secretaria de Estado*, 81.
12. Berninger, "Mexican Attitudes towards Immigration," 163; González Navarro reports different members of the junta: Juan de Dios Pérez Gálvez and Mariano Riva Palacio. See *Los extranjeros en México*, 1:254.
13. The obvious corpus is to be found in these two recompilations: de la Maza, *Código de colonización*; and Manuel Dublán and José María Lozano, *Legislación mexicana o colección completa de las disposiciones legislativas . . .* (México: Imprenta de Comercio, 1876).
14. See Article 1 of "Decreto de 27 de Noviembre de 1846, estableciendo la Dirección de Colonización," in de la Maza, *Código de colonización*, 345–47.
15. See "Ley—Aprobando el convenio celebrado en Londres el 17 de Septiembre de 1837."
16. Salvucci, *Politics, Markets, and Mexico's "London Debt."*
17. "Ley—Aprobando el convenio celebrado en Londres el 17 de Septiembre de 1837," in Dublán and Lozano, *Legislación mexicana o colección completa de las disposiciones legislativas*, 624–31.
18. My point here is that while these negotiations were taking place in London, the areas under consideration were under the control of a Comanche empire that was not invited to the negotiating table. Then again, neither were the Apaches.
19. "Ley—Aprobando el convenio celebrado en Londres el 17 de Septiembre de 1837."
20. These battles were the Battle of Palo Alto (8 May 1846), the Battle of Resaca de la Palma (9 May 1846), and the Battle of Monterrey (20–24 September 1846).

21. Irving W. Levinson, *Wars within War: Mexican Guerrillas, Domestic Elites, and the United States of America, 1846–1848* (Fort Worth: Texas Christian University Press, 2005), xiii–xviii.
22. Other military plans for colonization emerged in the years to come, not to mention dozens of essays giving various propositions on how best to colonize and settle the northern frontiers of the republic. This decree was the first iteration of the colonization issue, but it would not be the last. See Article 1 of "Decreto de 27 de Noviembre de 1846," in de la Maza, *Código de colonización*, 345–47.
23. "Decreto de 19 de Agosto de 1848; para que familias mexicanas que se encuentren en los Estados Unidos puedan emigrar a su patria," in de la Maza, *Código de colonización*, 407–12.
24. An excellent overview of several of the colonies founded during this period is González Milea, *El silencio de las aldeas.*
25. See "Reglamento de 4 de Diciembre de 1846 para la Dirección de Colonización" and "Circular de 4 de Diciembre de 1846, recomendando la exacta observancia de las medidas que contiene el decreto expedido para el establecimiento de la Dirección de Colonización," in de la Maza, *Código de colonización*, 347–64.
26. "Reglamento de 4 de Diciembre de 1846" in de la Maza, *Código de colonización*, 347–48.
27. Wilson, *Social Conquest of Earth*, chap. 10.
28. This is merely an observation, not a critique. Some examples in the historiography are David K. Burden, "La idea Salvadora: Immigration and Colonization Politics in Mexico, 1821–1857" (PhD diss., University of California, Santa Barbara, 2005); Berninger, "Mexican Attitudes towards Immigration," chap. 5; González-Polo y Acosta, "Colonización e inmigración extranjera," 4–7; Berninger, "Immigration and Religious Toleration"; Zilli Mánica, "Proyectos liberales de colonización"; Vos, "Una legislación de graves consecuencias"; González Navarro, *Los extranjeros en México*, 1:280–81.
29. For a detailed analysis of official government documents as "primary" documentation, the best source is still Guha, "Prose of Counter-Insurgency."
30. Ranajit Guha, *Dominance without Hegemony: History and Power in Colonial India* (Cambridge, MA: Harvard University Press, 1997), 6.
31. "Reglamento de 4 de Diciembre de 1846," in de la Maza, *Código de colonización*, 347–48.
32. Wolfe, "Settler Colonialism and the Elimination of the Native," 393.
33. *Junta Directiva de Colonización, México, Proyectos de colonización.*
34. See "Decreto de 27 de Noviembre de 1846; estableciendo la Dirección de Colonización" and "Decreto de 19 de Agosto de 1848; para que familias mexicanas que se encuentren en los Estados Unidos puedan emigrar a su patria," in de la Maza, *Código de colonización.*
35. *Junta Directiva de Colonización, México, Proyectos de colonización*, 11.
36. This article reads as follows: "Artículo 22 de la ley de 14 de junio de 1848: Queda autorizado el Gobierno para invertir hasta doscientos mil pesos del fondo de que habla el artículo 2° (el de indemnización que paguen los Estados Unidos) de esta ley en la traslación de las familias mexicanas que no quieran permanecer en el territorio cedido a los Estados Unidos y soliciten establecerse en la República. Esta cantidad podrá

aumentarse con presencia de los presupuestos respectivos, que el mismo Gobierno presentará al Congreso." Also, "Asunto: Ramón Ortiz—Nombramiento del citado para que pase a Nuevo México, comisionado para la traslación de familias a territorio de la República, 1848," exp. L-E-1975 (XXV), AHSRE.

37. "Decreto de 19 de Agosto de 1848," in de la Maza, *Código de colonización*.

38. Hernández, *Mexican American Colonization during the Nineteenth Century*, 225–31. For an excellent overview of these repatriation and national colonies, see González Milea, *El silencio de las aldeas*; Taylor, "La repatriación de mexicanos de 1848 a 1980"; and González de la Vara, "El traslado de familias de Nuevo México al norte de Chihuahua."

39. Carta de Menchaca al presidente de México, 4 diciembre 1850 in "El gobernador de Coahuila acompañando una solicitud de Don Antonio Menchaca vecino de Nacogdoches para trasladar a la República familias mexicanas. Se nombra comisionado al gobernador de Nuevo León, 1850," exp. 2-13-2975, AHSRE. See also "Sobre el establecimiento de 200 familias emigradas de Bejar en el punto del Remolino en Coahuila (1850)," exp. 1819, vol. SLVI, pp. 93–127, Archivo Histórico del Estado de Saltillo, Center for American History, University of Texas at Austin (hereafter SACAH).

40. González Milea, *El silencio de las aldeas*.

41. Carta de Menchaca al presidente de México, 4 diciembre 1850, exp. 2-13-2975, AHSRE.

42. González Milea, *El silencio de las aldeas*, 194, 195.

43. González Milea, *El silencio de las aldeas*, 194–96.

44. "Carta de Menchaca al presidente de México," 4 diciembre 1850," in exp. 2-13-2975, AHSRE.

45. González Milea points out that as late as 1863, Nuevo León and Coahuila were kept united as one state under one governing military chief. See "Colonias militares y civiles del siglo XIX: Una aproximación a las utopías urbanas del norte de Coahuila," *Estudios Fronterizos*13, no. 25 (January–June 2012): 191–219.

46. "Nombramiento para comisionado en Matamoros, hecho en Don Rafael de la Garza," Tesorero General del Estado de Nuevo León, 1850, exp. 2-13-2974, AHSRE.

47. "Carta de Joaquín S. de Castillo al Consulado de México en Brownsville," 25 octubre 1853, exp. 2-13-2975, AHSRE. See also "Sobre el establecimiento de 200 familias emigradas de Bejar en el punto del Remolino en Coahuila (1850)," exp. 1819, vol. SLVI, pp. 93–127, SACAH.

48. Hernández, "Decree of 19 August 1848."

49. "Sobre el establecimiento de 200 familias emigradas de Bejar en el punto del Remolino en Coahuila (1850)," exp. 1819, vol. SLVI, pp. 93–127, SACAH.

50. González Milea, "Colonias militares y civiles del siglo XIX," 206.

51. González Milea, *El silencio de las aldeas*, 197.

52. See "Sobre el establecimiento de 200 familias emigradas de Bejar en el punto del Remolino en Coahuila (1850)," exp. 1819, vol. SLVI, pp. 93–127, SACAH.

53. González Milea, "Colonias militares y civiles del siglo XIX," 209.

54. Statistics from "Congregación el Remolino (Zaragoza, Coahuila de Zaragoza)," PueblosAmerica.com, https://mexico.pueblosamerica.com/i/el-remolino-4/. For a

discussion of El Remolino and Indian raiding during the 1870s, see also the excellent work of González Quiroga, *War and Peace*, 268–73.

55. González Milea, *El silencio de las aldeas*, 194.

Chapter 4

1. *Memoria de la Secretaría de Estado . . . escrita por . . . Manuel Siliceo*; also Manero, *Documentos interesantes sobre colonización*, 43–52.
2. Patricia Galeana, *Juárez en la historia de México* (México: Editorial Miguel Ángel Porrúa, 2006), 58–59.
3. Florescano, *National Narratives in Mexico*, xi.
4. In his lectures on the philosophy of world history, G. W. F. Hegel outlines different stages of historical development. Hegel initiates his exploration by delineating three principal forms of historical methodology: original history, composed contemporaneously with the period under scrutiny; reflective history, crafted subsequent to the era's conclusion, infused with contemplative thought and interpretation; and philosophic history, employing a priori philosophical reasoning to construe history as a rational progression. (Reflective history is further subdivided into universal history, pragmatic, critical, and specialized methodologies.) Hegel, *Lectures on the Philosophy of World History*, 11–24.
5. The quintessential example of this narrative of failure is the pioneering research of González Navarro, which is also the obligatory starting point for any historiography on colonization in Mexico. See "La política colonizadora del Porfiriato," *La colonización en México*, and *Los extranjeros en México*.
6. *Memoria de la Secretaría de Estado . . . escrita por . . . Manuel Siliceo*; Manero, *Documentos interesantes sobre colonización*, 37.
7. *Memoria de la Secretaría de Estado . . . escrita por . . . Manuel Siliceo*, 37; Manero, *Documentos interesantes sobre colonización*, 43–52.
8. Scott, *Art of Not Being Governed*, 7.
9. Justo Sierra, *The Political Evolution of the Mexican People*, trans. ed. (Austin: University of Texas Press, 1969), 281–97.
10. For a copy of and commentary on the constitution, see Galeana, *Juárez en la historia de México*, 47–58.
11. Ohland Morton, "Life of General Don Manuel de Mier y Terán: As It Affected Texas-Mexican Relations," *Southwestern Historical Quarterly* 48, no. 4 (1945): 499–546.
12. Robert Bernasconi, "Hegel at the Court of the Ashanti," in *Hegel after Derrida*, ed. Stuart Barnett (New York: Routledge, 1998), 41–63. https://philpapers.org/rec/BERHAT-7
13. *Memoria de la Secretaría de Estado . . . escrita por . . . Manuel Siliceo*, 39–40; Manero, *Documentos interesantes sobre colonización*, 43–52. Original: "como el número de los conquistadores era corto respecto a la inmensa extensión del país que habían sujetado a su dominio, resultó que aun tomando sin limitación la tierra que querían, quedaban siempre grandes huecos que iban agregando a sus posesiones a medida

que enajenaban parte de ellas, o que tomaban incremento las labores a que las destinaban. De aquí resultó la aglomeración en pocas manos de la propiedad territorial; la increíble extensión de algunas fincas rústicas que contienen más superficie que la de varias soberanías europeas; y finalmente que cuando por cálculo se había creído que contenían cinco o seis leguas, se han encontrado después con treinta o cuarenta."

14. Francois Chevalier, *Land and Society in Colonial Mexico: The Great Hacienda* (Berkeley and Los Angeles: University of California Press, 1963), 308–14.
15. Galeana, *Juárez en la historia de México*, 44.
16. Berninger, "Mexican Attitudes towards Immigration," 166.
17. *Encyclopaedia Britannica Online*, s.v. "La Reforma," https://www.britannica.com/event/La-Reforma.
18. Walter V. Scholes, *Mexican Politics during the Juárez Regime, 1855–1872* (Columbia: University of Missouri Press, 1957), 92.
19. Robert H. Duncan, "Political Legitimation and Maximilian's Second Empire in Mexico, 1864–1867," *Mexican Studies/Estudios Mexicanos* 12, no. 1 (Winter, 1996): 27–66.
20. Find examples of the implementation of various colonization policy prescriptions in several decrees in de la Maza, *Código de colonización*, 718–44.
21. Scholes, *Mexican Politics during the Juárez Regime*, 117.
22. *Encyclopaedia Britannica Online*, s.v. "Maximilian," https://www.britannica.com/biography/Maximilian-archduke-of-Austria-and-emperor-of-Mexico; my italics.
23. Lomnitz-Adler, *Deep Mexico, Silent Mexico*, 88.
24. Scholes, *Mexican Politics during the Juárez Regime*, 117.
25. Burden, "Reform before La Reforma."
26. Erika Pani, "Dreaming of a Mexican Empire: The Political Projects of the 'Imperialistas,'" *Hispanic American Historical Review* 82, no. 1 (February 2002): 3–4.
27. Graham Burchell et al., *The Foucault Effect: Studies in Governmentality, with Two Lectures by and an Interview with Michel Foucault* (Chicago: University of Chicago Press, 1991).
28. María de la Paz Ramos Lara and Rigoberto Rodríguez Benítez, eds., *Formación de ingenieros en el México del siglo XIX* (Culiacán: Facultad de Historia, Universidad Autónoma de Sinaloa, 2007).
29. *Memoria presentada á S.M. el Emperador por el Ministro de Fomento Luis Robles Pezuela de los trabajos ejecutados en su ramo el año de 1865* (México: Imprenta de J. M. Andrade y F. Escalante, 1866), 98.
30. Burden, "Reform before La Reforma."
31. Beatriz Bernal Gómez, "México y las leyes liberales de Maximiliano de Habsburgo," *Hechos y Derechos* 11 (2 November 2012), https://revistas.juridicas.unam.mx/index.php/hechos-y-derechos/article/view/6731/8667.
32. *Memoria presentada á S.M. el Emperador*, 99; also Manero, *Documentos interesantes sobre colonización*, 53–57.
33. Jesús Islas, "Situación de los Hispano-Americanos en California," *El Clamor Público*, 23 October 1855.

34. Arnoldo De León, *They Called them Greasers: Anglo Attitudes towards Mexicans in Texas, 1821–1900* (Austin: University of Texas Press, 1983), 14–23.
35. Vanessa Heggie, "Blood, Race and Indigenous Peoples in Twentieth Century Extreme Physiology," *History and Philosophy of the Life Sciences* 41, article 26 (2019), DOI: 10.1007/s40656-019-0264-z; Mark Harrison, "'The Tender Frame of Man': Disease, Climate, and Racial Difference in India and the West Indies, 1760–1860," *Bulletin of the History of Medicine* 70, no. 1 (1996): 68–93, https://muse.jhu.edu/article/3659.
36. *Memoria presentada á S.M. el Emperador*, 98–99; also Manero, *Documentos interesantes sobre colonización*, 53–57. Original: "No me detendré en recomendar las ventajas que en todos tiempos ha producido á. las naciones que con franqueza la han adoptado, porque no hay quien ignore que la introducción de nuevos brazos, de nuevos capitales, y de nuevas industrias, dan un vigor desconocido a cualquier parte que se dirigen, de la misma manera que por medio de la trasfusión de la sangre se reanima y cobra alientos un cuerpo a quien las enfermedades han reducido al último extremo de debilidad."
37. N. S. R. Maluf, "History of Blood Transfusion: The Use of Blood from Antiquity through the Eighteenth Century," *Journal of the History of Medicine and Allied Sciences* 9, no. 1 (January 1954): 59–107, DOI: 10.1093/jhmas/IX.1.59.
38. Burden, "Reform before La Reforma."

Chapter 5

1. For an analysis of the campaign, see Paul Garner, *Porfirio Díaz: Profiles in Power* (London: Pearson, 2001), 61–65.
2. González Quiroga, *War and Peace*, 341–53.
3. Garner, *Porfirio Díaz*, 69.
4. Mora-Torres, *Making of the Mexican Border*, 59.
5. *Memoria presentada al Congreso de la Unión por el Secretario de Estado y del Despacho de Fomento, Colonización, Industria y Comercio de la República Mexicana, Vicente Riva Palacio, corresponde al año trascurrido de diciembre de 1876 a noviembre de 1877* (México: Imprenta de Francisco Diaz de León, 1877), 6.
6. For an interesting overview of this coup, see Sierra, *Political Evolution of the Mexican People*, 355–60.
7. Leopoldo Zea, *Positivism in Mexico*, trans. Josephine Schulte (Austin: University of Texas Press, 1974).
8. Vicente Riva Palacio et al., *México a través de los siglos*, 5 vols. (México and Barcelona: Espasa y Comp., Editores, 1884).
9. *Memoria presentada al Congreso de la Unión por . . . Vicente Riva Palacio*, 443–44; also Manero, *Documentos interesantes sobre colonización*, 70–73.
10. *Memoria presentada al Congreso de la Unión por . . . Vicente Riva Palacio*, 443; also Manero, *Documentos interesantes sobre colonización*, 70.
11. For the phrase "menos política y más administración," see *De cómo vino Huerta y cómo se fue: apuntes para la historia de un régimen militar* (México: Libreria General, 1914), 1:224.

12. Sierra, *Political Evolution of the Mexican People*, 365; Garner, *Porfirio Díaz*, 70.
13. *Memoria presentada al Congreso de la Unión por . . . Vicente Riva Palacio*, 443–44; also Manero, *Documentos interesantes sobre colonización*, 70–73.
14. "Ley de 31 de mayo de 1875, autorizando al Ejecutivo Federal para que haga efectiva la colonización," in de la Maza, *Código de colonización*, 826–28.
15. For the history of Tecate, the best study is L. Bibiana Santiago Guerrero, *La gente al pie del Cuchumá: memoria histórica de Tecate* (Mexicali, BC: Fundación La Puerta, Instituto de Investigaciones Históricas, Universidad Autónoma de Baja California, 2005).
16. Dennis Thurber Proffitt III, "The Symbiotic Frontier: The Emergence of Tijuana since 1769" (PhD diss., UCLA, 1988), 192–231.
17. Guerrero, *La gente al pie del Cuchumá*, 109–10.
18. John A. Price, "Tecate: An Industrial City on the Mexican Border," *Urban Anthropology* 2, no. 1 (1973): 35–47, http://www.jstor.org/stable/40552637.
19. *El Lunes*, 4 July 1881, 1–2, quoted in Don M. Coerver, "The Porfirian Interregnum: The Presidency of Manuel Gonzalez of Mexico, 1880–1884" (PhD diss., Tulane University, 1973), 57.
20. Rafael González Bartrina, "General Carlos Pacheco: héroe nacional incomprendido," *Ensenada.net*, 21 January 2016, https://www.ensenada.net/noticias/nota_CU.php?id=34779. Porfirio Díaz was initially appointed to Fomento but served only from 1 December 1880 to 27 June 1881.
21. "Colección Porfirio Díaz VII," 1058–60, quoted in Coerver, "Porfirian Interregnum," 57.
22. Coerver, "Porfirian Interregnum," 299. See also the budgetary chart for the agency in Mireya Blanco Martínez and José Moncada Maya, "El Ministerio de Fomento, impulsor del estudio y el reconocimiento del territorio mexicano (1877–1898)," *Investigaciones Geográficas, Boletín del Instituto de Geografía, UNAM* 74, (2011): 77.
23. *Memoria . . . años trascurridos de diciembre de 1877 a diciembre de 1882*, 1:3. Original: "el ejemplo rápido y prodigioso desarrollo que, debido a la colonización, había realizado la Republica de los Estados Unidos de Norte America, aguijoneaba los deseos que, desde un principio, concibieron los gobernantes Mexicanos de colonizar nuestras vastas y fértiles regiones."
24. *Memoria . . . años trascurridos de diciembre de 1877 a diciembre de 1882*, 1:3.
25. *Memoria . . . años trascurridos de diciembre de 1877 a diciembre de 1882*, 1:3–4.
26. *Memoria . . . años trascurridos de diciembre de 1877 a diciembre de 1882*, 1:5.
27. The spontaneous immigration that Mexico did experience was from Central America and the Caribbean, and most of these sojourners migrated to Mexico only as way to travel on to the United States, especially in the 1990s and well into the first two decades of the twenty-first century. Pew Research Center, "Rise in U.S. Immigrants From El Salvador, Guatemala and Honduras Outpaces Growth from Elsewhere," December 7, 2017, https://www.pewresearch.org/hispanic/2017/12/07/rise-in-u-s-immigrants-from-el-salvador-guatemala-and-honduras-outpaces-growth-from-elsewhere/.
28. *Memoria . . . años trascurridos de diciembre de 1877 a diciembre de 1882*, 1:7–9. Note, there could well be a typographical error in the law cited here. The obvious mistake could be that he is referring to the colonization law of 31 May 1875, not 1857.

29. *Memoria . . . años trascurridos de diciembre de 1877 a diciembre de 1882*, 1:7–8.
30. Debate on the law started in earnest in the session on 29 November 1883, then it was introduced intermittently until its passage in the Chamber of Deputies on 10 December 1883. The text of the law is located in *Diario de los debates de la Cámara de Diputados, undécima legislatura constitucional de la unión*, vol. 3, *Correspondiente a las sesiones ordinarias y extraordinarias durante el primer periodo del segundo año* (México: Imprenta de G. Horcasitas, 1883), 289–410. The senate then took up the law on 14 December 1883. See *Diario de los debates de la Cámara de Senadores, undécimo congreso constitucional*, vol. 3, *Correspondiente al tercer periodo de sesiones ordinarias de 16 de septiembre a 15 de diciembre de 1883* (México: Imprenta del Gobierno, 1886),179–88. Another copy can be found in "Ley de 15 de Diciembre de 1883, mandando deslindar, medir, fraccionar y valuar los terrenos baldíos o de propiedad nacional, para obtener los necesarios para el establecimiento de colonos," in de la Maza, *Código de colonización*, 936–45.
31. See Articles 18–26 in "Ley de 15 de Diciembre de 1883," in de la Maza, *Código de colonización*, 936–45. These companies were dissolved with the Decreto de 18 de diciembre de 1909.
32. For an analysis of the history of this scientific survey, see Raymond B. Craib, *Cartographic Mexico: A History of State Fixations and Fugitive Landscapes* (Durham, NC: Duke University Press, 2004).
33. See chap. 2, "De los colonos," which outlines the social contract, especially Article 16, in de la Maza, *Código de colonización*, 941.
34. Ramón Eduardo Ruiz, *The Great Rebellion: Mexico, 1905–1924*. (New York: Norton, 1980). For a good chronology of the changing nature of these pieces of legislation, including the 1894 amendments to the 1883 law, see Vos, "Una legislación de graves consecuencias," 76–113; also Hernández, *Mexican American Colonization during the Nineteenth Century*, 25–93; José C. Moya, "A Continent of Immigrants: Postcolonial Shifts in the Western Hemisphere," *Hispanic American Historical Review* 86, no. 1 (February 2006): 1–28; McKeown, "Global Migration"; Magnus Mörner, *Adventurers and Proletarians: The Story of Migrants in Latin America* (Pittsburgh, PA: University of Pittsburgh Press; Paris: UNESCO, 1985); Germán Carrera, "Sobre la Colonomanía," *Historia Mexicana* 6, no. 4 (April–June 1957): 597–610; also Zilli Mánica, "Proyectos liberales de colonización."
35. "Ley de 15 de Diciembre de 1883," in de la Maza, *Código de colonización*, 941.
36. The most reliable, if not Spenglerian, sources are still González Navarro, *La política colonizadora del Porfiriato, La colonización en México*, and *Los extranjeros en México*.
37. Mark Wasserman, *Pesos and Politics: Business, Elites, Foreigners, and Government in Mexico, 1854–1940* (Stanford, CA: Stanford University Press, 2015), especially chap. 4.
38. Article 3, Section III in "Ley de 15 de Diciembre de 1883," in de la Maza, *Código de colonización*, 936–45.
39. Robert H. Holden, "Priorities of the State in the Survey of the Public Land in Mexico, 1876–1911," *Hispanic American Historical Review* 70, no. 4 (1990): 579–608.

40. Holden, "Priorities of the State in the Survey of the Public Land in Mexico." The total land mass of Mexico is almost 200 million hectares.
41. Cortés, "Mexican Colonies during the Porfiriato," 3–12.
42. González Navarro and Holden use these numbers based on the reports from the Ministerio de Fomento. What neither of these authors points out is the number of contracts that were never fulfilled or were rescinded or cancelled. This is very important to recognize because the correspondence and requests for colonization contracts from companies and even individual settler-colonists are quite numerous and have yet to be analyzed in their totality. Some of these requests certainly came to fruition before, during, and after 1883, but a more robust research agenda is required before we can make more concrete statements.
43. *Memoria presentada al Congreso de la Unión por el Secretario de Estado y del Despacho de Fomento, Colonización e Industria de la República Mexicana, ingeniero Manuel Fernández Leal. Corresponde a los años transcurridos de 1892 a 1896* (México: Oficina Tipográfica de la Secretaría de Fomento, 1897), 20.
44. González Navarro, *Los extranjeros en México*, 2:134.
45. Scott, *Art of Not Being Governed*, 11.
46. For an empirical analysis of European immigration to Latin America, see Moya, *Cousins and Strangers*, 45–47.
47. González Navarro, *Los extranjeros en México*, 2:134; some of these statistics also appear in González's earlier work, *La colonización en México*, 35.

Chapter 6

1. "Carta de Luis Siliceo a ciudadano ministro de Fomento, Colonización, e Industria," 5 July 1895, in "Siliceo y todo relativo a colonización," exp. 452, 1.29 (32) AHTN, p. 150. My italics.
2. "Siliceo y todo relativo a colonización," exp. 452, 1.29 (32), AHTN. The final version of the contract is also available at "Contrato celebrado con el Sr. Luis Siliceo para la compra-venta y colonización de terrenos baldíos y nacionales en los Estados de Chihuahua, Coahuila, Guerrero, México, Michoacán, Puebla, y Veracruz, 1895," exp. 365, 1.29 (06), AHTN.
3. This fact can be established with much confidence because Siliceo's business card as a repatriation agent for the Mexican government is advertised in the popular Hispano newspaper *La Prensa* at least until the 1920s.
4. By 1895, the agency had gone through several name changes and another modification as Secretario de Estado y del Despacho de Fomento, Colonización, e Industria.
5. "Siliceo y todo relativo a colonización," exp. 452, 1.29 (32), AHTN.
6. *Anales del ministerio de fomento de la República mexicana* is an example.
7. "Siliceo y todo relativo a colonización," exp. 452, 1.29 (32), AHTN.
8. "Disposición de 13 de Febrero de 1856: Promoviendo la emigración de la raza hispano-americana existente en la Alta California, para aprovecharla en la colonización del Estado de Sonora," in de la Maza *Código de colonización*, 608.

9. Almost every point of contention raised by the Científicos in the bureaucracy was backed by some legal minutiae in the 1883 Land and Colonization Law. Find several handwritten contracts with amendments in "Siliceo y todo relativo a colonización," exp. 452, 1.29 (32), AHTN, pp. 1–28.
10. Sánchez, "Regresar a la madre patria, 259–82.
11. María Elena Martínez, *Genealogical Fictions: Limpieza de Sangre, Religion, and Gender in Colonial Mexico* (Stanford, CA: Stanford University Press, 2008).
12. "Siliceo y todo relativo a colonización," exp. 452, 1.29 (32), AHTN, pp. 1–12.
13. "Siliceo y todo relativo a colonización," exp. 452, 1.29 (32), AHTN, pp. 1–2, 14–28.
14. Siliceo was a well-traveled man, but his two long-term residences appear to have been in New Orleans, Louisiana, and San Antonio, Texas.
15. González Navarro, *La colonización en México* and *Los extranjeros en México*, 2:356, 367–69; also see Cortés, "Mexican Colonies during the Porfiriato"; Sánchez, "Regresar a la madre patria."
16. The marriage certificate of Luis's parents, José Ma. Siliceo and Helena Chousal, dated 26 November 1851 establishes that José and Manuel were brothers (available on Ancestry .com, https://www.ancestry.com/discoveryui-content/view/5862028:60013, accessed 5 January 2024).
17. Joseph Allen Stout, *Schemers and Dreamers: Filibustering in Mexico, 1848–1921* (Fort Worth: Texas Christian University Press, 2002).
18. *Memoria de la Secretaría de Estado . . . escrita por . . . Manuel Siliceo.* Part of the report is reproduced in Manero, *Documentos interesantes sobre colonización*, 43–52.
19. Guillermina Peralta Santiago, "Manuel Siliceo: un liberal moderado en acción" (licentiate thesis, Escuela Nacional de Estudios Profesionales Acatlán, UNAM, 2000).
20. Lawrence Douglas Taylor Hansen, "La fiebre de oro en Sonora durante la década de 1850 y sus repercusiones diplomáticas con Estados Unidos," *Revista de El Colegio de Sonora* 7, no. 12 (1996): 107–41.
21. Standart, "Sonoran Migration to California."
22. "Disposición de 13 de Febrero de 1856," in de la Maza, *Código de colonización*, 607–12.
23. "Disposición de 13 de Febrero de 1856," in de la Maza, *Código de colonización*, 607–12. Original: "si el supremo gobierno se decide a impartir su protección al Proyecto iniciado por D. Jesús Islas, se parece que sería conveniente nombrar a este individuo agente de colonización conforme a la ley de 16 de Febrero de 1854, para que procurarse la traslación a Sonora de la población hispano-americana, poniéndose de acuerdo con el Gobierno del nuevo Estado y con el acuerdo con el agente en Hermosillo, para los terrenos que se han de dar según el número de individuos que emigren, lugar en donde se han de colocar las colonias y auxilios que se han de ministrar a los que no puedan trasladarse por su cuenta."
24. The territories of California, Sonora, Arizona, Baja California, and Sinaloa constituted this northwestern military zone/region. See Hernández, "Decree of 19 August 1848."
25. "Disposición de 13 de Febrero de 1856," in de la Maza, *Código de colonización*, 607–12. Original: "que sabedores los habitantes de Sonora de este Proyecto lo han acogido con regocijo, porque además de los beneficios que les resultaran de una población que los

ayude a cultivar sus vastos desiertos y a defenderse de los barbaros, se consiguiera que vuelvan al seno de la patria porción de sonorenses que existen en la California y que por falta de recursos no pueden regresar al país donde vieron la luz primera."

26. Wolfe, "Settler Colonialism and the Elimination of the Native," 393–94.
27. "Disposición de 13 de Febrero de 1856," en de la Maza, *Código de colonización*, 608.
28. Sociologists Alejandro Portes and Ruben Rumbaut describe "reactive ethnicity" as originating in a "confrontation with an adverse native mainstream and the rise of defensive identities and solidarities to counter it." *Legacies: The Story of the Immigrant Second Generation* (Berkeley: University of California Press, 2001), 284.
29. Stout, *Schemers and Dreamers*, 38–55. Ressentiment is a concept encompassing intense resentment and bitterness that individuals feel when they perceive themselves as socially or morally disadvantaged, particularly by others or society. It goes beyond regular resentment, involving a belief in the victim's moral superiority and attribution of one's suffering to the perceived moral failings of others. This term is often used to analyze the psychological and emotional dynamics behind social and political movements rooted in a sense of victimization that seek retribution or revenge. On ressentiment, see Deleuze, *Nietzsche and Philosophy* (London: Bloomsbury Academic, 2006), 107.
30. "Disposición de 13 de Febrero de 1856," en de la Maza, *Código de colonización*, 608.
31. "Desautorización de José de Aguilar, gobernador de Sonora, para que Jesús Islas, quien se supone agente de colonización, envíe a sonorenses radicados en California a colonizar terrenos en Sonora. Ures, 1 julio 1856." Fondo Pablo Herrera Carrillo, 1.74, Archivo del Instituto de Investigaciones Históricas, Universidad Autónoma de Baja California.
32. Robert Humphrey Forbes, *Crabb's Filibustering Expedition into Sonora, 1857* (Tucson: Arizona Silhouettes, 1952). Much of the primary information is drawn from "Execution of Colonel Crabb and Associates: Message from the President of the United States communicating official information and correspondence [supplied by the secretary of state] in relation to the execution of Colonel Crabb and his associates (Washington, DC: US Congress, House: 1858). A list of government officials making this claim can be found in "Desautorización de José de Aguilar," 1.74, Archivo del Instituto de Investigaciones Históricas.
33. "La Repatriación," *El Fronterizo*, 29 June 1895, 2.
34. Cortés, "Mexican Colonies during the Porfiriato," 8.
35. For some of Manuel Siliceo's familial and political background, see Guillermina Peralta Santiago, "Manuel Siliceo: un liberal moderado en acción," (Licentiate thesis, Escuela Nacional de Estudios Profesionales Acatlán, UNAM, 2000).
36. Baptism certificate for Luis Gonzaga Homobano Siliceo, from ancestry.com, p. 260.
37. Anything from the Mexican Migration Project is an excellent and obligatory starting point for anyone seeking information on this topic. A good starting point would be Jorge Durand and Douglas S. Massey, *Crossing the Border: Research from the Mexican Migration Project* (New York: Russell Sage Foundation, 2004).
38. Entry for Marie Camelia Debat in 1880 census, City of New Orleans, Louisiana, 2 June 1880, New Orleans State Archives, p. 4, Sup. Dist. 4, Enum. Dist. 27.

39. Cortés, "Mexican Colonies during the Porfiriato," 1–14; Sánchez, "Regresar a la madre patria; González Navarro, *La política colonizadora del Porfiriato*, *La colonización en México*, and *Los extranjeros en México* 2:356, 367–70.
40. As per the agreement in the colonization contract, Díaz administration officials terminated the subsidy of *El Colono* in 1900. See "Carta de Primera Sección Iª a Luis Siliceo," 21 Julio 1900, in "Siliceo y todo relativo a colonización," exp. 452, 1.29 (32), p. 360, AHTN.
41. "De viaje," *El Colono*, 10 April 1896; Sánchez, "Regresar a la madre patria."
42. The affiliation with *La Repatriación* is described in "La Repatriación. Suspensión de facultades y urgencia de resolución," *El Colono*, vol. 2, no. 15, 7 June 1897, 1. For more details on Siliceo's newspaper business, see Evelyne Sánchez, "Regresar a la madre patria."
43. Dozens of Siliceo's advertisements for his Repatriation Agency appear in *La Prensa* of San Antonio throughout the 1920s. For one example, see the edition of 15 October 1920.
44. Advertisement in *La Prensa*, 24 September 1920.
45. "C. W. Wampler solicita celebrar un contrato para la extracción de aluminio y la aplicación de ese metal a la fabricación de artefactos . . . ," 26 April 1897, exp. 4, caja 34, and "Luis Siliceo a nombre del Sr. C. W. Wampler solicita establecer—un contrato para establecer fábricas de carburo de calcio," . . . ," 12 January 1897, exp. 3, caja 34, both in Fondo Fomento, Serie: Industrias Nuevas, Archivo General de la Nacion (hereafter AGN).
46. "Luis Siliceo solicita celebrar un contrato para la fabricación de artefactos de metal esmaltado, galvanizado, etc.," 29 July 1897, exp. 2, caja 35, Fondo Fomento, Serie: Nuevas Industrias, AGN.
47. "Carta de Luis Siliceo al Director del Conservatorio Nacional de Música," 25 September 1901, and "Carta de J. Rivas a Secretario de Justicia e Instrucción Pública," 25 September 1901, both in exp. 2, caja 35, Fondo Fomento, Nuevas Industrias, AGN.
48. Florescano, *National Narratives in Mexico*, 310–50.

Chapter 7

1. "Ley de 15 de Diciembre de 1883," in de la Maza, *Código de colonización*, 936–45. For references to the 1894 law, see Vos, "Una legislación de graves consecuencias," 87–91.
2. Nicolás Kanellos and Helvetia Martell, *Hispanic Periodicals in the United States, Origins to 1960: A Brief History and Comprehensive Bibliography* (Houston: Arte Público Press, 2000), 304.
3. "Condición de los mexicanos del otro lado del Bravo." *El Correo de Laredo. Periódico Imparcial y de Noticias*, no. 193, 19 April 1892, 1. This is the first article in the series.
4. "Condición de los Mexicanos del otro lado del Bravo."
5. Portes and Rumbaut, *Legacies*, 284.
6. *Encyclopaedia Britannica Online*, s.v., "yellow journalism," https://www.britannica.com/topic/yellow-journalism; Matthew Robert Kerbel, *If It Bleeds, It Leads: An Anatomy of Television News* (New York: Taylor & Francis, 2018).

7. Édouard René Lefèbvre de Laboulaye has an extensive biography, but the reference here is to his role in gifting the Statue of Liberty, the quintessential symbol of American freedom, to the United States.
8. "Condición de los mexicanos del otro lado del Bravo," *El Correo de Laredo*, 19 April 1892, 1–2.
9. "Condición de los mexicanos del otro lado del Bravo." *El Correo de Laredo*, 19 April 1892, 1–2.
10. "Los mexicanos en Estados Unidos. La repatriación. ¿Porque no se van a México?" parts 1 and 2, *El Correo de Laredo*, no. 194, 21 April 1892, 1–7, and no. 195, 23 April 1892, 1–2.
11. Audrey Smedley, "History of the Idea of Race . . . and Why it Matters," paper presented at the Race, Human Variation and Disease: Consensus and Frontiers conference, sponsored by the American Anthropological Association, Warrenton, VA, 14–17 March 2007.
12. "Los mexicanos en Estados Unidos. La repatriación. ¿Porque no se van a México?" part 3, *El Correo de Laredo*, no. 196, 26 April 1892, pp. 1–2.
13. "¿Porque no se van a México?" part 1, *El Correo de Laredo*, 21 April 1892, 1–7. The statement that fifty newspapers claim to be Mexican seems like a significant exaggeration.
14. Moyano Pahissa, *Antología*.
15. Charles B. Guignon, "Heidegger's 'Authenticity' Revisited." *Review of Metaphysics* 38, no. 2 (1984): 321–39, https://www.jstor.org/stable/20128154.
16. "¿Porque no se van a México?" part 2, *El Correo de Laredo*, 23 April 1892, 1–2.
17. Lawrence Douglas Taylor Hansen, "La repatriación de mexicanos de 1848 a 1980 y su papel en la colonización de la región fronteriza septentrional de México," *Relaciones* 18, no. 69 (1997): 198–212.
18. "¿Porque no se van a México?" part 2, *El Correo de Laredo*, 23 April 1892, 1–2.
19. "¿Porque no se van a México?" part 3, *El Correo de Laredo*, 26 April 1892, 1–2.
20. "¿Porque no se van a México?" part 3, *El Correo de Laredo*, 26 April 1892, 1–2.
21. Richard A. Garcia, *Rise of the Mexican American Middle Class: San Antonio, 1929–1941* (College Station: Texas A&M University Press, 1991).
22. "¿Porque no se van a México?" part 3, *El Correo de Laredo*, 26 April 1892, 1–2.
23. *El Correo* did not use the term "gente decente" but did suggest similar understandings of social and cultural hierarchies. For an excellent analysis, see Leticia Magda Garza-Falcón, *Gente Decente: A Borderlands Response to the Rhetoric of Dominance* (Austin: University of Texas Press, 2010).
24. "¿Porque no se van a México?" part 3, *El Correo de Laredo*, 26 April 1892, 1–2.
25. "¿Porque no se van a México?" part 3, *El Correo de Laredo*, 26 April 1892, 1–2.
26. "Condición de los Mexicanos," *El Correo de Laredo*, 19 April 1892, 1–2; "¿Porque no se van a México?" part 3, *El Correo de Laredo*, 26 April 1892, 1–2.
27. Carta de Lic. Ignacio Mariscal a M. Fernández Leal, 24 June 1892, in "Manuel A. Saldaña propone traer inmigrantes a la República repatriando mexicanos que han eludido la acción de la justicia," Año de 1892, no. 103, 3742-33, AHSRE.

28. Australia and New Zealand immediately come to mind. Veracini, *World Turned Inside Out*, 73, 78, 186, 210–18, 245, 268.
29. On "thick description" see Clifford Geertz, *The Interpretation of Cultures* (London: Basic Books, 1973).
30. "¿Porque no se van a México?" part 3, *El Correo de Laredo*, 26 April 1892, 1–2.
31. Carta de Manuel A. Saldaña a Señor General Hinojosa, 28 March 1892, no. 103, 2742-33, AHSRE.
32. Colonia Patria in Tamaulipas is a good example of honorific naming. See "La Colonia Patria," *El Colono*, vol. 2, no. 7, 10 April 1897, 4–5.
33. Carta de Manuel A. Saldaña a Señor General Hinojosa, 28 March 1892, no. 103, 2742-33, AHSRE.
34. Attila L. Nemesi, "What Discourse Goals Can Be Accomplished by the Use of Hyperbole?" *Acta Linguistica Hungarica* 51, nos. 3–4 (2004): 351–78, DOI: 10.1556/aling.51.2004.3-4.6
35. Carta de Manuel A. Saldaña a Señor General Hinojosa. On common sense ideas, see Arun K. Patnaik, "Gramsci's Concept of Common Sense: Towards a Theory of Subaltern Consciousness in Hegemony Processes," *Economic and Political Weekly* 23, no. 5 (1988): 2–10. https://www.jstor.org/stable/4378042.
36. Carta de Manuel A. Saldaña a Señor General Hinojosa, 28 March 1892, no. 103, 2742-33, AHSRE.
37. Carta de Manuel A. Saldaña a Señor General Hinojosa.
38. "Al vuelo," *El Colono*, vol. 3, no. 15, 7 June 1898, 1–4.
39. Guha, "Prose of Counter-Insurgency."
40. Carta de Manuel A. Saldaña a Señor General Hinojosa, 28 March 1892, no. 103, 2742-33, AHSRE.
41. Carta de Manuel A. Saldaña a Señor General Hinojosa.
42. "Proyectos de colonización presentados por la junta directiva del ramo," in de la Maza, *Código de colonización*, 368–98.
43. Moyano Pahissa, *Antología*.
44. An excellent example of the many debates and positions that are generated with these large movements of people, please see Fernando Saul Alanis Enciso, *They Should Stay There*.

Chapter 8

1. The year 1892 generated renewed interest in Mexico resettlement projects, and the activities of Lorenzo Abeyta of Colorado and Luis Siliceo of Texas certainly prompted this new wave of debates in the Greater Mexico public sphere. "La emigración a México," *El Correo de Laredo*, no. 197, 28 April 1892, 1–2, mentions the case of Abeyta (spelled Abeitia in the piece).
2. Because of the common practice of reprinting articles, we have information from and knowledge of many newspapers (like *La Repatriación*) without having any physical

evidence of their existence. In other words, we know that they existed, but do not have any archived copies of them.

3. "Repatriación: Los mexicanos residentes en Texas," *El Fronterizo*, no. 864, 29 June 1895, 1. Simultaneously, the newspaper *El País* of Mexico City was running some positive articles on repatriation. Interestingly given the importance of familial networks to colonization, the editor of *El País* was José Irineo Paz Flores (1836–1924), grandfather of the Nobel Prize–winning Mexican writer Octavio Paz. The younger Paz wrote quite disparagingly of the diaspora in the United States in his depiction of the pachuco. But I digress. . . .
4. "Repatriación: Los mexicanos residentes en Texas," *El Fronterizo*, 29 June 1895, 1.
5. "Repatriación: Los mexicanos residentes en Texas," *El Fronterizo*, 29 June 1895, 1.
6. "Repatriación: Los mexicanos residentes en Texas," *El Fronterizo*, 29 June 1895, 1.
7. In other words, and paraphrasing Hegel, you need others to identify your consciousness and identity is influenced by how others see you. The best exposition of this idea can be read in Francis Fukuyama, *Identity: The Demand for Dignity and the Politics of Resentment* (New York: Farrar, Straus, and Giroux, 2018).
8. "Repatriación: Los mexicanos residentes en Texas," *El Fronterizo*, 29 June 1895, 1.
9. "Repatriación: Los mexicanos residentes en Texas," *El Fronterizo*, 29 June 1895, 1.
10. José A. Chacón, "Octaviano Larrazolo: New Mexico's Greatest Governor," *La Luz* 1, no. 7 (November 1972).
11. The twenty-first-century media have a historical memory of about two weeks. See Edward S. Herman and Noam Chomsky, *Manufacturing Consent: The Political Economy of the Mass Media* (New York: Pantheon, 1988).
12. "La repatriación," 29 June 1895, *El Fronterizo*, 2.
13. "La repatriación," 29 June 1895, *El Fronterizo*, 2.
14. "Disposición de 13 de Febrero de 1856," in de la Maza *Código de colonización*, 607–12. Also published in *Ministerio de Fomento*, 10 May 1856.
15. "La repatriación," *El Fronterizo*, 29 June 1895, 2.
16. For a brief overview of the 1856 repatriations from Alta California to Sonora, see Hernández, "Decree of 19 August 1848."
17. "La repatriación," 29 June 1895, *El Fronterizo*, 2.
18. See Friedrich Katz, *The Life and Times of Pancho Villa* (Stanford, CA: Stanford University Press, 1998), 11–19; Ana María Alonso, *Thread of Blood: Colonialism, Revolution, and Gender on Mexico's Northern Frontier* (Tucson: University of Arizona Press, 1995); Daniel Nugent: *Spent Cartridges of Revolution: An Anthropological History of Namiquipa, Chihuahua* (Chicago: University of Chicago Press, 1994); Jane-Dale Lloyd, *Cinco ensayos sobre cultura material de rancheros y medieros del noroeste de Chihuahua, 1886–1910* (México: Universidad Iberoamericana, 2001), also *El proceso de modernización capitalista en el noroeste de Chihuahua, 1880–1910* (México: Universidad Iberoamericana, 1987); Daniel Nugent, ed., *Rural Revolt in Mexico and U.S. Intervention* (San Diego: Center for U.S.-Mexican Studies, University of California, 1988); María Teresa Koreck, "Espacio y revolución en el noreste de Chihuahua," *Iztapalapa: Revista de Ciencias Sociales y Humanidades* 17 (1989): 103–22; José Angel Hernández, "Violence

as Communication: The Revolt of La Ascensión, Chihuahua (1892)," *Landscapes of Violence* 2, no. 1, art. 6 (2012).

19. Frederick Jackson Turner, *The Significance of the Frontier in American History* (Madison: State Historical Society of Wisconsin, 1894).
20. Ernest Renan, "What Is a Nation?" in *Qu'est-ce qu'une nation? et autres essais politiques* (Paris: Presses-Pocket, 1992).
21. "La repatriación," *El Fronterizo*, 29 June 1895, 2.
22. "La repatriación," *El Fronterizo*, 29 June 1895, 2.
23. Aviezer Tucker, *Our Knowledge of the Past: A Philosophy of Historiography* (New York: Cambridge University Press, 2004), 85.
24. "La repatriación," *El Fronterizo*, 29 June 1895, 2.
25. On the human impulse to constantly seek an "elsewhere," read Lorenzo Veracini's excellent work, *The World Turned Inside Out*, 1–26.
26. "La repatriación," *El Fronterizo*, 27 July 1895, 1.
27. "Carta de Luis Siliceo a Ciudadano Ministro de Fomento Colonización e Industria, 5 Julio 1895," exp. 452, "Siliceo y todo relativo a Colonización," 1.29 (32) AHTN.
28. "La repatriación," *El Fronterizo*, 27 July 1895, 1.
29. "La repatriación," *El Fronterizo*, 27 July 1895, 1.
30. "La repatriación," *El Fronterizo*, 27 July 1895, 1.
31. See "Ley de 15 de Diciembre de 1883," in de la Maza, *Código de colonización*, 936–45.
32. "La Repatriación," *El Fronterizo*, 27 July 1895, 1.
33. Brian Bow and Arturo Santa-Cruz, "Mexican Anti-Americanism and Regional Integration in North America," *Norteamérica* 6, no. 2, (2011): 35–66.
34. "La repatriación," *El Fronterizo*, 27 July 1895, 1.
35. "La repatriación," *El Fronterizo*, 27 July 1895, 1
36. Arnoldo De León and Kenneth L. Stewart, *Tejanos and the Numbers Game: A Socio-Historical Interpretation from the Federal Censuses, 1850–1900* (Albuquerque: University of New Mexico Press, 1989), 20.

Chapter 9

1. "Gracias estimables colegas," *El Colono*, vol. 1, no. 1, 10 November 1895, 1–2.
2. Copies of *El Colono* dating from November 1895 to October 1898 are located UNAM, Fondo Reservado.
3. By "propaganda," I mean "information, ideas, opinions, or images, often only giving one part of an argument, that are broadcast, published, or in some other way spread with the intention of influencing people's opinions." *Cambridge Advanced Learner's Dictionary and Thesaurus*, s.v. "propaganda," https://dictionary.cambridge.org/us/dictionary/english/propaganda.
4. Moya, *Cousins and Strangers*, 35, 38.
5. Data from Peter J. Hugill, *World Trade since 1431* (Baltimore, MD: Johns Hopkins University Press, 1993), 128; also, Martin Stopford, *Maritime Economics*, 3rd ed. (London: Routledge, 2009).

6. Lester D. Langley, *The Americas in the Age of Revolution, 1750–1850* (New Haven, CT: Yale University Press, 1996).
7. Moya, "Continent of Immigrants," 1–28.
8. Adam McKeown reminds us that between forty-eight and fifty-two million Indians and southern Chinese migrated to Southeast Asia, the coast of the Indian Ocean, and the islands of the South Pacific, while forty-six to fifty-one million Russians and northeastern Asians migrated to various points in Manchuria, Siberia, Central Asia, and Japan. See "Global Migration."
9. "Nuestro propósito," *El Colono* vol. 1, no. 1, 10 November 1895.
10. Exp. 365, "Contrato Celebrado con el Sr. Luis Siliceo para la compra-venta y colonización de terrenos baldíos y nacionales en los Estados de Chihuahua, Coahuila, Guerrero, México, Michoacán, Puebla, y Veracruz, 1895," 1.29 (06) AHTN. All handwritten contracts with amendments are in exp. 452, "Siliceo y todo relativo a colonización," 1.29 (32), AHTN, 1–28.
11. As per the contractual agreement, Díaz administration officials terminated the subsidy for *El Colono* after five years. I have located a complete set of bimonthly publications from 10 November 1895 to 22 October 1898, so it is possible that there are later editions that have disappeared. For the correspondence terminating the subsidy for *El Colono*, see "Carta de Primera Sección Iª a Luis Siliceo, 21 Julio 1900," exp. 452, "Siliceo y todo relativo a colonización," 1.29 (32), no. 360, ATHN. Siliceo pleaded with the administration to continue subsidizing the newspaper, but in their response, the Científicos at Fomento refused his request based simply on the formalities of the contract.
12. Every article of the "La repatriación" series in *El Colono* is either a reprint from a newspaper of a similar mindset or is republished in Siliceo's other newspaper, *La Repatriación*.
13. Cortés, "Mexican Colonies during the Porfiriato," 3–12.
14. Kunitsugu Kosaka, "The Kyoto School and the Issue of "Overcoming Modernity," In *The Philosophy of the Kyoto School*, ed. Masakatsu Fujita (Singapore: Springer, 2018), 233–51.
15. Harry Harootunian, *Overcome by Modernity: History, Culture, and Commodity in Interwar Japan* (Princeton, NJ: Princeton University Press, 2000).
16. Benedict Anderson, *Imagined Communities: Reflections on the Origin and Spread of Nationalism*, reprint ed. (New York: Verso, 2003), 36, 44; also Lomnitz-Adler, *Deep Mexico, Silent Mexico*, 3–34.
17. Lomnitz-Adler, *Deep Mexico, Silent Mexico*, 5.
18. E. J. Hobsbawm, *Nations and Nationalism since 1780: Programme, Myth, Reality* (Cambridge: Cambridge University Press, 1990), 92.
19. Wolfe, "Settler Colonialism and the Elimination of the Native."
20. José Angel Hernández, "*El México Perdido y Anhelado:* The Prose of Settler Colonialism amidst the Diaspora," in *Writing/Righting History: Twenty-Five Years of Recovering the US Hispanic Literary Heritage*, ed. Clara Lomas and Antonia Castañeda (Houston: Arte Público Press, 2020): 185–224.
21. Lomnitz-Adler, *Deep Mexico, Silent Mexico*, 3–34.

22. "De a aquí y de allá. El amor a la patria," *El Colono* vol. 1, no. 2, 25 November 1895, 13–14.
23. *Cambridge Advanced Learner's Dictionary and Thesaurus*, s.v., "nostalgia," https://dictionary.cambridge.org/us/dictionary/english/nostalgia.
24. "De a aquí y de allá. El amor a la patria." *El Colono,* 25 November 1895, 13–14.
25. "El país del porvenir. The Country of the Future," *El Colono*, vol. 1, no. 2, 25 November 1895, 15–16.
26. Georg Wilhelm Friedrich Hegel, *Phenomenology of Spirit* (Oxford: Oxford University Press, 1979); Vilém Flusser, *The Freedom of the Migrant: Objections to Nationalism* (Chicago: University of Illinois Press, 2003), 16–20.
27. "De aquí y de allá. El amor a la patria." *El Colono*, 25 November 1895, 13–14.
28. "De aquí y de allá. El amor a la patria." *El Colono*, 25 November 1895, 13–14. Original: "pasados algunos años de vicisitudes y de trastornos, de seguir tras el fantasma que se llama felicidad, de haber gozado de todas las diversiones que ofrece la vida, de haber recorrido provincias y naciones diversas, y de haberse proporcionado una subsistencia cómoda y asegurado su porvenir, un sentimiento permanece incesante en el fondo de su alma: el de volver al lugar en que ha respirado por la primera vez."
29. "De aquí y de allá. El amor a la patria." *El Colono*, 25 November 1895, 13–14. Original: "feliz el hombre que al fin de sus días se halla rodeado de su familia en el pueblo en que ha nacido, que recuerda con orgullo en sus pasadas glorias consagradas a su patria; que ve aproximarse la hora de bajar al sepulcro, en medio de los encantos del bienestar, teniendo una mano amiga que vaya a cerrar sus ojos, y personas queridas que reciben su último suspiro y derramen una lágrima sobre la loza de su tumba."
30. Renan, "What Is a Nation," in *Qu'est-ce qu'une nation?* 9–10.
31. "De aquí y de allá. El amor a la patria," *El Colono*, 25 November 1895, 13–14.
32. Hegel, *Lectures on the Philosophy of World History*, 136.
33. "Al vuelo," *El Colono*, vol. 3, no. 14, 23 May 1898, 3–5. *Al vuelo* could have any number of meanings, and the authors never clarify their intention, but a rough translation would be "on the fly," "to fly," "prepare to fly," or "on the return," rather like saying "I'll circle back to you."
34. Cortés, "Mexican Colonies during the Porfiriato," 3–12.
35. Land clearing in the nineteenth century would today fall under the category of deforestation or something like the discourse of modern-day environmentalism. There was little of this discourse in *El Colono*, in fact, quite the opposite.
36. "Al vuelo," *El Colono*, 23 May 1898, 3–5.
37. "Al vuelo," *El Colono*, 23 May 1898, 3–5.
38. "Al vuelo," *El Colono*, 23 May 1898, 3–5.
39. Today, Güémez has gained municipal status: http://www.guemez.gob.mx/.
40. "Al vuelo," *El Colono*, vol. 3, no. 15, 7 June 1898, 1–4. Original: "¡Soldados del Progreso, sostenerse firmes, mano a las manceras, vuelta y media a las tierras, paso del caballo y marchen . . . !
41. "Al vuelo," *El Colono*, 7 June 1898, 1–4.
42. Veracini, *World Turned Inside Out*, 1–20.

43. "Al vuelo," *El Colono*, 7 June 1898, 1–4.
44. By "positive," I mean not only the quality of not being negative, but also the epistemological thinking that emerged from positivist philosophy à la August Comte. The hierarchy of supposed "human superiority" is one of hallmarks of this nineteenth-century philosophy.

Chapter 10

1. For an excellent analysis and exposition of this question, see John R. Chávez, *The Lost Land: The Chicano Image of the Southwest* (Albuquerque: University of New Mexico Press, 1984), 1–22.
2. Siliceo's affiliation with the newspaper *La Repatriación* is described in "La Repatriación. Suspensión de facultades y urgencia de resolución," *El Colono*, vol. 2, no. 15, 7 June 1897, 1; Sánchez, "Regresar a la madre patria."
3. Gilles Deleuze and Félix Guattari, *A Thousand Plateaus: Capitalism and Schizophrenia* (Minneapolis: University of Minnesota Press, 1987).
4. "Nuestro propósito," *El Colono*, vol. 1, no. 2, 10 November 1895.
5. Anthony Gabriel Meléndez, *So All Is Not Lost: The Poetics of Print in Nuevomexicano Communities, 1834–1958* (Albuquerque: University of New Mexico Press, 1997), 14, 21, 30.
6. Kanellos, *Hispanic Immigrant Literature.*
7. For examples of coverage in *El Clamor Público*, see "Emigración a Sonora. A los mexicanos, hispano americanos y californios: Manifiesto," *El Clamor Público*, 16 February 1856.
8. Kanellos, *Hispanic Immigrant Literature*, chap. 3.
9. González Navarro, *Los extranjeros en México*, 2:367–69.
10. Dirk Hoerder, *Cultures in Contact: World Migrations in the Second Millennium* (Durham, NC: Duke University Press, 2002), 339–44.
11. William J. Bernstein, *The Delusions of Crowds: Why People Go Mad in Groups* (New York: Grove/Atlantic, 2021).
12. For a study of "calidad," during the so-called colonial period, see Douglas R. Cope, *The Limits of Racial Domination: Plebeian Society in Colonial Mexico City, 1660–1720* (Madison: University of Wisconsin Press, 1994).
13. Moyano Pahissa, *Antología.*
14. El Director [Luis Siliceo], "La repatriación," *El Colono*, 10 November 1895, 2.
15. El Director [Luis Siliceo], "La repatriación," *El Colono*, 10 November 1895, 1.
16. Hayden V. White, *Metahistory: The Historical Imagination in Nineteenth-Century Europe* (Baltimore, MD: Johns Hopkins University Press, 2014).
17. In 1895–1900, Mexican GDP grew at around 5 percent per year, which for a few years was considerably better than U.S. economic performance. Siliceo himself made this observation in "200,000," *El Colono*, vol. 2, no. 5, 10 January 1897, 1–3. On annual GDP growth, see Edward Beatty, *Institutions and Investment: The Political Basis of*

Industrialization in Mexico before 1911 (Stanford, CA: Stanford University Press, 2011), 23.

18. Kanellos, *Hispanic Immigrant Literature*, 52.
19. For the 1872 case in New Mexico, see Hernández, *Mexican American Colonization during the Nineteenth Century*, 165–79.
20. Richard Hofstadter, *Social Darwinism in American Thought* (Boston: Beacon Press, 1964), 85–104.
21. "La repatriación," *El Colono*, vol. 1, no. 2, s25 November 1895, 1–2.
22. These ideas are folk beliefs elevated to scientific jargon. See Audrey Smedley, *Race in North America: Origin and Evolution of a Worldview* (New York: Taylor & Francis, 2018).
23. Moisés González Navarro and Dirección General de Estadística, *Estadísticas sociales del Porfiriato: 1877–1910* (México: Talleres Gráficos de la Nación, 1956), 150.
24. "El país del porvenir. The Country of the Future," *El Colono*, vol. 1, no. 2, 25 November 1895, 15–16. For an earlier reference from overseas, see Thomas Unett Brocklehurst, *Mexico To-day: A Country with a Great Future, and a Glance at the Prehistoric Remains and Antiquities of the Montezumas* (London: J. Murray, 1883).
25. "La repatriación," *El Colono*, 25 November 1895, 1–2.
26. Stabb, "Indigenism and Racism in Mexican Thought"; Powell, "Mexican Intellectuals and the Indian Question." On Porfirian indigenism, see Tenorio-Trillo, *Mexico at the World's Fairs*, 170, 239, 250.
27. Terry G. Jordan, "The German Settlement of Texas after 1865," *Southwestern Historical Quarterly* 73, no. 2 (1969): 193–212.
28. "La colonización que conviene a México," *El Colono*, vol. 1, no. 2, 10 November 1895, 3.
29. "Contrato celebrado con el Sr. Luis Siliceo para la compra-venta y colonización de terrenos baldíos . . . ," exp. 365, 1.29 (06), AHTN.
30. "La repatriación," *El Colono*, 25 November 1895, 1.
31. "Siliceo y todo relativo a colonización," exp. 452, 1.29 (32) AHTN, pp. 1–28, 180–82.
32. On "cultural capital," see Pierre Bourdieu, *Distinction: A Social Critique of the Judgement of Taste* (London: Taylor & Francis, 2013).
33. "Ley de 15 de Diciembre de 1883, mandando deslindar, medir, fraccionar y valuar los terrenos baldíos ó de propiedad nacional, para obtener los necesarios para el establecimiento de colonos," In *Código de colonización*, 941.
34. Perhaps Luis Siliceo's family connection to Manuel Siliceo, a previous secretary of fomento, could have influenced engineer Fernández Leal to award him such an impressive contract.
35. Katz, *Life and Times of Pancho Villa*, 16.
36. "La repatriación," *El Colono*, 25 November 1895, 1–2.
37. Siliceo's maternal grandparents were from France, and his first wife from Spain, based on the database of birth and baptismal records on Ancestry.com.
38. Loïc Wacquant, "A Concise Genealogy and Anatomy of Habitus," *Sociological Review* 64 (2016): 64–72.

39. For an analysis of anti-Spanish sentiment during this era, particularly among the Francophile Científico classes, see González Navarro, *Los extranjeros en México*, 2:135–202.
40. "La colonización que conviene a México," *El Colono*, 10 November 1895, 3.
41. José C. Moya, "The Positive Side of Stereotypes: Jewish Anarchists in Early-Twentieth-Century Buenos Aires," *Jewish History* 18 (2004): 19–48. DOI: 10.1023/B:JEHI.0000005735.80946.27.
42. "La repatriación," *El Colono* 25 November 1895, 1–2.
43. Harootunian, *Overcome by Modernity*, 34–94.
44. "La repatriación," *El Colono*, 25 November 1895, 1–2.
45. Stabb, "Indigenism and Racism in Mexican Thought; Powell, "Mexican Intellectuals and the Indian Question."
46. "Siliceo y todo relativo a Colonización," exp. 452, 1.29 (32) AHTN, pp. 1–28.
47. Wolfe, "Settler Colonialism and the Elimination of the Native," 393–94.
48. Edward Reynolds, "The Alabama Negro Colony in Mexico," *Journal of Negro History* 53, no. 3 (1968): 243–68.
49. Cortés, "Mexican Colonies during the Porfiriato," 8; John McKiernan-González, *Fevered Measures: Public Health and Race at the Texas-Mexico Border, 1848–1942* (Durham, NC: Duke University Press, 2012), especially chaps. 2–4; Reynolds, "Alabama Negro Colony in Mexico."
50. "La repatriación," *El Colono*, 25 November 1895, 1–2.
51. For some reports on epidemics in the Italian colonies, consult *Memoria presentada al Congreso de la Unión por . . . General Carlos Pacheco*, 1:16–20.
52. "La repatriación," *El Colono*, 25 November 1895, 1–2.
53. *El Colono* also reflected the ideas of a particular social class. See Ana María Carrillo, "Economía, política, y salud pública en el México porfiriano (1876–1910)," *História, Ciências, Saúde Manguinhos* 9 (2002): 67–87.
54. Joseph Stalin, *Dialectical and Historical Materialism (September 1938)* (Moscow: Foreign Languages Publishing House, 1949), 3.
55. Hofstadter, *Social Darwinism in American Thought*, 123–24.
56. "La repatriación," *El Colono*, 25 November 1895, 1–2.
57. "La repatriación," *El Colono*, 25 November 1895, 1–2.
58. Übermensch is from Friedrich Nietzsche, *Thus Spake Zarathustra, A Book for All and None*, trans. Thomas Common (New York: Modern Library, 1883).
59. Natalia Priego, "Microbiology in Mexico and Brazil in the Late XIX and Early XX Centuries," *Horizontes, Bragança Paulista* 21 (2003): 27–35.
60. "La repatriación," *El Colono* 25 November 1895, 1–2.
61. Luis Siliceo is buried in San Fernando Cemetery, San Antonio; his headstone bears the dates 1856–1928.
62. De León, *The Tejano Community*, 81.
63. "Al vuelo," *El Colono*, vol. 3, no. 15, 7 June 1898, 1–4.
64. For a reference to "prodigal sons" returning to the homeland, see "La repatriación: mexicanos que volverán pronto," *El Colono*, 25 June 1896, 1.

Chapter 11

1. For an explanation of the term "Mexico-Texano," see note 1 in the introduction.
2. For Mexico, see Beatty, *Institutions, and Investment*, 23. For the United States, David O. Whitten, "Depression of 1893," in *EH.Net Encyclopedia*, ed. Robert Whaples, August 14, 2001, http://eh.net/encyclopedia/the-depression-of-1893/.
3. Whitten, "Depression of 1893."
4. Siliceo himself made this observation in "200,000," *El Colono*, vol. 2, no. 5, 10 January 1897, 1–3.
5. Donald B. Keesing, "Structural Change Early in Development: Mexico's Changing Industrial and Occupational Structure from 1895 to 1950," *Journal of Economic History* 29, no. 4 (1969): 716–38, http://www.jstor.org/stable/2115707; also see Oscar Alfredo Erquizio Espinal, *Ciclos económicos de México* (México: USON, 2006).
6. Arjun Appadurai, *Modernity at Large: Cultural Dimensions of Globalization* (Minneapolis: University of Minnesota Press, 1996).
7. Whitten, "Depression of 1893."
8. Mora-Torres, *Making of the Mexican Border*, 128–33; González Navarro and Dirección General de Estadística, *Estadísticas sociales del Porfiriato.*
9. "200,000," *El Colono*, 10 January 1897, 1.
10. "Muy interesante aviso. A los mexicanos que quieren inscribirse para volver a la patria," *El Colono*, vol. 2, no. 5, 25 March 1897, 7–8.
11. See "La Junta de Prairie Lea," "La Junta Auxiliar de Taylor," "La Junta Auxiliar de Manor," and "La Junta Auxiliar de Repatriación de Corpus Christi" *El Colono*, vol. 2, no. 17, 7 July 1897, 4–5.
12. See, for example, "Nuevas juntas de repatriación; acta de la Junta de Repatriación de San Antonio, Texas," *El Colono*, vol. 3, no. 13, 7 May 1898, 5.
13. "La repatriación," *El Colono*, 25 November 1895, 1–2.
14. "200,000," *El Colono*, 10 January 1897, 1.
15. David Montejano, *Anglos and Mexicans in the Making of Texas,1836–1986* (Austin: University of Texas Press, 1987), 66–67.
16. "Muy interesante aviso. A los mexicanos que quieren inscribirse para volver a la patria," *El Colono*, 25 March 1897, 7.
17. "Carta de Ignacio Tovar, Miguel Guido, y Librado M. Carranza a Luis Siliceo," *El Colono*, vol. 2, no. 5, 25 March 1897, 6–7.
18. "Condiciones necesarias para asegurar un éxito en las empresas de colonización," *El Colono*, vol. 2, no. 20, 23 August 1897, 4–5.
19. For an overview of these colonization experts, especially engineers, see González Milea, "El 'poblamiento español' en la colonización," 105–15.
20. See Aboites Aguilar, "La Comisión Nacional de Colonización."
21. Hernández, "Indios Bárbaros and the Making of Mexican Colonization Policy after Independence."
22. Katz, *Life and Times of Pancho Villa*, 16–20.

23. "Condiciones necesarias para asegurar un éxito en las empresas de colonización," *El Colono*, 23 August 1897, 4–5.
24. Government officials, newspapers, and politicians frequently leveled accusations of inexperience, ignorance, laziness, and abandonment against colonists. The Italian case is particularly notable, as one recurring trope revolved around the colonists' perceived deficiency in agricultural knowledge. See González Navarro, *La colonización en México*, 42.
25. Marcela Martínez Rodríguez, *Colonizzazione al Messico! Las colonias agrícolas de italianos en México, 1881–1910* (San Luis Potosí: El Colegio de San Luis, 2013); José Benigno Zilli Mánica, *Italianos en México: documentos para la historia de los colonos italianos en México* (Xalapa: Ediciones Concilio; Instituto de Estudios Superiores, 2002); Anna Mario Flavia Colle, *Destinazione Messico: 1882 parte un vapore da Genova* (Belluno: Grafiche Trabella, 1998).
26. "Condiciones necesarias para asegurar un éxito en las empresas de colonización," *El Colono*, 23 August 1897.
27. González Navarro, *Los extranjeros en México*, 2:203–25.
28. *Memoria presentada al Congreso de la Unión por . . . General Carlos Pacheco*, 1:33.
29. Domenech J. Figueroa, *Guía general descriptiva de la República Mexicana: história, geografía, estadística, etc. . . .* (México: R. de S. N. Araluce, 1899), 368.
30. "Condiciones necesarias para asegurar un éxito en las empresas de colonización," *El Colono*, 23 August 1897.
31. "Condiciones necesarias para asegurar un éxito en las empresas de colonización," *El Colono*, 23 August 1897.
32. Richard Griswold del Castillo, *The Los Angeles Barrio: A Social History, 1850–1890* (Berkeley: University of California Press, 1979), 119–24; Hernández, *Mexican American Colonization during the Nineteenth Century*, 149–56.
33. "Nuevas juntas auxiliares," *El Colono*, vol. 2, no. 17, 7 July 1897, 4.
34. Emilio Zamora, *The World of the Mexican Worker in Texas* (College Station: Texas A&M University Press, 1993), 86–87.
35. "Reglamento de la Unión Fraternal de Repatriación," *El Colono*, vol. 3, no. 3, 7 December 1897, 1–5. I have been unable to locate any primary records of these fraternal organizations.
36. Zamora, *World of the Mexican Worker in Texas*, 86–87.
37. José Amaro Hernández, *Mutual Aid for Survival: The Case of the Mexican American* (Malabar, FL: Krieger, 1983), 15–59. Chapters 4 and 5 detail the proliferation of mutual-aid societies in Texas, Illinois, and California.
38. "Reglamento de la Unión Fraternal de Repatriación," *El Colono*, 7 December 1897, 1–5.
39. "Reglamento de la Unión Fraternal de Repatriación," *El Colono*, 7 December 1897, 1–5.
40. "Reglamento de la Unión Fraternal de Repatriación," *El Colono*, 7 December 1897, 1–5.
41. Beatty, *Institutions and Investment*, 23.

Chapter 12

1. Nicholas B. Dirks, "The Ethnographic State," in *Castes of Mind: Colonialism and the Making of Modern India* (Princeton, NJ: Princeton University Press, 2001), 43–60.
2. On the 1857 rebellion see Darshan Perusek, "Subaltern Consciousness and Historiography of Indian Rebellion of 1857," *Economic and Political Weekly* 28, no. 37 (1993): 1931–36. http://www.jstor.org/stable/4400141.
3. Scott, *Seeing Like a State*, especially chaps. 1 and 2.
4. Dirks, "Ethnographic State."
5. Mario Luis Fuentes Alcalá and Saúl Arellano Almanza, *Nuevo ensayo político-social de la República Mexicana. Recuento de las desigualdades y la pobreza en México, 1790–1930* (México: UNAM, 2019); Mario Luis Fuentes Alcalá, "El censo y su visión política," *Excelsior*, n.d., https://www.excelsior.com.mx/opinion/mario-luis-fuentes/el-censo-y-su-vision-politica/1363170.
6. This file, along with dozens of others of a related nature, are archived in Mexico City's Archivo Histórico de Terrenos Nacionales (AHTN) as part of the materials from the First Section of Fomento, which is to say everything related to colonization, land surveys, and inspections of colonies in Mexico during the Porfiriato. The newest manifestation of Fomento is Secretaría de Desarrollo Agrario, Territorial y Urbano, or SEDATU.
7. These rules are designed to prevent the entry of invasive species and to avoid spreading bacteria, viruses, and potentially other diseases. https://www.cbp.gov/travel/clearing-cbp/traveler-entry-form.
8. See chapter 2, "De Los Colonos," Art. VII, Sección 3, in "Ley de 15 de Diciembre de 1883," in de la Maza, *Código de Colonización*, 936–45.
9. Settlers clearly colonized other locations beyond these three; however, these are the three that can be extrapolated from the documentary record and the newspaper *El Colono*.
10. Jacques Derrida and Eric Prenowitz, "Archive Fever: A Freudian Impression." *Diacritics* 25, no. 2 (1995): 9–63, DOI: 10.2307/465144.
11. Arnoldo De León and Kenneth L. Stewart, *Tejanos and the Numbers Game: A Socio-Historical Interpretation from the Federal Censuses, 1850–1900* (Albuquerque: University of New Mexico Press, 1989), x.
12. For example, José María Rodríguez self-identified as "Mexico-Texano" with a birthplace of "Texas." Teodora Castillo Garza of Laredo, Texas, was one of the few widows who self-identified as "Mexico-Tejana"; she was born in "Texas." See, respectively, informe no. 38, folio 123 and informe no. 45, folio 143, in "Luis Siliceo. Contrato sobre compra-venta y colonización de terrenos en varios Estados de la República, y todo relativo a dicho contrato," 8 July 1895, exp. 453, 1.29 (32), AHTN.
13. In regard to birthplace, 501 were born in Mexico proper and 369 in the United States. Thirty-eight-year-old Maria de Galván of Lockhart, Texas, wrote down "Germany" as her place of birth. She was married to Martín Galván (age 50) from Tamaulipas. The

other person who was not of Mexican origin was William Spencer of Luling, Texas. See informe no. 137 grupo 3, folio 517, in exp. 453, 1.29 (32), AHTN .

14. "Siliceo y todo relativo a colonización," exp. 452, 1.29 (32), AHTN.
15. Stewart and De León, *Tejanos and the Numbers Game*, 15, 24.
16. I believe that there are thousands more declaraciones like these, but they are not always organized and frequently this sort of information was recorded in a letter. Aside from the relatively modern appearance of the forms Siliceo's colonists completed, the declaration requirements were par for the course and required for every case of resettlement I have examined. See Articles V and VI in "Ley de 15 de Diciembre de 1883," in de la Maza, *Código de colonización*, 936–45.
17. Friedrich Engels, *The Origin of the Family, Private Property, and the State* (London: Penguin Books, 2010 [1884]).
18. "Luis Siliceo. Contrato sobre compra-venta . . . y todo relativo a dicho contrato," 8 July 1895, pp. 72–145, 361–580, exp. 452, 1.29 (32), AHTN.
19. De León and Stewart, *Tejanos and the Numbers Game*, 51, especially table 4.1, 50.
20. It was common for resettlers to declare only their horse and rifle. See "Luis Siliceo. Contrato sobre compra-venta . . . y todo relativo a dicho contrato," 72–145, 361–580.
21. De León and Stewart, *Tejanos and the Numbers Game*, 51, especially table 4.1.
22. "Luis Siliceo. Contrato sobre compra-venta . . . y todo relativo a dicho contrato."
23. De León and Stewart, *Tejanos and the Numbers Game*, 54.
24. The six locations were all clustered along a north-south axis in the center of the state and close to railroad lines. The numbers for the top three cities are as follows: San Antonio, 32 families, 101 individuals; Manor, 37 families, 150 individuals, and Georgetown, 29 families, 85 individuals.
25. Vivian Elizabeth Smyrl, "Caldwell County," *Handbook of Texas Online*, updated October 19, 2020, https://www.tshaonline.org/handbook/entries/caldwell-county.
26. "The City of Manor, founded in 1872, was located on the Houston and Texas Central Railway, giving residents easy access to markets. By the mid-1880s Manor had a district school, three churches, six general stores, and a population of 125. Cotton, cottonseed, and grain were the principal commodities shipped from the area. The community grew rapidly in the late nineteenth and early centuries, with population estimates reaching 500 by 1892 and 900 by 1914." "Manor History," City of Manor, accessed February 24, 2024, https://www.cityofmanor.org/page/header_about_manor.
27. For the 75 declarants who did not declare an occupation, I inferred their occupation based on the material history and farming tools they imported. Moreover, this data also fits within the larger pattern (structure if you prefer) of the other declaraciones and is in line with contractual obligations, news reports, and the words of Siliceo himself.
28. Neil Foley, *The White Scourge: Mexicans, Blacks, and Poor Whites in Texas Cotton Culture* (Berkeley: University of California Press, 1997), 10.
29. "Luis Siliceo. Contrato sobre compra-venta . . . y todo relativo a dicho contrato"
30. Foley, *White Scourge*, 10.

31. El Director, "La repatriación," *El Colono*, 10 November 1895, p. 2. Original: "Los que durante mi permanencia en San Antonio fueron inscritos, y a quienes iniciaron mi proyecto de repatriación, son indudablemente la clase de individuos que se hacen necesarios en nuestros campos, pues además de ser laboriosos, son gente moralizada y en gran parte bastante ilustrados; no son, ni mucho menos, lo que la gran masa de emigrados a los Estados Unidos fue, hace algunos años, pues la mayoría de estos mexicanos, cuenta con todos los útiles e instrumentos necesarios modernos para la agricultura, muchos de ellos tienen algunas cabezas de ganado vacuno y caballar, y por últimos estos brazos no son peones de campo, sino más bien medieros que viven con algún desahogo pero que por mil circunstancias anhelan el regreso al lugar que los vio nacer."
32. Many immigrants arriving in the United States in 1890s were from central and southern Europe. See, for instance, Hoerder, *Cultures in Contact*, chap. 14 (pp. 331–65).
33. "Arrendamiento," *El Colono*, 10 November 1895, 2–3.
34. "Arrendamiento," *El Colono*, 10 November 1895, 2–3; my italics on "to both."
35. Foley, *White Scourge*, map 3, "Zone of Central Texas Cotton Culture," 16, 29 (quotation from Meinig, *Imperial Texas*), 30.
36. "Luis Siliceo. Contrato sobre compra-venta . . . y todo relativo a dicho contrato." For González's declaration, see informe 730; for Luna's, see informe 14630.
37. Foley, *White Scourge*, 10.

Chapter 13

1. After asking for the name of the colono, the questionnaire proceeds to document demographic information on (as applicable) the declarant's wife, his children, and his extended family.
2. Unless otherwise noted, all figures in this chapter are calculated from data in "Luis Siliceo. Contrato sobre compra-venta y colonización de terrenos en varios Estados de la República, y todo relativo a dicho contrato," 8 July 1895, exp. 452, 1.29 (32), AHTN, pp. 72–145, 361–580.
3. Jorge Durand, *Política, modelos y patrón migratorios: el trabajo y los trabajadores mexicanos en Estados Unidos* (San Luis Potosí: El Colegio de San Luis, 1998); Alexander Monto, *The Roots of Labor Migration* (Westport, CT: Praeger, 1994).
4. González Quiroga, *War and Peace*, 360.
5. For the "mixed-status" reference, see Cassaundra Rodriguez, "Experiencing 'Illegality' as a Family? Immigration Enforcement, Social Policies, and Discourses Targeting Mexican Mixed-Status Families," *Sociology Compass* 10, no. 8 (August 2016): 706–17, DOI: 10.1111/soc4.12393. For contemporary discussions around "mixed-status" families see Heide Castañeda, *Borders of Belonging: Struggle and Solidarity in Mixed-Status Immigrant Families* (Stanford, CA: Stanford University Press, 2019).
6. José Narro Robles and David Moctezuma Navarro, "Analfabetismo en México: una deuda social," *Realidad, Datos, y Espacio: Revista Internacional de Estadística y Geografía* 3, no. 3 (September–December 2012), 10. The 50 percent literacy figure for Mexico

City is from Edward Beatty, *Technology and the Search for Progress and Modernity in Mexico* (Berkeley: University of California Press, 2015), 193–202.

7. Steven Mintz, "Statistics: Education in America, 1860–1950," Gilder Lehrman Institute of American History, https://www.gilderlehrman.org/history-resources/teacher-resources/statistics-education-america-1860-1950.
8. De León and Stewart, *Tejanos and the Numbers Game*, 36.
9. Several of the declarants did not record their spouses' places of birth, but at least one spouse each came from Germany (Maria de Galván of Lockhart, Texas), New Mexico (Andrea G. De Jurado), and Louisiana (Marcelina Cárdenas of Dunlap, Texas).
10. Richard Griswold del Castillo, *La Familia: Chicano Families in the Urban Southwest: 1848 to Present* (Notre Dame, IN: Notre Dame University Press, 1984), 56–71.
11. Recall that 44 percent of married male declarants stated they had been born in these states. There was a total of 58/155 wives in the sample.
12. The states were San Luis Potosí (22), Zacatecas (9), Guanajuato (5), and Jalisco (10), totaling 46/155 wives.
13. For an excellent overview of technical education during this period, see Beatty, *Technology and the Search for Progress and Modernity in Mexico*, 193–202.
14. Narro Robles and Moctezuma Navarro, "Analfabetismo en México," 10.
15. De León and Stewart, *Tejanos and the Numbers Game*, 86.
16. Héctor Díaz Zermeño, *El origen y desarrollo de la escuela primaria mexicana y su magisterio, de la Independencia a la Revolución Mexicana* (México: Escuela Nacional de Estudios Profesionales Acatlán, UNAM, 1997), 41–68.
17. "49. Escuelas primarias y alumnos existentes en ellas, por sexo y edad, en las entidades federativas Años de 1878 a 1907. Primera parte." In González Navarro and Dirección General de Estadística, *Estadísticas sociales del Porfiriato, 1877–1910* (México: Talleres Gráficos de la Nación, 1956), 42.
18. De León and Stewart, *Tejanos and the Numbers Game*, 86.
19. Arnoldo De León and Kenneth L. Stewart, *Not Room Enough: Mexicans, Anglos, and Socioeconomic Change in Texas, 1850–1900* (Albuquerque: University of New Mexico Press, 1993), 70–71.
20. De León and Stewart, *Not Room Enough*, 66–67.
21. More than 95% of the declarants were born in Mexico, and many of their children and spouses were born in Texas. From the available data, one could presumably calculate the year of migration to the United States and extrapolate earlier migration patterns from states or regions.

Chapter 14

1. See Arjun Appadurai, "The Thing Itself," *Public Culture* 18, no. 1 (January 2006): 15; Alexey Golubev, *The Things of Life: Materiality in Late Soviet Russia* (Ithaca, NY: Cornell University Press, 2020), 24.
2. Bruce G. Trigger, *A History of Archaeological Thought*, 2nd ed. (New York: Cambridge University Press, 2014).

3. From which Marx developed his theories of historical materialism. See Tom Rockmore, "Marx," chap. 44 in *A Companion to the Philosophy of History and Historiography*, ed. Aviezer Tucker, 488–97.
4. Stalin, *Dialectical and Historical Materialism*, 3.
5. Nico Randeraad, *States and Statistics in the Nineteenth Century: Europe by Numbers* (Manchester, UK: Manchester University Press, 2010).
6. Herman Hollerith, "The Electrical Tabulating Machine," *Journal of the Royal Statistical Society* 57, no. 4 (1894): 678–89, DOI: 10.2307/2979610. I understand one could historicize this machine with the difference and analytical engines of Charles Babbage (1791–1871), in which case why not go back even further to the Antikythera mechanism (87 BCE)?
7. Lawrence Goldman, *Victorians and Numbers: Statistics and Society in Nineteenth-Century Britain* (Oxford: Oxford University Press, 2022), xix.
8. Turner, *Significance of the Frontier in American History*.
9. I am unsure who created and printed these forms: Siliceo, Fomento, Aduana, or a combination of these. Siliceo owned three newspapers, and thus a print shop, which he could have used to create these forms.
10. Foley, *White Scourge*, 10.
11. "Automobiles in San Antonio, 1899–1916," Texas Transportation Museum website, https://www.txtransportationmuseum.org/history-automobile.
12. Thor Hanson, *The Triumph of Seeds: How Grains, Nuts, Kernels, Pulses, and Pips Conquered the Plant Kingdom and Shaped Human History* (New York: Basic Books, 2015).
13. Unless otherwise noted, all figures in this chapter are calculated from data in "Luis Siliceo. Contrato sobre compra-venta y colonización de terrenos en varios Estados de la República, y todo relativo a dicho contrato," 8 July 1895, exp. 452, 1.29 (32), AHTN, pp. 72–145; 361–580.
14. Jonathan Saha, *Colonizing Animals: Interspecies Empire in Myanmar* (Cambridge: Cambridge University Press, 2021).
15. Edward O. Wilson, *Half-Earth: Our Planet's Fight for Life* (New York: Liveright, 2016).
16. Crosby, *Ecological Imperialism*.
17. Luis Duque, *Spanish in Spanish; or Spanish as a Living Language: A Practical Method of Making Spanish the Means of Its Own Mastery* (Boston: Allyn & Bacon, 1894), 392.
18. Carriages: 92; carts: 66; wagons: 26.
19. Early declaration forms did not have categories for these animals, but as more settlers signed on, the variety of animals that accompanied them increased.
20. Informe 130 in "Luis Siliceo. Contrato sobre compra-venta . . . y todo relativo a dicho contrato," 8 July 1895, exp. 452, 1.29 (32), AHTN.
21. Of the declarants, 25 percent (60) were bachelors (*solteros*) and that the proportion jumps to 33 percent when the eighteen widowers are included. One of out of three heads of household was an unmarried or widowed man, with an average age of 39.5 years.

22. Aaron Karp, "Estimating Global Civilian-Held Firearms Numbers," briefing paper, Small Arms Survey, June 2018. https://www.smallarmssurvey.org/sites/default/files/resources/SAS-BP-Civilian-Firearms-Numbers.pdf.
23. Harari, *Sapiens*, 3–19.
24. *Homo habilis* literally means "handy man" or "tool maker." See Hands, *Cosmosapiens*, 439.
25. Benjamin B. Beck, *Animal Tool Behavior: The Use and Manufacture of Tools by Animals* (New York: Garland Science, 1980), 10.
26. For Martin Heidegger, "equipment" meant all material things that make up our world. See G. Harman, "Technology, Objects, and Things in Heidegger," *Cambridge Journal of Economics* 34, no. 1 (2010): 17–25, http://www.jstor.org/stable/24232017.
27. Richard L. Currier, *Unbound: How Eight Technologies Made Us Human and Brought Our World to the Brink* (New York: Arcade, 2015), especially chaps. 2 and 3.
28. Edward Beatty, "Approaches to Technology Transfer in History and the Case of Nineteenth-Century Mexico," *Comparative Technology Transfer and Society* 1, no. 2 (January 2003), 167–200.
29. In other words, *aduanas* and other ports of entry are potential reservoirs of data for analyzing amounts and kinds of technology transfer.
30. The best study on sewing machines and their relationship to technology transfer is Beatty, *Technology and the Search for Progress and Modernity in Mexico*, 83–106.
31. For a typical advertisement, see *El Colono*, vol. 2, no. 2, 25 March 1897, 15.
32. "Machinery Milestones: The World's First Tractors," *Farmers Weekly*, https://www.fwi.co.uk/machinery/tractors/machinery-milestones-the-worlds-first-tractors.
33. "Editorial: Evolution of the Plow over 10,000 years and the Rationale for No-Till Farming," *Soil and Tillage Research* 93 (2007) 1–12.
34. Foley, *White Scourge*, 10.
35. This is one of many arguments Richard C. Francis made in *Domesticated: Evolution in a Man-Made World* (New York: W. W. Norton, 2015).
36. Saha, *Colonizing Animals*.

Epilogue

1. "Carta de Luis Siliceo a Secretario de Fomento y Colonización," 14 May 1900, in "Siliceo y todo relativo a Colonización, 1895." exp. 452, 1.29 (32), AHTN.
2. González Navarro, *Los extranjeros en México* 2:354–69.
3. By 1895, the agency had gone through several name changes and another modification as Secretario de Estado y del Despacho de Fomento, Colonización, e Industria.
4. Cortés, "Mexican Colonies during the Porfiriato," 10; also Junta Organizadora del Partido Liberal Mexicano, Article 35, "A los mexicanos residentes en el extranjero que lo soliciten los repatriará el Gobierno pagándoles los gastos de viaje y les proporcionará tierras para su cultivo," http://www.ordenjuridico.gob.mx/Constitucion/CH6.pdf.
5. González Navarro, *Los extranjeros en México* 2:354–69.

6. "Al vuelo," *El Colono* vol. 3, no. 15, 7 June 1898, 1–4. Original: "¡Soldados del Progreso, sostenerse firmes, mano a las manceras, vuelta y media a las tierras, paso del caballo y marchen . . . !
7. "Carta de Luis Siliceo a Secretario de Fomento y Colonización," 14 May 1900, in "Siliceo y todo relativo a colonización, 1895," exp. 452, 1.29 (32), AHTN.
8. The best study of this epidemic in Laredo is McKiernan-González, *Fevered Measures* especially chaps. 2–4.
9. Carta de Luis Siliceo a Secretario de Fomento y Colonización," 14 May 1900, in "Siliceo y todo relativo a colonización, 1895," exp. 452, 1.29 (32), AHTN.
10. See "Contrato celebrado con el Sr. Luis Siliceo para la compra-venta y colonización de terrenos baldíos y nacionales en los Estados de Chihuahua, Coahuila, Guerrero, México, Michoacán, Puebla, y Veracruz, 1895," exp. 365, 1.29 (06), AHTN.
11. "Carta de Luis Siliceo a Secretario de Fomento y Colonización," 14 May 1900, in "Siliceo y todo relativo a Colonización, 1895." exp. 452, 1.29 (32), AHTN.
12. "Carta de Luis Siliceo a Secretario de Fomento y Colonización," 14 May 1900, in "Siliceo y todo relativo a Colonización, 1895." exp. 452, 1.29 (32), AHTN.
13. Historiographically speaking, a considerable amount of ink has been spilled on explaining how land displacement and dispossession were some of the primary structural factors leading to the Mexican Revolution in 1910. It is fair to say that no researcher has studied *all* these contracts collectively to see which were accepted, cancelled, rescinded, or like Siliceo's, were finalized and completed.
14. *Memoria presentada al Congreso de la Unión por . . . Manuel Fernández Leal*, 22.
15. One of the few scholars to remain as skeptical as I am is Holden, "Priorities of the State in the Survey of the Public Land."
16. "Carta de Luis Siliceo al director del Conservatorio Nacional de Música," 25 September 1901, exp. 2, "Luis Siliceo solicita celebrar un contrato para la fabricación de artefactos de metal esmaltado, galvanizado, etc." caja 35, Fondo Fomento, Nuevas Industrias, 29 July 1897, AGN.
17. Fernando Saúl Alanís Enciso, *El primer programa bracero y el gobierno de México, 1917–1918* (San Luis Potosí: Colegio de San Luis, 1999).
18. Covarrubias, "La inmigración y colonización en las Américas." The same study was also published as "La inmigración y colonización en las Américas IV. La inmigración y colonización en la República Argentina," and later as "La inmigración y colonización en las Américas V. La colonización artificial."
19. Covarrubias, *Algunas observaciones acera la inmigración y de la colonización*, 155–57. On Porfirian indigenism, see Tenorio-Trillo, *Mexico at the World's Fairs*.
20. Andrés Molina Enríquez, *Los grandes problemas nacionales* (México: Imprenta de A. Carranza e Hijos, 1909), 248.
21. Ignacio Mariscal, "Los trabajadores Mexicanos en los EU," *Boletín de la Secretaría de Fomento* 4, no. 3 (October 1906), 234–35.
22. Rómulo Escobar Zerman, "La emigración de nuestros peones," *Boletín de la Secretaría de Fomento* 6, no. 1 (August 1906), 28–41.

23. Victor S. Clark, *Mexican Labor in the United States* Bureau of Labor Bulletin (Washington, DC: US Government Printing Office, 1909), 471.
24. Hernández, "Contemporary Deportation Raids and Historical Memory: Mexican Expulsions in the Nineteenth Century." *Aztlán: A Journal of Chicano Studies* 52 (2) (Fall 2010): 115–141.
25. Hernández, "Contemporary Deportation Raids"; Clark, *Mexican Labor in the United States*, 520–21.
26. Katz, *Life and Times of Pancho Villa*, 49.

BIBLIOGRAPHY

Archives and Libraries

Mexico

Archivo del Instituto de Investigaciones Históricas, Universidad Autónoma de Baja California
Archivo General de la Nación (AGN)
Biblioteca, Archivo General de la Nación
Archivo Histórico Genaro Estrada, Secretaría de Relaciones Exteriores (AHSRE)
Archivo Histórico de Terrenos Nacionales, Secretaría de la Reforma Agraria (AHTN)
Biblioteca Nacional, Universidad Nacional Autónoma de México (UNAM)
Fondo Reservado
Hemeroteca Nacional de México (HNM)

United States

Center for American History, University of Texas at Austin
Archivo Histórico del Estado de Saltillo (SACAH)

Newspapers and Magazines

Boletín de la Secretaría de Fomento
El Clamor Público
El Colono
El Correo de Laredo
El Fronterizo
El Imparcial
El Lunes
El Mundo
El País
La Prensa
La Repatriación
Nature
New York Times

Revista Positiva: Científica, Filosófica, Social y Política. Órgano del Positivismo en México
Science

Published Primary Sources

Anales del Ministerio de Fomento de la República Mexicana. Mexico: Imprenta de Francisco Díaz de León, 1891.

Colonization and Naturalization Laws of the Republic of Mexico with Amendments (México: American Book & Printing Co., 1905.

De cómo vino Huerta y cómo se fue: apuntes para la historia de un régimen militar, vol. 1 Mexico: Libreria General, 1914.

De la Maza, Francisco F., ed. *Código de colonización y terrenos baldíos de la República Mexicana, formado por Francisco F. de la Maza y publicado según el acuerdo del presidente de la república, por conducta de la secretaría de estado y del despacho de fomento, años de 1451 a 1892*. México: Oficina Tipográfica de la Secretaria de Fomento, 1893.

Diario de los debates de la Cámara de Diputados, undécima legislatura constitucional de la unión. Vol. 3, *Correspondiente á las sesiones ordinarias y extraordinarias durante el primer periodo del segundo año*. México: Imprenta de G. Horcasitas, 1883.

Diario de los debates de la Cámara de Senadores, undécimo congreso constitucional. Vol. 3, *Correspondiente al tercer periodo de sesiones ordinarias de 16 de septiembre a 15 de diciembre de 1883*. México: Imprenta del Gobierno, 1886.

Dublán, Manuel, and José María Lozano. *Legislación mexicana, o colección completa de las disposiciones legislativas expedidas desde la independencia de la República, ordenada por los licenciados Manuel Dublán y José María Lozano*. Edición oficial. México: Imprenta de Comercio, a Carga de Dublán y Lozano, Hijos, 1876.

Galicia, Severiano. *La auto-colonización en México. Discurso del señor ingeniero Severiano Galicia, en apoyo de su proyecto de ley sobre la colonización de los terrenos despoblados de la república por los mismos mexicanos, pronunciado en la sesión del Congreso Nacional de Agricultura efectuada la tarde del día ocho de marzo de 1893 en el congreso de la unión*. México: Tipografía de "El Correo Español," 1893.

González, José E. *Algunos apuntes y datos estadísticos que pueden servir de base para formar una estadística del estado de Nuevo León*. Monterrey: Imprenta del Gobierno, 1873.

Junta Directiva de Colonización, México. *Proyectos de colonización presentados por la Junta Directiva del Ramo, al Ministerio de Relaciones de la República Mexicana en 5 de Julio de 1848*. México: Imprenta de Vicente García Torres, 1848.

Manero, Vicente E. *Documentos interesantes sobre colonización: los ha reunido, puesto en orden cronológico y los publica, Vicente E. Manero, gefe de la Sección 1ª del Ministerio de Fomento*. México: Imprenta de la V. E Hijos de Murguía, 1878.

Memoria de la primera Secretaria de Estado y del Despacho de Relaciones Interiores y Esteriores de los Estados Unidos Mexicanos, leída al soberano Congreso constituyente en los días 14, 15, y 16 de diciembre de 1846. México: Imprenta de Vicente García Torres, 1847.

Memoria de la Secretaría de Estado y del Despacho de Fomento, Colonización, Industria y Comercio de la República Mexicana, escrita por el Ministro del Ramo, D. Manuel Siliceo, para dar cuenta con ella al Soberano Congreso Constitucional. México: Imprenta de Vicente García Torres, 1857.

Memoria del Ministro de Relaciones Interiores y Esteriores D. Luis G. Cuevas leída en la Cámara de Diputados el 5 y en la de Senadores el 8 de Enero de 1849. México: Imprenta de Vicente García Torres, Ex-Convento del Espíritu Santo, 1849.

Memoria presentada á S.M. el Emperador por el Ministro de Fomento Luis Robles Pezuela de los trabajos ejecutados en su ramo el año de 1865. México: Imprenta de J. M. Andrade y F. Escalante, 1866.

Memoria presentada al Congreso de la Unión por el Secretario de Estado y del Despacho de Fomento, Colonización, Industria y Comercio de la República Mexicana, General Carlos Pacheco, corresponde a los años trascurridos de diciembre de 1877 a diciembre de 1882. 3 vols. México: Oficina Tipográfica de la Secretaria de Fomento, 1885.

Memoria presentada al Congreso de la Unión por el Secretario de Estado y del Despacho de Fomento, Colonización e Industria de la República Mexicana, ingeniero Manuel Fernández Leal. Corresponde a los años transcurridos de 1892 a 1896. México: Oficina Tipográfica de la Secretaría de Fomento, 1897.

Memoria presentada al Congreso de la Unión por el Secretario de Estado y del Despacho de Fomento, Colonización, Industria, y Comercio de la República Mexicana, Vicente Riva Palacio, Corresponde al Año Trascurrido de Diciembre de 1876 a Noviembre de 1877. México: Imprenta de Francisco Diaz de León, 1877.

Moyano Pahissa, Ángela. *Antología: Protección consular a mexicanos en los Estados Unidos, 1849–1900.* México: Archivo Histórico Diplomático Mexicano, 1989.

Orozco, Wistano Luis. *Legislación y jurisprudencia sobre terrenos baldíos.* México: Imprenta El Tiempo, 1895.

Ortiz de Ayala, Simón Tadeo. *Resumen de la estadística del imperio mexicano, 1822: estudio preliminar, revisión de texto, notas y anexos de Tarsicio García Díaz.* Reprint ed. México: Biblioteca Nacional, UNAM, 1968.

Riva Palacio, Vicente, Alfredo Chavero, Julio Zárate, Enrique Olavarría y Ferrari, and José María Vigíl. *México a través de los siglos.* 5 vols. México and Barcelona: Espasa y Comp., Editores, 1884.

Secretaría de Fomento. *Ley sobre ocupación y enajenación de terrenos baldíos de los Estados Unidos Mexicanos.* México: Oficina Tipográfica de la Secretaría de Fomento, 1894.

Theses and Dissertations

Adams, David Bergen. "The Tlaxcalan Colonies of Spanish Coahuila and Nuevo León: An Aspect of the Settlement of Northern Mexico." PhD diss., University of Texas, 1971.

Águila, Jaime R. "Protecting 'México de Afuera': Mexican Emigration Policy, 1876–1928." PhD diss., Arizona State University, 2000.

Berninger, George Dieter. "Mexican Attitudes towards Immigration 1821–1857." PhD diss., University of Wisconsin, Madison, 1972.

Burden, David K. "La idea Salvadora: Immigration and Colonization Politics in Mexico, 1821–1857." PhD diss., University of California, Santa Barbara, 2005.

Coerver, Don M. "The Porfirian Interregnum: The Presidency of Manuel Gonzalez of Mexico, 1880–1884." PhD diss., Tulane University, 1973.

Peralta Santiago, Guillermina. "Manuel Siliceo: un liberal moderado en acción." Licentiate thesis, UNAM, 2000.

Proffitt, Dennis Thurber III. "The Symbiotic Frontier: The Emergence of Tijuana since 1769." PhD diss., UCLA, 1988.

Sego Eugene B. "Six Tlaxcalan Colonies on New Spain's Northern Frontier: A Comparison of Success and Failure." PhD diss., Indiana University, 1990.

Stern, Peter A. "Social Marginality and Acculturation on the Northern Frontier of New Spain." PhD diss., University of California, Berkeley, 1985.

Secondary Sources

Aboites Aguilar, Luis. "La Comisión Nacional de Colonización y la Expansión de la pequeña propiedad rural en México, 1947–1963." *Historia Mexicana* 68, no. 3 (January–March 2019): 1165–1204.

Alanís Enciso, Fernando Saúl. *El primer programa bracero y el gobierno de México, 1917–1918.* San Luis Potosí: Colegio de San Luis, 1999.

———. *They Should Stay There: The Story of Mexican Migration and Repatriation during the Great Depression.* Translated by Russ Davidson. Chapel Hill: University of North Carolina Press, 2017.

Alberdi, Juan Bautista. *Bases y puntos de partida para la organización política de la República Argentina.* Buenos Aires, 1852.

Alonso, Ana María. *Thread of Blood: Colonialism, Revolution, and Gender on Mexico's Northern Frontier.* Tucson: University of Arizona Press, 1995.

Almaguer, Tomás. *Racial Fault-Lines: The Historical Origins of White Supremacy in California.* Berkeley: University of California Press, 1994.

Altman, Ida. *The War for Mexico's West: Indians and Spaniards in New Galicia, 1524–1550.* Albuquerque: University of New Mexico Press, 2010.

Anderson, Benedict. *Imagined Communities: Reflections on the Origin and Spread of Nationalism.* Reprint ed. New York: Verso, 2003.

Andrews, George Reid. *Blacks and Whites in São Paulo, Brazil, 1888–1988.* Madison: University of Wisconsin Press, 1991.

Appadurai, Arjun. *Modernity at Large: Cultural Dimensions of Globalization.* Minneapolis: University of Minnesota Press, 1996.

———. "The Thing Itself." *Public Culture* 18, no. 1 (January 2006): 15–22.

Aquino Sánchez, Faustino A. *Intervención francesa, 1838–1839. La diplomacia mexicana y el imperialismo del libre comercio* (México: Instituto Nacional de Antropología e Historia, 1997).

Ardelean, C. F., et al. "Evidence of Human Occupation in Mexico around the Last Glacial Maximum." *Nature* 584 (2020): 87–92. DOI: 10.1038/s41586-020-2509-0.

Baily, Samuel L., and Eduardo José Míguez. *Mass Migration to Modern Latin America.* London: Rowman & Littlefield, 2003.

Bansak, Cynthia, Nicole Simpson, and Madeline Zavodny. *The Economics of Immigration.* 2nd ed. New York: Routledge, 2020.

Barrera, Mario. *Race and Class in the Southwest: A Theory of Racial Inequality.* South Bend, IN: Notre Dame University Press, 1979.

Bartra, Roger. *Anatomía del mexicano.* México: Plaza y Janés, 2002.

Beatty, Edward. "Approaches to Technology Transfer in History and the Case of Nineteenth-Century Mexico." *Comparative Technology Transfer and Society* 1, no. 2 (January 2003): 167–200. DOI: 10.1353/ctt.2003.0013.

———. *Institutions and Investment: The Political Basis of Industrialization in Mexico before 1911.* Stanford, CA: Stanford University Press, 2011.

———. *Technology and the Search for Progress and Modernity in Mexico.* Berkeley: University of California Press, 2015.

Becerra-Valdivia, Lorena, and Thomas Higham. "The Timing and Effect of the Earliest Human Arrivals in North America." *Nature* 584 (2020): 93–97. DOI: 10.1038/s41586-020-2491-6.

Beck, Benjamin B. *Animal Tool Behavior: The Use and Manufacture of Tools by Animals.* New York: Garland Science, 1980.

Beezley, William H., and Michael C. Meyer, eds. *The Oxford History of Mexico.* New York: Oxford University Press, 2010.

Bellwood, Peter, ed. *The Global Prehistory of Human Migration.* New York: John Wiley & Sons, 2014.

Benton, Bradley J. *The Lords of Tetzcoco: The Transformation of Indigenous Rule in Post-conquest Central Mexico.* Cambridge: Cambridge University Press, 2017.

Berdán, Frances F., Richard E. Blanton, Elizabeth Hill Boone, Mary G. Hodge, Michael E. Smith, and Emily Umberger, eds. *Aztec Imperial Strategies.* Washington, DC: Dumbarton Oaks Research Library and Collection, 1996.

Bernal, Rafael. *México en Filipinas: Estudio de una transculturación.* México: UNAM, 1965.

Bernal Gómez, Beatriz. "México y las leyes liberales de Maximiliano de Habsburgo." *Hechos y Derechos* 11 (2 November 2012). https://revistas.juridicas.unam.mx/index.php/hechos-y-derechos/article/view/6731/8667.

Bernasconi, Robert. "Hegel at the Court of the Ashanti." In *Hegel after Derrida*, edited by Stuart Barnett. New York: Routledge, 1998.

Berninger, Dieter. "Immigration and Religious Toleration: A Mexican Dilemma, 1821–1860." *The Americas* 32(4) (April 1976): 549–65.

Bernstein, William J. *The Delusions of Crowds: Why People Go Mad in Groups.* New York: Grove/Atlantic, 2021.

Blanco Martínez, Mireya, and José Moncada Maya. "El Ministerio de Fomento, impulsor del estudio y el reconocimiento del territorio mexicano (1877–1898)." *Investigaciones Geográficas, Boletín del Instituto de Geografía, UNAM* 74 (2011): 77.

Blyth, Lance R. *Chiricahua and Janos: Communities of Violence in the Southwestern Borderlands, 1680–1880.* Lincoln: University of Nebraska Press, 2012.

Bodner, Martin, Ugo A. Perego, J. Edgar Gomez, Ricardo M. Cerda-Flores, Nicola Rambaldi Migliore, Scott R. Woodward, Walther Parson, and Alessandro Achilli. "The

Mitochondrial DNA Landscape of Modern Mexico." *Genes (Basel)* 12, no. 9 (21 September 2021): 1453. DOI: 10.3390/genes12091453.

Bonfil Batalla, Guillermo. *México Profundo: Reclaiming a Civilization.* Austin: University of Texas Press, 1996.

Bourdieu, Pierre. *Distinction: A Social Critique of the Judgement of Taste.* London: Taylor & Francis, 2013.

———. *Outline of a Theory of Practice.* New York: Cambridge University Press, 1977.

Bow, Brian, and Arturo Santa-Cruz. "Mexican Anti-Americanism and Regional Integration in North America." *Norteamérica* 6, no. 2 (2011): 35–66.

Bower, Bruce. "An Indigenous People in the Philippines Have the Most Denisovan DNA." *Science News*, 12 August 2021. https://www.sciencenews.org/article/indigenous-people-philippines-denisovan-dna-genetics.

Bradley, Guy, and John Paul Wilson, eds. *Greek and Roman Colonization: Origins, Ideologies and Interactions.* Swansea, UK: Classical Press of Wales, 2006.

Brocklehurst, Thomas Unett. *Mexico To-day: A Country with a Great Future, and a Glance at the Prehistoric Remains and Antiquities of the Montezumas.* London: J. Murray, 1883.

Brokaw, Galen, and Jongsoo Lee, eds. *Fernando de Alva Ixtlilxochitl and His Legacy.* Tucson: University of Arizona Press, 2016.

Bueno, Christina. *The Pursuit of Ruins: Archaeology, History, and the Making of Modern Mexico.* Albuquerque: University of New Mexico Press, 2016.

Burchell, Graham, Colin Gordon, and Peter Miller, eds. *The Foucault Effect: Studies in Governmentality: With Two Lectures by and an Interview with Michel Foucault.* Chicago: University of Chicago Press, 1991.

Burden, David K. "Reform before La Reforma: Liberals, Conservatives, and the Debate over Immigration, 1846–1855." *Mexican Studies/Estudios Mexicanos* 23, no. 2 (Summer 2007): 283–316.

Burrough, Bryan, Chris Tomlinson, and Jason Stanford. *Forget the Alamo: The Rise and Fall of an American Myth.* New York: Penguin Random House, 2021.

Cañizares-Esguerra, Jorge. *How to Write the History of the New World: Histories, Epistemologies, and Identities in the Eighteenth-Century Atlantic World.* Stanford, CA: Stanford University Press, 2001.

Carrera, Germán. "Sobre la Colonomanía," *Historia Mexicana* 6, no. 4 (April–June 1957): 597–610.

Carrillo, Ana María. "Economía, política y salud pública en el México porfiriano (1876–1910)." *História, Ciências, Saúde Manguinhos* 9 (2002): 67–87.

Castañeda, Heide. *Borders of Belonging: Struggle and Solidarity in Mixed-Status Immigrant Families.* Stanford, CA: Stanford University Press, 2019.

Ceballos Ramírez, Manuel. "Consecuencias de la guerra entre México y Estados Unidos. La traslación de mexicanos y la fundación de Nuevo Laredo." In *Nuestra frontera norte*, edited by Patricia Galeana, 39–59. México: AGN, 1997.

Chacón-Duque, Juan-Camilo, et al. "Latin Americans Show Wide-Spread Converso Ancestry and Imprint of Local Native Ancestry on Physical Appearance." *Nature Communications* 9, no. 5388 (2018). DOI: 10.1038/s41467-018-07748-z.

Chávez, John R. "Aliens in Their Native Lands: The Persistence of Internal Colonial Theory." *Journal of World History* 22, no. 4 (December 2011): 785–809.

———. *The Lost Land: The Chicano Image of the Southwest.* Albuquerque: University of New Mexico Press, 1984.

Chávez Chávez, Jorge. *Los indios en la formación de la identidad nacional Mexicana.* Ciudad Juárez, Chih: Universidad Autónoma de Ciudad Juárez, 2003.

Chevalier, Francois. *Land and Society in Colonial Mexico: The Great Hacienda.* Berkeley and Los Angeles: University of California Press, 1963.

Christian, David. *Maps of Time: An Introduction to Big History.* Berkeley: University of California Press, 2011.

Clark, Victor S. *Mexican Labor in the United States.* Bureau of Labor Bulletin. Washington, DC: US Government Printing Office, 1909.

Clarke, Mary Whatley. *Chief Bowles and the Texas Cherokees.* Norman: University of Oklahoma Press, 1971.

Clendinnen, Inga. *Ambivalent Conquests: Maya and Spaniard in Yucatan, 1517–1570.* Cambridge: Cambridge University Press, 2003.

Colle, Anna Mario Flavia. *Destinazione Messico: 1882 parte un vapore da Genova.* Belluno: Grafiche Trabella, 1998.

Cope, Douglas R. *The Limits of Racial Domination: Plebeian Society in Colonial Mexico City, 1660–1720.* Madison: University of Wisconsin Press, 1994.

Cortés, Enrique. "Mexican Colonies during the Porfiriato." *Aztlán* 10 (Fall 1979): 1–14.

Cortés, José. *Views from the Apache Frontier: Report on the Northern Province of New Spain.* Edited by Elizabeth A. H. John. Translated by John Wheat. Norman: University of Oklahoma Press, 1989.

Covarrubias, José. *Algunas observaciones acerca la inmigración y de la colonización en las naciones independientes de América.* N.p., 1906.

———. "La inmigración y colonización en las Américas." *Revista Positiva: Científica, Filosófica, Social, y Política* 7, no. 77 (1907): 4–14, 94–121.

———. "La inmigración y colonización en las Américas IV. La inmigración y colonización en la República Argentina." *Revista Positiva: Científica, Filosófica, Social, y Política* 7, no. 81 (23 April 1907): 297–325.

———. "La inmigración y colonización en las Américas V. La colonización artificial." *Revista Positiva: Científica, Filosófica, Social, y Política* 7, no. 81 (23 April 1907): 363–98.

Craib, Raymond B. *Cartographic Mexico: A History of State Fixations and Fugitive Landscapes.* Durham, NC: Duke University Press, 2004.

Crosby, Alfred W. *Ecological Imperialism: The Biological Expansion of Europe, 900–1900.* Cambridge: Cambridge University Press, 1986.

Croix, Teodoro de. *Teodoro de Croix and the Northern Frontier of New Spain, 1776–1783: From the Original Document in the Archives of the Indies, Seville.* Norman: University of Oklahoma Press, 1941.

Cruciani, Fulvio, et al. "Tracing Past Human Male Movements in Northern/Eastern Africa and Western Eurasia: New Clues from Y-Chromosomal Haplogroups E-M78 and J-M12." *Molecular Biology and Evolution* 24, no. 6 (June 2007): 1300–11.

Currier, Richard L. *Unbound: How Eight Technologies Made Us Human and Brought Our World to the Brink.* New York: Arcade, 2015.

De León, Arnoldo. *The Tejano Community, 1836–1900.* Albuquerque: University of New Mexico Press, 1982.

———. *They Called them Greasers: Anglo Attitudes towards Mexicans in Texas, 1821–1900.* Austin: University of Texas Press, 1983.

De León, Arnoldo, and Kenneth L. Stewart. *Not Room Enough: Mexicans, Anglos, and Socioeconomic Change in Texas, 1850–1900.* Albuquerque: University of New Mexico Press, 1993.

———. *Tejanos and the Numbers Game: A Socio-Historical Interpretation from the Federal Censuses, 1850–1900.* Albuquerque: University of New Mexico Press, 1989.

Deleuze, Gilles. *Nietzsche and Philosophy.* London: Bloomsbury Academic, 2006.

Deleuze, Gilles, and Félix Guattari. *Anti-Oedipus: Capitalism and Schizophrenia.* New York: Viking Press, 1977.

———. *Nomadology: The War Machine.* Translated by Brian Massumi. Seattle, WA: Wormwood Distribution, 2010.

———. *A Thousand Plateaus: Capitalism and Schizophrenia.* Minneapolis: University of Minnesota Press.

Delgado López, Enrique. "El clima y la raza como parte de la historia de México en la primera mitad del siglo XIX." *Revista de Historia de América* 146 (January–June 2012): 113–33.

Derrida, Jacques, and Eric Prenowitz. "Archive Fever: A Freudian Impression." *Diacritics* 25, no. 2 (1995): 9–63. DOI: 10.2307/465144.

Diamond, Jared. *Guns, Germs, and Steel: The Fates of Human Societies.* New York: W. W. Norton, 1997.

Díaz Zermeño, Héctor. *El origen y desarrollo de la escuela primaria mexicana y su magisterio, de la Independencia a la Revolución Mexicana.* México: Escuela Nacional de Estudios Profesionales Acatlán, UNAM, 1997.

Dirks, Nicholas B. *Castes of Mind: Colonialism and the Making of Modern India.* Princeton, NJ: Princeton University Press, 2001.

Duara, Prasenjit. *Rescuing History from the Nation: Questioning Narratives of Modern China.* Chicago: University of Chicago Press, 1996.

Duncan, Robert H. "Political Legitimation and Maximilian's Second Empire in Mexico, 1864–1867." *Mexican Studies/Estudios Mexicanos* 12, no. 1 (Winter 1996): 27–66.

Duque, Luis. *Spanish in Spanish; or Spanish as a Living Language: A Practical Method of Making Spanish the Means of Its Own Mastery.* Boston: Allyn & Bacon, 1894.

Durand, Jorge. *Política, modelos y patrón migratorios: el trabajo y los trabajadores mexicanos en Estados Unidos.* San Luis Potosí: El Colegio de San Luis, 1998.

Durand, Jorge, and Douglas S. Massey. *Crossing the Border: Research from the Mexican Migration Project.* New York: Russell Sage Foundation, 2004.

Durvasula, Arun, and Sriram Sankararaman. "Recovering Signals of Ghost Archaic Introgression in African Populations." *Science Advances* 6, no. 7 (2020). DOI: 10.1126/sciadv.aax5097.

Duverger, Christian. *El primer mestizaje: La clave para entender el pasado Mesoamericano.* México: Taurus, 2007.

"Editorial: Evolution of the Plow over 10,000 Years and the Rationale for No-Till Farming." *Soil and Tillage Research* 93 (2007): 1–12.

Elizondo, Virgilio. *The Future Is Mestizo: Life Where Cultures Meet.* Revised ed. Denver: University Press of Colorado, 2000.

Engels, Friedrich. *The Origin of the Family, Private Property, and the State.* London: Penguin Books, 2010 [1884].

Erquizio Espinal, Oscar Alfredo. *Ciclos económicos de México.* México: USON, 2006.

Escobar Zerman, Rómulo. "La emigración de nuestros peones." *Boletín de la Secretaría de Fomento* 6, no. 1 (August 1906): 28–41.

Everett, Dianna. *The Texas Cherokees: A People between Two Fires, 1819–1840.* Norman: University of Oklahoma Press, 1990.

Figueroa, Domenech J. *Guía general descriptiva de la República Mexicana: históría, geografía, estadística, etc. . . .* México: R. de S. N. Araluce, 1899.

Fitzgerald, David. *A Nation of Emigrants: How Mexico Manages Its Migration.* Berkeley: University of California Press, 2009.

Florescano, Enrique. *Historia de las historias de la nación mexicana.* México: Taurus, 2002.

———. *National Narratives in Mexico: A History.* Translated by Nancy T. Hancock. Norman: University of Oklahoma Press, 2002.

Flusser, Vilém. *The Freedom of the Migrant: Objections to Nationalism.* Chicago: University of Illinois Press, 2003.

Foley, Neil. *The White Scourge: Mexicans, Blacks, and Poor Whites in Texas Cotton Culture.* Berkeley: University of California Press, 1997.

Forbes, Robert Humphrey. *Crabb's Filibustering Expedition into Sonora, 1857.* Tucson: Arizona Silhouettes, 1952.

Francis, Richard C. *Domesticated: Evolution in a Man-Made World.* New York: W. W. Norton, 2015.

Fuentes Alcalá, Mario Luis, and Saúl Arellano Almanza. *Nuevo ensayo político-social de la República Mexicana. Recuento de las desigualdades y la pobreza en México, 1790–1930.* México: UNAM, 2019.

Fukuyama, Francis. *Identity: The Demand for Dignity and the Politics of Resentment.* New York: Farrar, Straus, and Giroux, 2018.

Galeana, Patricia. *Juárez en la historia de México.* México: Editorial Miguel Ángel Porrúa, 2006.

Gamio, Manuel. *The Influence of Migrations on Mexican Life.* N.p., 1931. Nettie Lee Benson Latin American Collection.

Garcia, Richard A. *Rise of the Mexican American Middle Class: San Antonio, 1929–1941.* College Station: Texas A&M University Press, 1991.

Garner, Paul. *Porfirio Díaz: Profiles in Power.* London: Pearson, 2001.

Garza-Falcón, Leticia Magda. *Gente Decente: A Borderlands Response to the Rhetoric of Dominance.* Austin: University of Texas Press, 2010.

Geertz, Clifford. *The Interpretation of Cultures.* London: Basic Books, 1973.

Gibson, Charles. *Tlaxcala in the Sixteenth Century.* New Haven, CT: Yale University Press, 1952.

Goldman, Lawrence. *Victorians and Numbers: Statistics and Society in Nineteenth-Century Britain.* Oxford: Oxford University Press, 2022.

Golubev, Alexey. *The Things of Life: Materiality in Late Soviet Russia.* Ithaca, NY: Cornell University Press, 2020.

Gómez, Rocío, Miguel G. Vilar, Marco Antonio Meraz-Ríos, David Véliz, Gerardo Zúñiga, Esther Alheli Hernández-Tobías, María del Pilar Figueroa-Corona, Amanda C. Owings, Jill B. Gaieski, Theodore G. Schurr, and the Genographic Consortium. "Y Chromosome Diversity in Aztlán Descendants and Its Implications for the History of Central Mexico." *iScience* 24, no. 5, 102487. DOI: 10.1016/j.isci.2021.102487.

González Casanova, Pablo. "El colonialismo interno." In *De la sociología del poder a la sociología de la explotación: pensar América Latina en el siglo XXI*, edited by Marcos Roitman Rosenmann. México: Siglo XXI Editores, 2015.

González de la Vara, Martín. "El traslado de familias de Nuevo México al norte de Chihuahua y la conformación de una región fronteriza, 1848–1854." *Frontera Norte* 6, no. 11 (January–June 1994): 9–21.

González Milea, Alejandro. "Colonias militares y civiles del siglo XIX: una aproximación a las utopías urbanas del norte de Coahuila." *Estudios Fronterizos* 13, no. 25 (2012): 191–219.

———. "El 'poblamiento español' en la colonización del norte mexicano: la voz de los ingenieros entre la Independencia y la Posrevolución." *edA Esempi di Architettura* 7, no. 2 (2020): 105–15.

———. *El silencio de las aldeas. Urbanismo militar y civil del noreste mexicano, siglo XIX.* Monterrey: Consejo Nacional para la Cultura y las Artes, 2014.

González Navarro, Moisés. *La colonización en México, 1877–1910.* México: Talleres de Impresión de Estampillas y Valores, 1960.

———. "La política colonizadora del Porfiriato." *Estudios Históricos Americanos* (1953): 183–239.

———. *Los extranjeros en México y los mexicanos en el extranjero.* 3 vols. México: El Colegio de México, 1993.

González Navarro, Moisés, and Dirección General de Estadística. *Estadísticas sociales del Porfiriato: 1877–1910.* México: Talleres Gráficos de la Nación, 1956.

González-Polo y Acosta, Ignacio. "Colonización e inmigración extranjera durante las primeras décadas del siglo XIX." *Boletín Bibliográfico de la Secretaria de Hacienda y Crédito* 412 (1973): 4–7.

González-Quiroga, Miguel Ángel. *War and Peace on the Rio Grande Frontier, 1830–1880.* Norman: University of Oklahoma Press, 2020.

Gregory, Timothy A. *A History of Byzantium.* Oxford: Blackwell, 2005.

Griswold del Castillo, Richard. *La Familia: Chicano Families in the Urban Southwest: 1848 to Present.* Notre Dame, IN: Notre Dame University Press, 1984.

———. *The Los Angeles Barrio: A Social History, 1850–1890.* Berkeley: University of California Press, 1979.

Guardino, Peter. *The Dead March: A History of the Mexican American War.* Cambridge, MA: Harvard University Press, 2017.

Güereca Durán, Raquel E. "Las milicias tlaxcaltecas en Saltillo y Colotlán." *Estudios de Historia Novohispana* 54 (January–June 2016): 50–73.

Guerrero, L. Bibiana Santiago. *La gente al pie del Cuchumá: memoria histórica de Tecate.* Mexicali, BC: Fundación La Puerta, Instituto de Investigaciones Históricas, Universidad Autónoma de Baja California, 2005.

Guha, Ranajit. *Dominance without Hegemony: History and Power in Colonial India.* Cambridge, MA: Harvard University Press, 1997.

———. "On Some Aspects of the Historiography of Colonial India." In *Selected Subaltern Studies,* edited by Ranajit Guha and Gayatri Chakravorty Spivak, 37–43. Oxford: Oxford University Press, 1988.

———. "The Prose of Counter-Insurgency." In *Subaltern Studies II: Writings of South Asian History and Society,* 2–42. Oxford: Oxford University Press, 1983.

Guignon, Charles B. "Heidegger's 'Authenticity' Revisited." *Review of Metaphysics* 38, no. 2 (1984): 321–39. http://www.jstor.org/stable/20128154.

Hämäläinen, Pekka. *The Comanche Empire.* New Haven, CT: Yale University Press, 2008.

———. *Indigenous Continent: The Epic Contest for North America.* London: W. W. Norton, 2022.

———. *Lakota America: A New History of Indigenous Power.* New Haven, CT: Yale University Press, 2019.

Hamnett, Brian. "The Comonfort Presidency, 1855–1857." *Bulletin of Latin American Research* 15, no. 1 (1996): 81–100.

Hands, John. *Cosmosapiens: Human Evolution from the Origin to the Universe.* New York: Abrams, 2017.

Hanson, Thor. *The Triumph of Seeds: How Grains, Nuts, Kernels, Pulses, and Pips Conquered the Plant Kingdom and Shaped Human History.* New York: Basic Books, 2015.

Harari, Yuval Noah. *Sapiens: A Brief History of Humankind.* New York: Harper, 2015.

Harman, G. "Technology, Objects, and Things in Heidegger." *Cambridge Journal of Economics* 34, no. 1 (2010): 17–25. http://www.jstor.org/stable/24232017.

Harootunian, Harry. *Overcome by Modernity: History, Culture, and Commodity in Interwar Japan.* Princeton, NJ: Princeton University Press, 2000.

Harrison, Mark. "'The Tender Frame of Man': Disease, Climate, and Racial Difference in India and the West Indies, 1760–1860." *Bulletin of the History of Medicine* 70, no. 1 (1996): 68–93. https://muse.jhu.edu/article/3659.

Hassig, Ross. *Aztec Warfare: Imperial Expansion and Political Control.* Norman: University of Oklahoma Press, 1995.

Hegel, Georg Wilhelm Friedrich. *Lectures on the Philosophy of World History.* Translated by H. B. Nisbet. Cambridge: Cambridge University Press, 1975.

———. *Phenomenology of Spirit.* Oxford: Oxford University Press, 1979.

Heggie, Vanessa. "Blood, Race, and Indigenous Peoples in Twentieth-Century Extreme Physiology." *History and Philosophy of the Life Sciences* 41, article 26 (2019). DOI: 10.1007/s40656-019-0264-z.

Herman, Edward S., and Noam Chomsky. *Manufacturing Consent: The Political Economy of the Mass Media*. New York: Pantheon, 1988.

Hernández, José Amaro. *Mutual Aid for Survival: The Case of the Mexican American*. Malabar, FL: Krieger, 1983.

Hernández, José Angel. "Contemporary Deportation Raids and Historical Memory: Mexican Expulsions in the Nineteenth Century." *Aztlán* 52, no. 2 (Fall 2010): 115–41.

———. "The Decree of 19 August 1848: First Repatriation Commissions and Postwar Settlements along the US-Mexico Borderlands." *Maryland Journal of International Law* 33, no. 1 (2018): 1–37.

———. "*El México Perdido y Anhelado:* The Prose of Settler Colonialism amidst the Diaspora." In *Writing/Righting History: Twenty-Five Years of Recovering the US Hispanic Literary Heritage*, edited by Clara Lomas and Antonia Castañeda, 185–224. Houston, TX: Arte Público Press, 2020.

———. "From Conquest to Colonization: Indios and Colonization Policies after Mexican Independence." *Mexican Studies/Estudios Mexicanos* 26, no. 2 (Summer 2010): 285–315.

———. "Indios Bárbaros and the Making of Mexican Colonization Policy after Independence: From Conquest to Colonization." In *Transnational Indians in the North American West*, edited by Andrae M. Marak and Clarissa Confer, 89–117. College Station: Texas A&M University Press, 2015.

———. *Mexican American Colonization during the Nineteenth Century: A History of the US-Mexico Borderlands*. Cambridge: Cambridge University Press, 2012.

———. "Mexican Expulsions and Indian Removal during the Early Period of Global Mass Immigrations." *World History Bulletin* 30, no. 2 (Fall 2014): 30–34.

———. "Violence as Communication: The Revolt of La Ascensión, Chihuahua (1892)." *Landscapes of Violence* 2, no. 1, art. 6 (2012). DOI: 10.7275/R52Z13F8.

Hietala, Thomas R. *Manifest Design: American Exceptionalism and Empire*. Rev. ed. Ithaca, NY: Cornell University Press, 2003.

Hobsbawm, E. J. *Nations and Nationalism since 1780: Programme, Myth, Reality*, Cambridge: Cambridge University Press, 1990.

Hoerder, Dirk. *Cultures in Contact: World Migrations in the Second Millennium*. Durham, NC: Duke University Press, 2002.

Hofstadter, Richard. *Social Darwinism in American Thought*. Boston: Beacon Press, 1964.

Holden, Robert H. "Priorities of the State in the Survey of the Public Land in Mexico, 1876–1911." *Hispanic American Historical Review* 70, no. 4 (1990): 579–608.

Hollerith, Herman. "The Electrical Tabulating Machine." *Journal of the Royal Statistical Society* 57, no. 4 (1894): 678–89. DOI: 10.2307/2979610.

Hublin, Jean-Jaques, Abdelouahed Ben-Ncer, Shara E. Bailey, Sarah E. Freidline, Simon Neubauer, Matthew M. Skinner, Inga Bergmann, Adeline Le Cabec, Stefano Benazzi, Katerina Harvati, and Philipp Gunz. "New Fossils from Jebel Irhoud, Morocco and the Pan-African Origin of *Homo sapiens*." *Nature* 546 (2017): 289–92. DOI: 10.1038/nature22336.

Hugill, Peter J. *World Trade since 1431*. Baltimore, MD: Johns Hopkins University Press, 1993.

Huntington, Samuel P. *Who Are We? The Challenges to America's National Identity.* New York: Simon & Schuster, 2005.

Jordan, Terry G. "The German Settlement of Texas after 1865." *Southwestern Historical Quarterly* 73, no. 2 (1969): 193–212.

Kanellos, Nicolás. *Hispanic Immigrant Literature: el sueño del retorno.* Austin: University of Texas Press, 2011.

Kanellos, Nicolás, and Helvetia Martell. *Hispanic Periodicals in the United States, Origins to 1960: A Brief History and Comprehensive Bibliography.* Houston, TX: Arte Público Press, 2000.

Katz, Friedrich. "Labor Conditions on Haciendas in Porfirian Mexico: Some Trends and Tendencies." *Hispanic American Historical Review* 54, no. 1 (February 1974): 1–47.

———. *The Life and Times of Pancho Villa.* Stanford, CA: Stanford University Press, 1998.

Keesing, Donald B. "Structural Change Early in Development: Mexico's Changing Industrial and Occupational Structure from 1895 to 1950." *Journal of Economic History* 29, no. 4 (1969): 716–38. http://www.jstor.org/stable/2115707.

Kerbel, Matthew Robert. *If It Bleeds, It Leads: An Anatomy of Television News.* New York: Taylor & Francis, 2018.

Knight, Alan. Review of *The Other Rebellion: Popular Violence, Ideology, and the Mexican Struggle for Independence, 1810–1821. The Americas* 59, no. 4 (April 2003): 606–11.

Koreck, María Teresa. "Espacio y revolución en el noreste de Chihuahua." *Iztapalapa: Revista de Ciencias Sociales y Humanidades* 17 (1989): 103–22.

Kosaka, Kunitsugu. "The Kyoto School and the Issue of 'Overcoming Modernity.'" In *The Philosophy of the Kyoto School*, edited by Masakatsu Fujita, 233–51. Singapore: Springer, 2018.

Krause, Johannes, and Thomas Trappe. *A Short History of Humanity: A New History of Old Europe.* New York: Random House, 2021.

Lack, Paul D. "The Córdova Revolt." In *Tejano Journey, 1770–1850*, edited by Gerald E. Poyo, 89–109. Austin: University of Texas Press, 1996.

Lang Aldon S., and Christopher Long. "Land Grants." *Handbook of Texas Online*, accessed April 13, 2022, https://www.tshaonline.org/handbook/entries/land-grants.

Langley, Lester D. *The Americas in the Age of Revolution, 1750–1850.* New Haven, CT: Yale University Press, 1996.

Levinson, Irving W. *Wars within War: Mexican Guerrillas, Domestic Elites, and the United States of America, 1846–1848.* Fort Worth: Texas Christian University Press, 2005.

Lieberman, Daniel. *The Story of the Human Body: Evolution, Health, and Disease.* New York: Knopf Doubleday, 2014.

Lockhart, James. *The Nahuas after Conquest: A Social and Cultural History of the Indians of Central Mexico, Sixteenth through Eighteenth Centuries.* Stanford, CA: Stanford University Press, 1992.

Lomnitz-Adler, Claudio. *Deep Mexico, Silent Mexico: An Anthropology of Nationalism.* Minneapolis: University of Minnesota Press, 2001.

López-Ruiz, Carolina, and Michael Dietler, eds. *Colonial Encounters in Ancient Iberia: Phoenician, Greek, and Indigenous Relations.* Chicago: University of Chicago Press, 2009.

Lloyd, Jane-Dale. *Cinco ensayos sobre cultura material de rancheros y medieros del noroeste de Chihuahua, 1886–1910*. México: Universidad Iberoamericana, 2001.

———. *El proceso de modernización capitalista en el noroeste de Chihuahua, 1880–1910*. México: Universidad Iberoamericana, 1987.

MacLachlan, Colin M. *Imperialism and the Origins of Mexican Culture*. Cambridge, MA: Harvard University Press, 2015.

Maluf, N. S. R. "History of Blood Transfusion: The Use of Blood from Antiquity through the Eighteenth Century." *Journal of the History of Medicine and Allied Sciences* 9, no. 1 (January 1954): 59–107. DOI: 10.1093/jhmas/IX.1.59.

Mariscal, Ignacio. "Los trabajadores Mexicanos en los EU." *Boletín de la Secretaría de Fomento* 4, no. 3 (October 1906), 234–35.

Martínez, María Elena. *Genealogical Fictions: Limpieza de Sangre, Religion, and Gender in Colonial Mexico*. Stanford, CA: Stanford University Press, 2008.

Martínez, Rubén. "Internal Colonialism: A Reconceptualization of Race Relations in the United States." *Humboldt Journal of Social Relations* 10, no. 1 (1982): 163–76.

Martínez Baracs, Andrea. "Colonizaciones tlaxcaltecas." *Historia Mexicana* 43, no. 2 (1993): 195–250. http://www.jstor.org/stable/25138897.

Martínez-Cortés, Gabriela, Joel Salazar-Flores, Laura Gabriela Fernández-Rodríguez, Rodrigo Rubi-Castellanos, Carmen Rodríguez-Loya, Jesús Salvador Velarde-Félix, José Francisco Muñoz-Valle, Isela Parra-Rojas, and Héctor Rangel-Villalobos. "Admixture and Population Structure in Mexican-Mestizos Based on Paternal Lineages." *Journal of Human Genetics* 57 (2012): 568–74. DOI: 10.1038/jhg.2012.67.

Martínez Rodríguez, Marcela. *Colonizzazione al Messico! Las colonias agrícolas de italianos en México, 1881–1910*. San Luis Potosí: El Colegio de San Luis, 2013.

Matthew, Laura E. *Memories of Conquest: Becoming Mexicano in Colonial Guatemala*. Chapel Hill: University of North Carolina Press, 2012.

Matthew, Laura E., and Michel R. Oudijk, eds. *Indian Conquistadors: Indigenous Allies in the Conquest of Mesoamerica*. Norman: University of Oklahoma Press, 2007.

McCornack, Richard Blaine. "The San Patricio Deserters in the Mexican War." *The Americas* 8, no. 2 (October 1951): 131–42.

McEnroe, Sean F. *From Colony to Nationhood in Mexico: Laying the Foundations, 1560–1840*. Cambridge: Cambridge University Press, 2014.

McKeown, Adam. "Global Migration, 1846–1940." *Journal of World History* 15, no. 2 (June 2004): 155–89.

McKiernan-González, John. *Fevered Measures: Public Health and Race at the Texas-Mexico Border, 1848–1942*. Durham, NC: Duke University Press, 2012.

Mehl, Eva Maria. *Forced Migration in the Spanish Pacific World: From Mexico to the Philippines, 1765–1811*. Cambridge: Cambridge University Press, 2016.

Meier, Matt S. *Mexican Americans: From Conquistadors to Chicanos*. New York: HarperCollins, 1972.

Meléndez, Anthony Gabriel. *So All Is Not Lost: The Poetics of Print in Nuevomexicano Communities, 1834–1958*. Albuquerque: University of New Mexico Press, 1997.

Meyer, Michael C., William H. Sherman, and Susan M. Deeds. *The Course of Mexican History.* New York: Oxford University Press, 2018.

Molina Enríquez, Andrés. *Los grandes problemas nacionales.* México: Imprenta de A. Carranza e Hijos, 1909.

Montejano, David. *Anglos and Mexicans in the Making of Texas, 1836–1986.* Austin: University of Texas Press, 1987.

Monto, Alexander. *The Roots of Labor Migration.* Westport, CT: Praeger, 1994.

Moorhead, Max L. *The Presidio: Bastion of the Spanish Borderlands.* Norman: University of Oklahoma Press, 1991.

Mora-Torres Juan. *The Making of the Mexican Border: The State, Capitalism, and Society in Nuevo León, 1848–1910.* Austin: University of Texas Press, 2001.

Mörner, Magnus. *Adventurers and Proletarians: The Story of Migrants in Latin America.* Pittsburgh, PA: University of Pittsburgh Press; Paris: UNESCO, 1985.

Morton, Ohland. "Life of General Don Manuel de Mier y Terán: As It Affected Texas-Mexican Relations." *Southwestern Historical Quarterly* 48, no. 4 (1945): 499–546.

Moya, José C. "A Continent of Immigrants: Postcolonial Shifts in the Western Hemisphere." *Hispanic American Historical Review* 86, no. 1 (February 2006): 1–28.

———. *Cousins and Strangers: Spanish Immigrants in Buenos Aires, 1850–1930.* Berkeley: University of California Press, 1998.

———. "The Positive Side of Stereotypes: Jewish Anarchists in Early-Twentieth-Century Buenos Aires." *Jewish History* 18 (2004): 19–48. DOI: 10.1023/B:JEHI.0000005735.80946.27.

Murillo, Dana Velasco. *Urban Indians in a Silver City: Zacatecas, Mexico, 1546–1810.* Stanford, CA: Stanford University Press, 2016.

Narro Robles, José, and David Moctezuma Navarro. "Analfabetismo en México: una deuda social." *Realidad, Datos, y Espacio: Revista Internacional de Estadística y Geografía* 3, no. 3 (September–December 2012).

Nelson, Jason C. "The Application of the International Law of State Succession to the United States: A Reassessment of the Treaty between the Republic of Texas and the Cherokee Indians." *Duke Journal of Comparative and International Law* 17, no. 1 (Fall 2006): 1–48.

Nemesi, Attila L. "What Discourse Goals Can Be Accomplished by the Use of Hyperbole?" *Acta Linguistica Hungarica* 51, nos. 3–4 (2004): 351–78. DOI: 10.1556/aling.51.2004.3-4.6.

Nichols, James David. *The Limits of Liberty: Mobility and the Making of the Eastern U.S.-Mexico Border.* Omaha: University of Nebraska Press, 2018.

Nietzsche, Friedrich Wilhem. *On the Advantage and Disadvantage of History for Life.* London: Hackett, [1872] 1980.

———. *Thus Spake Zarathustra: A Book for All and None.* Translated by Thomas Common. New York: Modern Library, 1883.

Nugent, Daniel, ed. *Rural Revolt in Mexico and U.S. Intervention.* San Diego: Center for U.S.-Mexican Studies, University of California, 1988.

———. *Spent Cartridges of Revolution: An Anthropological History of Namiquipa, Chihuahua.* Chicago: University of Chicago Press, 1994.

O'Dwyer, Conor. "Runaway State Building: How Political Parties Shape States in Post-communist Eastern Europe." *World Politics* 56, no. 4 (2004): 520–53. http://www.jstor.org/stable/25054274.

Olalde, Iñigo, et al. "The Genomic History of the Iberian Peninsula over the Past 8000 Years." *Science*, 15 March 2019: 1230–34.

Pääbo, Svante. *Neanderthal Man: In Search of Lost Genomes.* New York: Basic Books, 2014.

Pani, Erica. "Dreaming of a Mexican Empire: The Political Projects of the 'Imperialistas.'" *Hispanic American Historical Review* 82, no. 1 (February 2002): 1–31.

Paredes, Américo. *A Texas-Mexican Cancionero: Folksongs of the Lower Border.* Austin: University of Texas Press, 1995.

Patnaik, Arun K. "Gramsci's Concept of Common Sense: Towards a Theory of Subaltern Consciousness in Hegemony Processes." *Economic and Political Weekly* 23, no 5 (1988): 2–10. http://www.jstor.org/stable/4378042.

Pérez-Rocha, Emma, and Rafael Tena. *La nobleza indígena del centro de México después de la conquista.* México: Instituto Nacional de Antropología e Historia, 2000.

Pérez Zevallos, Juan Manuel, and Héctor Cuauhtémoc Hernández Silva. *México a través de los siglos: historia general y completa del desenvolvimiento social, político, religioso, militar, artístico, científico y literario de México desde la antigüedad más remota hasta la época actual: obra única en su género*, edited by Vicente Riva Palacio. México: Ballescá y Compañía; Barcelona Espasa y Compañía, 1882.

Perusek, Darshan. "Subaltern Consciousness and Historiography of Indian Rebellion of 1857." *Economic and Political Weekly* 28, no. 37 (1993): 1931–36. http://www.jstor.org/stable/4400141.

Portes, Alejandro, and Ruben Rumbaut. *Legacies: The Story of the Immigrant Second Generation.* Berkeley: University of California Press, 2001.

Powell, T. G. "Mexican Intellectuals and the Indian Question, 1876–1911." *Hispanic American Historical Review* 48, no. 1 (February 1968): 19–36.

Poyo, Gerald E., ed. *Tejano Journey, 1770–1850.* Austin: University of Texas Press, 1996.

Price, John A. "Tecate: An Industrial City on the Mexican Border." *Urban Anthropology* 2, no. 1 (1973): 35–47. http://www.jstor.org/stable/40552637.

Priego, Natalia. *Positivism, Science, and "The Scientists" in Porfirian Mexico: A Reappraisal.* Liverpool, UK: Liverpool University Press, 2016.

Ramos, Raul. *Beyond the Alamo: Forging Mexican Ethnicity in San Antonio, 1821–1861.* Chapel Hill: University of North Carolina Press, 2008.

Ramos Lara, María de la Paz, and Rigoberto Rodríguez Benítez, eds. *Formación de ingenieros en el México del siglo XIX.* Culiacán: Facultad de Historia, Universidad Autónoma de Sinaloa, 2007.

Randeraad, Nico. *States and Statistics in the Nineteenth Century: Europe by Numbers.* Manchester, UK: Manchester University Press, 2010.

Rangel Silva, José Alfredo. *Ave de las tempestades: Wistano Luis Orozco y las contradicciones del porfiriato en la provincia, 1884–1910*. San Luis Potosí: El Colegio de San Luis, 2019.

Reich, David. *Who We Are and How We Got Here: Archaeogenetics and the New Science of the Human Past.* New York: Pantheon Books, 2018.

Reisler, Mark. *By the Sweat of Their Brow: Mexican Immigrant Labor in the United States, 1900–1940*. Westport, CT: Greenwood Press, 1976.

Renan, Ernest. *Qu'est-ce qu'une nation? et autres essais politiques*. Paris: Presses-Pocket, 1992.

Reséndez Andrés. *Changing National Identities at the Frontier: Texas and New Mexico, 1800–1850*. Cambridge: Cambridge University Press, 2005.

———. *A Land So Strange: The Epic Journey of Cabeza de Vaca*. New York: Basic Books, 2007.

Restall, Matthew. *Maya Conquistador*. Boston: Beacon Press, 1998.

Reynolds, Edward. "The Alabama Negro Colony in Mexico." *Journal of Negro History* 53, no. 3 (1968): 243–68.

Rodriguez, Cassaundra. "Experiencing 'Illegality' as a Family? Immigration Enforcement, Social Policies, and Discourses Targeting Mexican Mixed-Status Families." *Sociology Compass* 10, no. 8 (August 2016): 706–17. DOI: 10.1111/soc4.12393.

Rodriguez, Gregory. *Mongrels, Bastards, Orphans, and Vagabonds: Mexican Immigration and the Future of Race in America*. New York: Vintage Books, 2008.

Rodríguez Martínez, María del Carmen, Ponciano Ortiz Ceballos, Michael D. Coe, and Richard Allen Diehl. "Oldest Writing in the New World." *Science* 313, no. 5793 (15 September 2006): 1610–14. DOI: 10.1126/science.1131492.

Rodríguez O., Jaime E. *"We Are Now the True Spaniards": Sovereignty, Revolution, Independence, and the Emergence of the Federal Republic of Mexico, 1808–1824*. Stanford, CA: Stanford University Press, 2012.

Rodríguez O., Jaime E., and Colin M. MacLachlan. *The Forging of the Cosmic Race: A Reinterpretation of Colonial Mexico*. Berkeley: University of California Press, 1990.

Rowse, Tim, and Len Smith. "The Limits of 'Elimination' in the Politics of Population." *Australian Historical Studies* 41, no. 1 (2010): 90–106. DOI: 10.1080/10314610903317598.

Ruiz, Ramón Eduardo. *The Great Rebellion: Mexico, 1905–1924*. New York: W. W. Norton, 1980.

Saha, Jonathan. *Colonizing Animals: Interspecies Empire in Myanmar*. Cambridge: Cambridge University Press, 2021.

Saler, Beth. *The Settlers' Empire: Colonialism and State Formation in America's Old Northwest*. Philadelphia: University of Pennsylvania Press, 2014.

Salvucci, Richard J. *Politics, Markets, and Mexico's "London Debt," 1823–1887*. Cambridge: Cambridge University Press, 2009.

Sánchez, Evelyne. "Regresar a la madre patria. La repatriación de los mexicanos durante el Porfiriato." In *Fronteras y sensibilidades en las Américas*, edited by Salvador Bernabeú and Frédérique Langue, 259–82. Madrid: MASCIPO-CNRS: 2011.

Scholes Walter V. *Mexican Politics during the Juárez Regime, 1855–1872*. Columbia: University of Missouri Press, 1957.

Schulman, Sam. "Juan Bautista Alberdi and His Influence on Immigration Policy in the Argentine Constitution of 1853." *The Americas* 5, no. 1 (July 1948): 3–17.

Scott, James C. *The Art of Not Being Governed: An Anarchist History of Upland Southeast Asia*. New Haven, CT: Yale University Press, 2009.

———. *Seeing Like a State: How Certain Schemes to Improve the Human Condition Have Failed.* New Haven, CT: Yale University Press, 1998.

Sewell, William H. *The Logics of History: Social Theory and Social Transformation.* Chicago: University of Chicago Press, 2005.

Shoemaker, Nancy. "Settler Colonialism: Universal Theory or English Heritage?" *William and Mary Quarterly* 76, no. 3 (July 2019): 369–74.

Sierra, Justo. *The Political Evolution of the Mexican People.* Trans. ed. Austin: University of Texas Press, 1969.

Sikora, Martin, et al. "The Population History of Northeastern Siberia since the Pleistocene." *Nature* 570 (5 June 2019): 182. DOI: 10.1038/s41586-019-1279-z.

Smedley, Audrey. *Race in North America: Origin and Evolution of a Worldview.* New York: Taylor & Francis, 2018.

Smithers, Gregory D. *The Cherokee Diaspora: An Indigenous History of Migration, Resettlement, and Identity.* New Haven, CT: Yale University Press, 2015.

Smyrl, Vivian Elizabeth. "Caldwell County." *Handbook of Texas Online.* Updated October 19, 2020. https://www.tshaonline.org/handbook/entries/caldwell-county.

Stabb, Martin S. "Indigenism and Racism in Mexican Thought: 1857–1911." *Journal of Inter-American Studies* 1, no. 4 (October 1959): 405–23.

Stalin, Joseph V. *Dialectical and Historical Materialism.* Moscow: Foreign Languages Publishing House, 1949.

Standart, M. Colette. "The Sonoran Migration to California, 1848–1856: A Study in Prejudice." *Southern California Quarterly* 58, no. 3 (Fall 1976): 333–57.

Stopford, Martin. *Maritime Economics.* 3rd ed. London: Routledge, 2009.

Stout Joseph Allen. *Schemers and Dreamers: Filibustering in Mexico, 1848–1921.* Fort Worth: Texas Christian University Press, 2002.

Taylor Hansen, Lawrence Douglas. "La fiebre de oro en Sonora durante la década de 1850 y sus repercusiones diplomáticas con Estados Unidos." *Revista de El Colegio de Sonora* 7, no. 12 (1996): 107–41.

———. "La repatriación de Mexicanos de 1848 a 1980 y su papel en la colonización de la región fronteriza septentrional de México." *Relaciones* 18, no. 69 (1997): 198–212.

Tenorio-Trillo, Mauricio. *Mexico at the World's Fairs: Crafting a Modern Nation.* Berkeley: University of California Press, 1996.

Thrapp, Dan L. *The Conquest of Apacheria.* Norman: University of Oklahoma Press, 1975.

Topolski, Jerzy. "Historical Narrative: Towards a Coherent Structure." *History and Theory* 26, no. 4 (1987): 75–86. DOI: 10.2307/2505046.

Tozer, Lilly. "Did Our Human Ancestors Eat Each Other? Carved-up Bone Offers Clues." *Nature News*, 26 June 2023. https://www.nature.com/articles/d41586-023-02082-x.

Trigger, Bruce G. *A History of Archaeological Thought.* 2nd ed. New York: Cambridge University Press, 2014.

Trouillot, Michel-Rolph. *Silencing the Past: Power and the Production of History.* London: Beacon Press, 1995.

Tsouras, Peter G. *Warlords of Ancient Mexico: How the Mayans and Aztecs Ruled for More Than a Thousand Years.* New York: Skyhorse, 2014.

Tucker, Aviezer, ed. *A Companion to the Philosophy of History and Historiography.* Chichester, UK: John Wiley & Sons.

———. *Our Knowledge of the Past: A Philosophy of Historiography.* New York: Cambridge University Press, 2004.

Turner, Frederick Jackson. *The Significance of the Frontier in American History.* Madison: State Historical Society of Wisconsin, 1894.

Van Young, Eric. *The Other Rebellion: Popular Violence, Ideology, and the Mexican Struggle for Independence, 1810–1821.* Stanford, CA: Stanford University Press, 2001.

Vargas Machuca, Captain Bernardo de. *The Indian Militia and Description of the Indies.* Durham, NC: Duke University Press, 2008.

Velázquez Becerril, César Arturo. "Intelectuales y poder en el Porfiriato. Una aproximación al grupo de los Científicos, 1892–1911." *Revista Fuentes Humanísticas* 22, no. 41 (2010): 7–23.

Veracini, Lorenzo. "Obituary: Patrick Wolfe (1949–2016)." *Settler Colonial Studies* 6, no. 3 (2016): 189–90. DOI: 10.1080/2201473X.2016.1176393.

———. "Settler Colonialism." In *The Palgrave Encyclopedia of Imperialism and Anti-Imperialism,* edited by Immanuel Ness and Zake Cope, 1–6. London: Palgrave Macmillan, 2019. https://link.springer.com/referenceworkentry/10.1007/978-3-319-91206-6_26-1.

———. *Settler Colonialism: A Theoretical Overview.* London: Palgrave Macmillan, 2010.

———. *The World Turned Inside Out: Settler Colonialism as a Political Idea.* London: Verso, 2021.

Vizcaya Canales, Isidro. *Incursiones de indios al noreste en el México independiente, 1821–1855.* Monterrey: Gobierno de Nuevo León, Archivo General del Estado, 1995.

Vos, Jan de. "Una legislación de graves consecuencias: el acaparamiento de tierras baldías en México con el pretexto de colonización, 1821–1910." *Historia Mexicana* 34, no. 1 (July–September 1984): 76–113.

Wacquant, Loïc. "A Concise Genealogy and Anatomy of Habitus." *Sociological Review Monographs* 64 (2016): 64–72.

Wakefield, Edward Gibbon, ed. *A View of the Art of Colonization; with Present Reference to the British Empire; in Letters between a Statesman and a Colonist.* London: John W. Parker, 1849.

Wasserman, Mark. *Pesos and Politics: Business, Elites, Foreigners, and Government in Mexico, 1854–1940.* Stanford, CA: Stanford University Press, 2015.

Weber David J. *Bárbaros: Spaniards and Their Savages in the Age of Enlightenment.* New Haven, CT: Yale University Press, 2005.

———. *The Mexican Frontier, 1821–1846: The American Southwest under Mexico.* Albuquerque: University of New Mexico Press, 1982.

Weber, Max. *Max Weber: Essays in Sociology.* London: Routledge, 1991.

White, Hayden V. *Metahistory: The Historical Imagination in Nineteenth-Century Europe.* Baltimore, MD: Johns Hopkins University Press, 1975.

Whitten, David O. "Depression of 1893," in *EH.Net Encyclopedia,* edited by Robert Whaples. August 14, 2001. http://eh.net/encyclopedia/the-depression-of-1893/.

Wilson, Edward O. *Half-Earth: Our Planet's Fight for Life*. New York: Liveright, 2016.

———. *The Social Conquest of Earth*. New York: Liveright, 2012.

Winkler Ernest William. "The Cherokee Indians in Texas." *Quarterly of the Texas State Historical Association* 7, no. 2 (October 1903): 95–165.

Wolfe, Patrick. "Settler Colonialism and the Elimination of the Native." *Journal of Genocide Research* 8, no. 4 (December 2006), 387–409.

———. "Settler Colonialism, Time, and the Question of Genocide." In *Empire, Colony, Genocide: Conquest, Occupation, and Subaltern Resistance in World History*, edited by A. Dirk Moses, 102–32. New York: Berghahn Books, 2008.

Wootton, David. *The Invention of Science: A New History of the Scientific Revolution*. New York: HarperCollins, 2015.

Zamora, Emilio. *The World of the Mexican Worker in Texas*. College Station: Texas A&M University Press, 1993.

Zea, Leopoldo. *Positivism in Mexico*. Translated by Josephine Schulte. Austin: University of Texas Press, 1974.

Zilli Mánica, José Benigno. *Italianos en México: documentos para la historia de los colonos italianos en México*. Xalapa: Ediciones Concilio: Instituto de Estudios Superiores, 2002.

———. "Proyectos liberales de colonización en el siglo XIX." *La Palabra y el Hombre* 52 (October–December 1984): 129–42.

INDEX

References to illustrations appear in italic type.

Printed in the USA
CPSIA information can be obtained
at www.ICGtesting.com
CBHW030926041024
15293CB00005BA/105/J

9 780806 194592